Ask a Suffragist

Stories and Wisdom from
America's First **Feminists**

Ask a Suffragist

Stories and Wisdom from
America's First **Feminists**

April Young Bennett

B3 Brown Blackwell Books

Published in the United States of America
by Brown Blackwell Books
Salt Lake City, Utah
Copyright © 2019 Brown Blackwell Books
All rights reserved.
Hardcover ISBN-13: 978-1-7338239-0-6
Paperback ISBN-13: 978-1-7338239-9-9
Ebook ISBN-13: 978-1-7338239-1-3
Large Print ISBN-13: 978-1-7338239-2-0

CONTENTS

PREFACE

"Is not this a wonderful time
and era long to be remembered?" [1]
–Susan B. Anthony, 1854

If nineteenth century suffragists were still alive today, watching us relax in our blue jeans while machines wash our dishes and laundry, they might be tempted to mock us with tweets about our #ModernWorldProblems. But they would also see how far we haven't come. Much has changed in the United States of America since the battle for women's suffrage, but human nature remains and so does patriarchy. A new generation of feminists is fighting to overcome overt and subtle sexism across the nation and the world—and we could learn a thing or two from the feminists who came before us.

I started researching the suffragist movement to inform my own activism. I wanted to know the suffragists better because I was walking a similar path, nearly two hundred years later. And I wanted to know more than what they said and did; I wanted to know who they were. What ignited their passion for women's rights? How did they devote their lives to such exhausting and often disappointing work? How did they balance their activism with their families, careers and personal lives?

American suffragists weren't called suffragettes, by the way, which is too bad because 'suffragettes' is so much easier for me to say without sounding like I have a lisp. In spite of the name, I can relate to suffragists. Like me, they were activists who nursed babies and pursued careers.

Suffragists were deliberate in their efforts to change society for the women who would follow them, but they weren't necessarily trying to live their everyday lives as examples. After coming home from their public advocacy efforts, they were minding their own business, attending to their own love lives, families, and occupations with no thought that a busybody like me might examine their personal affairs someday. I don't doubt that several of them would raise an eyebrow if they knew I was prying into their personal lives to find something to emulate.

But I am doing it anyway. Suffragists left us with a much less sexist world, but we still have work to do! If we can draw morality tales from the lives of the founding fathers, learning from stories about them that probably weren't even true—yes, George Washington, I'm talking about you and your cherry tree—how much more could we learn from the real lived experiences of those who founded liberty for women after the founding fathers neglected to?

And anyhow, they certainly won't object at this point.

This book shares the stories and wisdom of some of the first Americans to suggest that women should have equal rights with men. They fought for equality in the 1830s-1860s, when the idea was radical and its supporters were vilified. From the comfort of the twenty-first century, it can be tempting to skip ahead from this inhospitable beginning to 1920, when their efforts were rewarded with the Nineteenth Amendment granting (most) women the right to vote.

The women who lived through this era had no such luxury. Most of these women didn't live to see the Nineteenth Amendment's passage. None of them were around when the voting rights promised by the Nineteenth Amendment finally became a reality for Native American and Southern black women decades later.

Let's sit with them for a while in their own time, when victories were few and the ultimate outcome was unknown. We should be able to relate, since we are at that same, uncertain place with many of the modern causes we support today. How did suffragists cope with such challenging work through so many decades of minimal success? What kept them going? What can we learn from their accomplishments? How can we avoid their mistakes?

Let's meet them and see what they can teach us.

CHAPTER ONE
How can we make our voices heard?

"Sue for your rights and privileges. Know the reason you cannot attain them. Weary them with your importunities." [1]
–Maria W. Stewart, 1831

"We are exceeding careful in this matter and we all move on together step-by-step looking at principles and entirely forgetting the conclusions we must at length come to. Some will undoubtedly shrink back when they come to find where they stand and believe they must have been mistakened. Others will want moral courage to carry out what they know to be duty and a few, I hope and believe, will go out in the world pioneers in the great reform which is about to revolutionize society." [2]
–Antoinette Brown, 1847

"A thorough discontent with the existing wrong must be created, and this is done by depicting it in all its naked deformity—calling every crime and every criminal by the right name—and if anger most intense swell the bosom of the wrongdoer, it is proof the truth's barbed arrow is fast in the right place." [3]
–Lucy Stone, 1853

The suffrage movement began at a particularly trying time for female activists, when Paul's Biblical injunction to "let your women keep silent" was taken quite literally. [4] Maria W. Stewart, a young black woman who had been raised as an indentured servant in Boston, wasn't concerned about Paul's disapproval. [5] "Did St. Paul but know of our wrongs and deprivations, I presume he would make no objection to our pleading in public for our rights," she said. [6]

Maria may have been the first American woman to speak out for women's rights in "promiscuous company"—audiences of men and women—when norms of 1830s America limited female speeches to women-only audiences. [7]

Still, she wouldn't have broken the social taboos of her time if it hadn't been for the tragic deaths of two young men in Maria's life. Maria's husband died only three years after their wedding and shortly thereafter, the executors of her husband's will robbed her of her husband's estate, leaving her a penniless widow. [8]

According to Maria's abolitionist mentor, David Walker, Maria wasn't the first black woman in Boston to endure such treatment. "In this very city, when a man of color dies, if he owned any real estate it most generally falls into the hands of some white person," he reported.

Only a year later, David Walker died as well. David had been the author of a controversial manifesto, the title of each cheerful chapter beginning, "Our Wretchedness" and then listing something sure to make people mad, such as "Our Wretchedness in Consequence of the Preachers of the Religion of Jesus Christ." [9] He would plant his booklet in the pockets of clothing he sold to sailors headed to southern states. [10]

David's actions earned him enemies, and when he died, some suspected foul play. Determined to continue his legacy, Maria published her first political tract shortly thereafter, lamenting that "the fair daughters of Africa be compelled to bury their minds and talents beneath a load of iron pots and kettles." She urged her peers to band together to finance their own educations and rebuked the rich and powerful for their oppression. She was eloquent but not confident, admitting that she felt "almost unable to address you; almost incompetent to perform the task." [11]

By her next speech, the meekness had evaporated. Without mincing words, she abruptly opened with the question, "Why sit ye here and die?" and called upon her audience to combat not only slavery, but also prejudice, ignorance and poverty. [12]

Her speeches were fiery, but not nearly so inflammatory as the announcements that preceded them, such as this shocking notice: "The Hall is convenient to accommodate ladies and gentleman, and all who feel interested in the subject are respectfully invited to attend." [13]

A colored woman giving speeches? And with men in the audience? Even friends who agreed with her message opposed her choice to become the messenger. [14]

Only three years after her first speech, pushback led to Maria's early retirement. Maria realized that black Bostonians needed to work out issues among themselves before they would be ready to take on their oppressors—and she wasn't volunteering to be her community's personal therapist. She was tired of coping with the contempt and as far as she could observe, her efforts had been futile. "I find it is no use for me as an individual to try to make myself useful among my color in this city," she sighed. [15]

Her farewell speech drew big crowds. She used her last speaking platform to defend women's right to speak in public, even as she announced that she would stop doing so herself. [16]

"What if I am a woman?" she demanded, before schooling her audience about the outspoken women of the Bible and world history. [17]

Meanwhile, in Philadelphia, it didn't occur to anyone to include women in the newly organized American Anti-Slavery Society, but Lucretia Mott showed up anyway. [18]

Lucretia was a Quaker lay preacher known for her "peculiar testimony" about elevating the status of women. [19] Her diminutive stature and polite demeanor led many to assume that she was docile, as long as they didn't pay attention to the radical things she was actually saying. Paying attention to women wasn't in vogue at the time, so Lucretia and her tame, matronly image often went unchallenged.

At the Anti-Slavery Society meeting, Lucretia made several useful suggestions that were incorporated into the Society's platform. [20] She made such an impression on Society delegates that they resolved that women should also work for the abolitionist cause, even as they shooed them out the door: the ladies could go form anti-slavery societies of their own. [21]

A few days later, Lucretia and other female abolitionists began the Philadelphia Female Anti-Slavery Society, one of the first anti-slavery societies for women. [22] The Society was also groundbreaking in another way; it was racially integrated from its inception, including black women such as Charlotte Vandine Forten and her daughters: Margaretta, Harriet, and Sarah. [23]

Charlotte's husband James was a mid-ranking officer in the American Anti-Slavery Society, as was Harriet's husband Robert Purvis, but white men held most of the influence over the men's organization in the 1830s. In contrast, the Forten women were powerful figures in the Philadelphia Female Anti-Slavery Society. At the first meeting, Margaretta was appointed to a committee to write the new Society's charter. [24] She was later elected recording secretary and Sarah served on the board of managers. [25]

The Forten family had something of a celebrity status among abolitionists, as well as the uncomfortable position of being a novelty among these comparatively progressive but predominantly white people— "abolition property," as Robert put it. [26] They were flattered when the famous poet John Greenleaf Whittier wrote a tribute to the Forten sisters, but horrified when someone published the poem, which had been intended as a private gift, without the permission of Whittier or the Fortens. [27]

Sarah was a poet herself, publishing her first poem in an anti-slavery newspaper when she was only sixteen. Her most famous work, "An Appeal to Woman," called on white women to fight slavery and racism. [28] Sarah appreciated white people who joined the abolitionist cause, even as she acknowledged that abolitionists weren't free from the "dark mantle" of racial prejudice. [29]

White abolitionists were constantly pointing to the Forten family as evidence of black people's potential for education and refinement—and pointing can be quite rude. On one cringe-worthy occasion, a white abolitionist asked Margaretta to play the piano because he had "never heard a colored lady play."

On another, James asked Margaretta to translate a letter that was written in French for the benefit of a visitor. The white guest seemed to think that a black girl who spoke French was newsworthy enough to write about in an abolitionist paper. When the Fortens saw the article, they were understandably peeved that "our friends should wonder at our being like other people." [30]

Margaretta, a teacher, was particularly influential in the Philadelphia Female Anti-Slavery Society's decision to finance a school for black children. Sarah led petition drives, although their senator warned them that the impertinent act of petitioning could have the opposite of its intended effect; huffy elected officials might react by delaying abolition instead of granting it. [31] Supposedly, petty men would intentionally deny women's wishes if women were so bold as to express them, binding women into a patriarchy-fueled Catch-22.

In this case, their senator's prediction was prophetic. Congress passed a series of gag rules, tabling all anti-slavery petitions, which only increased petitioners' resolve to send more of them. [32] Anti-slavery advocates found new allies among proponents of free speech and collected more signatures than ever before. Even as Congressmen refused to read the petitions, the quantity of paper arriving in their offices made the message clear. [33]

"Women of Philadelphia!" shouted Angelina Grimké. "Allow me as a Southern woman, with much attachment to the land of my birth, to entreat you to come up to this work. Especially let me urge you to petition. Men may settle this and other questions at the ballot box, but you have no such right; it is only through petitions that you can reach the Legislature. It is therefore peculiarly your duty to petition." [34]

Angelina Grimké and her sister Sarah were transplants from South Carolina who rebelled against their slaveholding upbringing. [35] Growing up, Sarah had been interested in studying law so that she could "be a protector of the helpless and the unfortunate."

"You are a girl," her parents reminded her. Instead of law, they pushed her toward dancing, flirtation and fashion—pastimes that Sarah viewed as frivolous. [36]

As a young adult, Sarah moved to Philadelphia to help her father seek medical care. She never returned to her belle lifestyle, instead finding a home there and converting to Quakerism. The faith was refreshing to Sarah; their doctrinal emphasis on "inner light" encouraged independent thinking, they embraced more egalitarian marriage vows and encouraged both men and women to speak at religious services.

With Sarah gone, Angelina was left in South Carolina without the mentor she had always depended on. As a teenager, Sarah had taken on special responsibility for baby Angelina, who shared both her bedroom and her progressive views, but not her quiet personality. [37]

"It is hard for me to be and do nothing. My restless, ambitious temper, so different from dear sister's, craves high duties and high attainments," wrote Angelina. "I fear I am even proud of my pride." [38]

As a young adult, Angelina sometimes thought about escaping "this land of slavery" like Sarah had, but she hoped to make a difference among her own people. [39] "I feel that I am called with a high and holy calling and that I ought to be peculiar," she wrote in her diary. [40]

She pressured her minister to preach about the evils of slavery. When that didn't work, she approached members of her church individually and tried to convert them to abolitionism one by one. [41] When her family and friends vented about the people they were enslaving, Angelina would ask, "What made them so depraved?" She won no converts, but her efforts were occasionally rewarded with small victories, such as when she convinced her brother to stop beating one of the men he enslaved. [42] Even so, persistent nagging was hardly a strategy for large-scale, systemic change, and 22-year-old Angelina was too principled—and perhaps too immature—to choose her battles.

"It is very hard that I cannot give my children what food I choose or have a room papered, without being found fault with," complained her mother. "I am weary of being continually blamed about everything I do. I wish to be let alone. I see no sin in these things." [43]

Angelina was making a nuisance of herself and her community reciprocated with equal obnoxiousness. A rescue committee from her church came to her home to helpfully inquire about her sanity and question her righteousness. [44]

"They may love me with a feeling of pity but all respect for and confidence in me is destroyed. Such love is calculated to humble rather than gratify me," observed Angelina. [45]

When they finally gave up on saving her, they excommunicated her instead.

After a visit from Sarah, Angelina decided to try the local Quaker church, but it was hardly a refuge from the storm. The local Quaker congregation had only two members, elderly brothers who were not on speaking terms with each other. [46]

The kind of energy needed to rebel against her own family and community on a daily, hourly basis was not sustainable. Within two years of her abolitionist awakening, Angelina "exiled" herself from South Carolina and joined Sarah in Pennsylvania, where she hoped to find strangers who understood her better than her lifetime neighbors.

Angelina thought Northerners would share her passion for abolition, but she encountered only apathy until she joined the Philadelphia Female Anti-Slavery Society about a half-decade later. Like her new neighbors, once she was freed from the daily horrors of witnessing slavery firsthand, Angelina's abolitionism went dormant. [47]

When she finally found her allies, she wrote an *Appeal to the Christian Women of the South*, calling on other Southern women to consider her words "for the sake of former confidence and former friendship." [48] Not too many of her Southern friends actually read her appeal; in her hometown of Charleston, the postmaster burned the copies he found in the mail. The police informed her family that they would arrest Angelina if she ever attempted to visit home. But the appeal was so moving to Northerners that abolitionists from the American Anti-Slavery Society asked Angelina to become an abolitionist agent, although no woman had ever held such a post.

Sarah tried to talk her out of it. It would be hard, she would have no privacy, people would hate her. But Angelina's will was stronger. In the end, Sarah decided to work for the Anti-Slavery Society too, hoping that she could protect her little sister if she stayed with her. [49]

The Anti-Slavery Society originally intended for the Grimké sisters to talk only to women in their homes, but there were too many people interested to contain in someone's parlor. So a friendly minister offered the use of his church, leading to a scandalous rumor that women would give a public lecture—perhaps, even, with men in the audience.

Horrified by the accusation, the sisters almost canceled the engagement, until Theodore Weld, their trainer with the Anti-Slavery Society, persuaded them otherwise. During the meeting, the local minister stayed nearby to play the role of bouncer, ejecting men who tried to listen in.

"How supremely ridiculous!" scoffed Theodore. "To think of a man being shouldered out of a meeting for fear he should hear a woman speak!"

He wasn't the only man who felt that way. Soon, hordes of men started showing up at the Grimkés' speeches. The next time a clergyman offered his services as a bouncer, the sisters refused. After only a few speeches with men in the audience, they had become converted to the "fundamental principle" that women should speak to whomever they please, just as men always had.

Angelina was thrilled when Lucretia Mott followed their lead and gave a political speech to a mixed gender audience. She hoped that they were "only pioneers, going before a host of worthy women" who would break the taboo that silenced them. [50]

But her hope happened to be the deepest fear of many clergymen, who preferred to maintain a male monopoly on moral exhortation. The General Association of Congregational Ministers took a stand against the Grimké sisters, embarking on a campaign to keep the disease of outspokenness from spreading to other women. They barred women from giving speeches at churches, the primary meeting venue of the time, and issued a Pastoral Letter to be read in every congregation. [51]

The Pastoral Letter was a long anti-woman rant, calling parishioners' attention to dangers threatening "the female character with widespread and permanent injury." The female character, as far as these male ministers understood it, was dependent and weak, but when a woman becomes a public lecturer, "her character becomes unnatural," or in other words, independent and strong. [52]

That didn't sound like such a bad thing to a teenager named Lucy Stone, who endured a reading of the Pastoral Letter at her own local church. [53] But just in case the ladies were confused, the ministers helpfully continued on, invoking the venerable tradition of comparing women to inanimate objects to put them in their place: "If the vine, whose strength and beauty is to lean upon the trelliswork... thinks to assume the independence and the overshadowing nature of the elm, it will not only cease to bear fruit, but fall in shame and dishonor into the dust." [54]

Lucy was indignant; she had no intention of spending her life leaning like a pretty little vine. [55] (The phrase "lean in" had no feminist connotations 176 years before Sheryl Sandberg wrote her book. [56]) Lucy's cousin, unlucky enough to be seated beside Lucy at church that day, bore the brunt of her wrath. Lucy jabbed her and nudged her to attention as each offensive phrase was read, leaving her physically bruised.

"If I ever had anything to say in public, I should say it," young Lucy vowed indignantly, "And all the more because of that Pastoral Letter." [57]

For every woman who is motivated to feminist action by a showy patriarchal shutdown, there are other women who respond by supporting the patriarchy as co-conspirators in their own oppression. This time, it was a prominent opinion leader among American women named Catharine Beecher who heeded the call. She published a patronizing open letter to Angelina that raised questions about the appropriate "times, place and manner" for women to exert their influence. It took Catharine 152 pages to explain, but her answers can be summarized thus: almost never, hardly anywhere and not by any means that might possibly effect policy change. [58]

As made evident by her methods—most people would send letters privately by mail instead of publishing them in book form—Catharine happened to be an activist herself. To protest Andrew Jackson's Indian Removal Act, Catharine had organized the first nationwide petition drive by American women. Her bold activism was tempered by her apologetic wording; her petition acknowledged herself to be guilty of "presumptuous interference...wholly unbecoming the character of American females." [59] In some ways, Catharine Beecher was like the Phyllis Schlafly of her time—she loved women's pedestal and scorned female efforts outside the domestic sphere, all the while hopping off that pedestal herself to traverse the public sphere when she felt the need to spread her views. [60]

Angelina admired Catharine; she had signed that petition and had even considered attending Catharine's school at one point. [61] But she wasn't intimidated by her. "Whatever is morally right for a man to do, it is morally right for a woman to do," retorted Angelina. [62]

Sarah and Angelina adopted this motto as a sort of battle cry. Sarah even started writing it in all caps, which apparently was a thing even back then, and just as ineffective as it is today. [63]

Sarah expanded on this theme in her own series of open letters, which enumerated injustices toward women in cultures across the world and made a biblical argument for women's equality, including a sentence-by-sentence rebuttal to the Pastoral Letter. Her letters were later collated and published as the first book about feminism by an American woman. [64]

Their abolitionist mentor, Theodore Weld, was horrified by Sarah's feminist essays. As long as the sisters weren't expressing their feminism in words, there was a certain degree of plausible deniability about their actions; the group that hosted Angelina and Sarah only two days before the Pastoral Letter was released responded with a statement asserting that the Grimkés' lectures had been "designed for the ladies" and they should not be blamed because men happened to show up. [65] Theodore himself liked to excuse the sisters' tendency to speak to mixed audiences as a religious idiosyncrasy to be tolerated. Quakers were just like that. [66]

Angelina and Sarah wanted no excuses. They were breaking taboos on principle. Never one to shy from conflict, Angelina rejoiced in the controversy. "We have given great offense on account of our womanhood, which seems to be as objectionable as our abolitionism. The whole land seems aroused to discussion on the province of woman and I am glad of it. We are willing to bear the brunt of the storm, if we can only be the means of making a break in that wall of public opinion which lies right in the way of woman's rights, true dignity, honor and usefulness." [67]

But she didn't want the storm to come from Theodore, who had become something more than a friend. A book-length public rebuke from someone as "absurd" as Catharine Beecher was one thing, but 10 pages of private condemnation from her boyfriend was quite another.

Breaking the taboo against women speakers was actually quite simple, Theodore mansplained in his letters, although he had never actually tried to do it himself.

> Now, if instead of blowing a blast through the newspapers, sounding the onset, and summoning the ministers and churches to surrender, you had without any introductory flourish just gone right among them and lectured, when and where and as you could find opportunity, and paid no attention to criticism, but pushed right on, without making any ado about "attacks," and "invasions," and "opposition," and have let the barkers bark their bark out, within one year you might have practically brought over five hundred thousand persons of the very moral elite of New England. You may rely upon it.

How could the sisters have failed to come up with such a brilliant plan on their own? Theodore had some thoughts about that too:

You are both liable, it seems to me, from your structure of mind, to form your opinions upon too slight data, and too narrow a range of induction. …Both of you, but especially Angelina, unless I greatly mistake, are constitutionally tempted to push for present effect, and upon the suddenness and impulsiveness of the onset rely mainly for victory. Besides, from her strong resistiveness and constitutional obstinacy, she is liable every moment to turn short from the main point and spend her whole force upon some little one-side annoyance that might temporarily nettle her. In doing this she might win a single battle, but lose a whole campaign.

Most affectionately, your brother ever,

T.D. Weld.

For some reason, Angelina seemed offended by Theodore's affectionate epistles.

"Angelina is so wrathy that I think it will be unsafe to trust the pen in her hands to reply to thy two last good long letters," replied Sarah, who proceeded to educate her younger sister's beau on the evils of patriarchy with the patience of a schoolteacher instructing a slow but well-intentioned pupil.

I know the opposition to our views arises in part from the fact that women are habitually regarded as inferior beings, but chiefly I believe from a desire to keep them in unholy subjection to man, and one way of doing this is to deprive us of the means of becoming their equals by forbidding us the privileges of education which would fit us for the performance of duty. I am greatly mistaken if most men have not a desire that women should be silly.

She had to cut the lesson short when Angelina demanded the pen.

"I have not said half I wanted, but this must suffice for the present, as Angelina has concluded to try her hand at scolding," wrote Sarah before she passed off the partially written letter to her sister.

Despite her use of Quaker niceties like "thee" and "brother," Angelina proved herself quite proficient in scolding. "Sister seems very much afraid that my pen will be transformed into a venomous serpent when I employ it to address thee, my dear brother, and no wonder, for I like to pay my debts, and, as I received ten dollars' worth of scolding, I should be guilty of injustice did I not return the favor," she began. "Well! Such a lecture I never before had from anyone. What is the matter with thee?" [68]

Angelina got to the point:

Can you not see that women could do and would do a hundred times more for the slave if she were not fettered?" she asked. "If we surrender the right to speak to the public this year, we must surrender the right to petition the next year and the right to write the year after and so on.

What then can women do for the slave when she is herself under the feet of man and shamed into silence? [69]

Frustrated by opposition to women speaking in public, as well as by the futility of persuading women to sign abolition petitions who didn't dare do so without male permission, Sarah and Angelina sought to inject the abolition movement with a strong dose of feminism. [70]

At a national meeting for female abolitionists, Angelina proposed a new resolution for their platform, expanding their mission to encompass women's rights. The resolution passed, but some women were so offended by it that they took the unusual step of requesting that their names be formally recorded as having voted, "Nay." [71]

Philadelphia abolitionists and other reformers banded together to build a venue for their events called Pennsylvania Hall. According to Pennsylvania Hall Management Association records, a majority of the shareholders were "working men, and as is the case in almost every other good work," they interjected pointedly, "a number are females." [72] The Philadelphia Female Anti-Slavery Society was among the shareholders of the project and they held a convention there only a few days after its grand opening. [73]

On the same day that Pennsylvania Hall opened, Angelina and Theodore were married. Many of their wedding guests were black, which was unusual for a wedding of two white people at the time, and a rumor spread that Angelina had married a black man. Racist sentiment abounded around interracial marriage. When Harriet arrived with her husband Robert at the Hall's grand opening, onlookers became agitated by the sight of these two fair-skinned people of color. Was it possible that one of them was white and the other black? [74] Black and white women came in and out of the Hall with their arms linked together, perhaps as a sign of solidarity, perhaps as a safety measure, and one reporter wrote that "no doubt" those women were discussing their hopes of becoming sisters-in-law.

An anonymous group posted placards throughout Philadelphia, ironically urging all "who entertain a proper respect for the right of property and the preservation of the Constitution" to gather together to destroy the abolitionists' property and interfere with their constitutional rights of speech and assembly.

More than three thousand people came to hear Angelina speak at the Philadelphia Female Anti-Slavery Society's convention at Pennsylvania Hall. Both men and women crowded in, so Lucretia had to give a disclaimer on behalf of their National Women's Anti-Slavery Society affiliate, which did not sanction the scandalous practice of women giving speeches to men. She added, probably with an eye-roll, that "such false notions of delicacy and propriety would not long obtain in this enlightened country."

It soon became apparent that the country was not quite as enlightened as Lucretia would hope, because during Angelina's speech, a mob gathered outside the Hall, throwing rocks and shattering windows. Undaunted, Angelina shouted,

"What is a mob? What would the breaking of every window be? What would the leveling of this Hall be?"

She would soon find out.

The next day the Society convened again, but so did the ever-growing mob. By the time 15,000 people swarmed outside the Hall, the mayor, John Swift, convinced members of the Society to adjourn early for their own protection, promising that he would calm the mob as soon as the women had left.

The mayor did address the mob, but his words were no deterrent. After assuring the mob that the building had been evacuated and no one would summon the police, the mayor added, "I look upon you as my police and I trust you will abide by the laws and keep order." [75]

The mob loved this plan and cheered for Mayor Swift before they broke into the building and started destroying the furniture inside: a waste of time, since they soon set the whole building on fire. [76] Firefighters saved the surrounding buildings, but didn't even try to stop Pennsylvania Hall from burning.

After burning down the hall, they headed over to Lucretia's house, but in the end kindly decided not to burn down her home because Lucretia and the other residents refused to evacuate. Instead, they attacked an orphanage and then a church, both of which served black people. [77]

Before the next annual meeting of the Philadelphia Female Anti-Slavery Society, Mayor Swift called on Lucretia to discuss precautions they might take to avoid a repeat of last year's riots.

"Will the convention be confined to women?" he asked hopefully.

The delegates would be women.

"Just white women, or white and colored?"

The meeting would be racially integrated, so the mayor told Lucretia that attendees should not meet in the evening and should avoid unnecessary walking with colored people.

"We should not be likely to have evening meetings, for, to the shame of Philadelphia be it spoken, the only building we could procure of sufficient size has but a barn roof, is without a ceiling, and could not, therefore, easily be lighted for such a meeting," responded Lucretia. If only Philadelphia Hall were still standing!

Lucretia would not consider the mayor's other request. "We shall do as we have done before—walk with colored people as occasion offers. It is a principle with us, which we cannot yield, to make no distinction on account of color. I am expecting delegates from Boston of that complexion and will probably accompany them to the place of meeting." [78]

Inspired by the Grimké sisters and other female abolitionists, Lucy Stone decided to become an abolitionist herself. She wanted to prepare by seeking a college education. Her choice of schools was easy; only one college in the nation, Oberlin in Ohio, allowed women to attend. She would need to raise the funds herself because her father thought that educating a woman would be a bad investment. [79]

Unfortunately, he had a point. Women still struggle to pay back student loans on the measly 80¢ a woman can expect to earn for every dollar earned by a man— even less for a woman of color. [80] In the 1840s, the wage gap was more of a wage gorge. Lucy was offered a teaching job at a nearby town after a male teacher was fired, earning less than half of the salary of her incompetent predecessor. Much of that went toward helping to support her parents' household—including paying for the college educations of her brothers. After nearly a decade of saving, at the age of 25, she finally set off for college herself.

Oberlin was progressive for its time, but not enough so for Lucy, who quickly earned a reputation for herself. One man warned a new Oberlin student about Lucy Stone, describing her as "a young woman of strange and dangerous opinions...always talking about women's rights." He finished this frightening bio with a word of advice: "You'd better have nothing to do with her." [81]

That new student, Antoinette Brown, explained how this advice affected her: "Of course, she became the one person whose acquaintance I most desired to make." [82]

Lucy and Nette, as her friends called her, enrolled in the same public speaking course, where both were dismayed to find that women were expected to learn public speaking by silently listening to their male classmates. [83] They took matters into their own hands, organizing a "Ladies Literary Society" that met regularly to practice public speaking and debate. To prevent scholastic discipline, Society members met secretly at the home of a black woman, far from campus. They were careful to arrive separately so as not to attract attention.

Their nemesis was the Oberlin Ladies Board, a group of professors' wives assigned to supervise female students. With rebellious snark, Nette claimed that she actually enjoyed being called before the Ladies Board for disciplinary hearings, as it gave her an opportunity to air her views. [84]

At one point, Lucy and Nette managed to convince their professor to allow them to debate each other in class. In their own opinions, at least, the debate was brilliant, but the Ladies Board made sure nothing like that ever happened again. [85]

When it came time for commencement, Lucy was one of several students chosen to speak, sort of. Oberlin asked female students to write speeches to be read aloud by a man on their behalf. Lucy unsuccessfully petitioned the faculty and the Ladies Board to allow her to give her own speech. When that failed, she declined the honor. [86]

After graduation, Lucy marched down the path forged for female abolitionists by Angelina and Sarah, securing her dream job as an itinerant speaker for the Anti-Slavery Society. As she worked, scripture was regularly used against her, both by quotation and by hurling the holy books at her head. Launched rebuttals took other forms as well, such as eggs, dead fish and tobacco spit.

Lucy's feminism sometimes crowded out abolition in her speeches, leading to a rebuke from her employer. "The people came to hear anti-slavery, not women's rights," he said.

"I was a woman before I was an abolitionist," answered Lucy. "I must speak for the women."

That was certainly the case, but her employer had a valid point; she was getting paid to talk about abolition, not women's rights. Eventually, the two worked out a compromise. Lucy worked for the anti-slavery society on weekends only and spoke about women's rights at her own expense on weekdays. [87] At first, Lucy was reluctant to charge a fee because she was afraid it would prevent people from attending, but she soon found that between those who were sincerely interested and those too curious to miss a shocking spectacle of female impropriety, she rarely lacked an audience. [88] Reform became surprisingly profitable to Lucy, a fact of which her detractors cynically took note. [89]

A few years later, Nette also joined the lecture circuit as a temperance advocate. [90] Modern Americans, with our twenty-twenty hindsight vision of how well prohibition worked out, tend to wave off the temperance movement as unworthy of our collective memory. However, at a time when the wives and daughters of alcoholics had little recourse, many suffragists saw temperance as crucial to the cause of women's rights.

But not every temperance advocate reciprocated.

"I am reminded that in this temperance gathering, temperance is to be discussed in its length and breadth—nothing else and nothing more, not a word about Woman and her rights…although the world does disfranchise one half of its inhabitants…and although the other half have contributed to leave a [liquor] license to exist in almost the entire world," Nette scoffed at one particular temperance association meeting. "Not a word about the right of Woman to prevent an intemperate husband from taking her earnings and spending them for his grog bills and his legal right to do this. …What can all this have to do with the temperance cause?" [91]

A planning meeting for the World Temperance Convention was thrown into a tumult when someone nominated Susan B. Anthony for the business committee. Thomas Wentworth Higginson further baited the indignant men by moving that he step down from the committee so Lucy Stone could take his place. Attendees resolved the conflict by voting to eject women from the proceedings altogether.

"Think of it," gasped Lucy. "A World's Convention in which woman is voted not of the world!" [92]

The women and their male allies dubbed it the "Half World's Temperance Convention" since it would exclude the female half of the world population. They announced that they would host their own "Whole World's Temperance Convention" in protest. [93]

Organizers of the Half World's Temperance Convention backtracked. "Who has said a word about…excluding women from the Convention?" they asked, but they made no promises. The convention would "probably" allow participants of all demographics, they assured the public. [94]

Not feeling reassured, women's rights activists went ahead with their plan. "This is not a woman's rights convention," Thomas clarified in his opening remarks, but it would be "a convention in which woman is not wronged." [95]

When the so-called Half World's Temperance Convention convened a few days later, its organizers insisted that the Whole World's Temperance Convention had been a wasted exercise, protesting a nonexistent issue. If the women had attended their convention instead of going off and doing their own thing, they would have been "received without a doubt." Sure, that planning meeting had been something of a mess, but that was just "a preliminary gathering and its decisions were of no authority in the convention proper." And really, shame on those women for being so "unjust in saying that the men would not accept their cooperation before the question had been fairly tested."

But there was still time to test the question and Nette decided to do just that. [96] She arrived at the Half World's Convention shortly after hearing word of this apparent change of heart. The results were mixed; they let her in but forced her out as soon as she tried to speak.

She came back again the next day, determined to finish her remarks, but the other convention goers threw a collective tizzy fit. It started with a minister who was close enough to wag his finger in her face as he interrupted her to scream, "Shame on the woman!" He started shouting and stamping his feet to prevent her from being heard and others joined in, pounding their canes into the dirt and raising up a cloud of dust. [97]

The presiding officer tried to calm the crowd, but whenever Nette attempted to speak, someone would interrupt with a "point of order" of some sort and the rioting would begin again.

"Gentlemen," cried one exasperated delegate, using the term "gentlemen" very broadly to include these hooligans. "There can be no order when you are raising so many points of order. Take your seats!" [98]

A bewildered member of the audience pointed at the raging temperance advocates on the platform and asked, "Are those men drunk?" [99]

Nette stood her ground, or rather, sat her ground, because eventually someone offered her a chair. It was no use. [100]

Finally, Nette left and went to the Woman's Rights Convention, which was also in progress. The World's Fair was underway in New York and several reformers had scheduled their conventions to coincide with the festivities, hoping to take advantage of the crowds.

The crowds were certainly present, but not necessarily sympathetic. The Woman's Rights Convention had earned itself its own nickname—the Mob

Convention—due to the crowds of rowdy men who showed up to protest the proceedings. [101]

Lucy wooed the mob, praising women who take on traditional roles in the home before she moved on to talk about professional women. That was when the men started hissing.

Nette took a different approach, using her turn at the podium to call out the hecklers as "genuine bigots." They may or may not have actually heard the insult over their own cacophony. Still, Nette reserved her harshest criticism for "the most hopeless and spiteful" opponents of women's rights: "that large class of women whose merits are not their own; who have acquired some influence in society...by the accident of having fathers, brothers, or husbands."

Take that, Oberlin Ladies Board.

Lucretia was presiding over the convention and for the most part, benevolently tolerated the mob. She even let one of the men take the stand, because he desperately wanted "to show that there is at least one person to protest against the inalienable rights which [women] lay claim to" and apparently, the loud crowd of men drowning out the speakers had not accomplished that objective to his satisfaction. He took the stage and droned on until Lucretia interrupted to announce that the time for that session had elapsed.

"I am sorry we cannot satisfy the gentleman by answering his objections as intelligently (to his mind) as he seems to think he has stated them," she remarked as she closed the meeting. "However, perhaps even our dullness may be turned into an argument to give us the liberty we demand; because if we received that liberty, it is possible we might use it in such a way as, after due time, to be able to answer so learned an opponent as he is." [102]

At last, the women summoned the police to control the mob and the Woman's Rights Convention adjourned early. [103] On the bright side, the throngs of hecklers had paid admission to get in, so convention organizers enjoyed an unexpected fiscal surplus. [104]

A male ally tried to escort Lucretia through the rowdy crowd of protesters as they left, but she suggested that he help more "timid" people instead.

"But who will take care of you?" he asked.

"This man," she replied, and took the arm of a particularly vocal protester. He was startled but complied, and while he may have thought he was protecting an old lady, Lucretia managed to occupy him so he couldn't harass any of the other suffragists. [105]

While reports of the Woman's Rights Convention were mixed, depending largely on the reporter's attitude toward women's rights, coverage of the Half World's Temperance Convention was almost universally scathing. [106] Horace Greeley's summary in the *New York Tribune* was particularly fun:

> First Day—Crowding a woman off the platform.
> Second Day—Gagging her.

Third Day—Voting that she shall stay gagged. Having thus disposed of the main question, we presume the incidentals will be finished this morning. [107]

The press coverage proved to be "a most unexpected advertisement" for Nette. She found herself inundated with invitations for speaking engagements, many at "the highest lecture course prices." [108] Moreover, bad publicity proved to be a better motivator than ethics and reason to the pious gentlemen of the Temperance Society, who were more eager to integrate women into temperance activism going forward. [109]

Nette, on the other hand, was feeling less inclined to continue working with the temperance society after such treatment and refocused her efforts on "womanhood and its dawning uplift." [110]

Few Americans today would argue that women have no right to give speeches to men. Our predecessors already fought and won that particular battle. Yet speaking out is still challenging for women. Often, women simply aren't at the table. A century after winning the right to vote, American women still hold fewer than a quarter of the seats in Congress and no woman has ever become president of the United States. [111]

Women continue to be underrepresented within many businesses and professions. [112] Many religious congregations ban women from leadership roles altogether.

When women are present, bias may prevent people from listening to them. Women tend to stay quiet when outnumbered by men—which they often are in male-dominated avenues of life—and yet, they are perceived as talking too much, even when they speak less than their male peers. Women experience more tone critiques, backlash and interruptions than men. [113] Even female Supreme Court justices, arguably the most powerful women in the nation, are interrupted in the courtroom three times as often as their male colleagues. [114]

Suffragists didn't wait for invitations. Whether welcome or not, they inserted themselves into male-dominated spaces. They also created their own female spaces where they could work in their own way, avoiding both the sexist and racist pitfalls of their male counterparts.

Still, we can't assume that women will support feminism, just because they are women. Patriarchy isn't men; it's a system of power in which both men and women participate. Suffragists had to educate their peers in female anti-slavery societies about why they needed feminism to accomplish their other goals, and we need to do the same throughout our own modern endeavors. Likewise, modern feminist movements will not reach their full potential without diversity, and diversity cannot be achieved if feminist goals fail to reach beyond the needs of white, middle class women.

As we grapple with our own modern censorship problems, we can take comfort knowing that censorship backfires. Public indignation at Lucy Stone's speeches drove more people to attend, a Congressional petition ban motivated new people to sign, and the Temperance Society's bad behavior eventually proved embarrassing enough to drive change. The norms that continue to prevent women's voices from being heard—the prevalence of sexist tone critiques, male-dominated professional spheres, and patriarchal religious traditions—will eventually change if we persist.

Unless we don't want to persist. Maria W. Stewart did some great work in her three years of activism, and then she moved on, leaving those who followed her to finish the job. That's okay. But if I ever make an exit, I'd like to make it a grand exit, like Maria did. Never waste an opportunity to make yourself heard.

CHAPTER TWO
What is men's role in a feminist movement?

"All I ask of our brethren is that they will take their feet from our necks and permit us to stand on the ground which God has designed us to occupy." [1]
–Sarah Grimké, 1838

"The speedy success of our cause depends upon the zealous and untiring efforts of both men and women." [2]
–Lucretia Mott, 1848

"Woman herself must do this work; for woman alone can understand the height and the depth, the length and the breadth of her own degradation and woe." [3]
–Elizabeth Cady Stanton, 1848

"This is, in our opinion, an uncalled for interference, though made with holiest intentions," declared William Lloyd Garrison, when he learned that hundreds of Pennsylvania women had signed a petition in protest of the Indian Removal Act. "We should be sorry to have this practice become general. There would then be no question agitated in Congress without eliciting the informal and contrarian opinions of the softer sex." [4]

William wasn't usually afraid of contrarian opinions. He himself had just been released from jail after angering a slave dealer who accused him of libel and inciting slave rebellion. Fortunately, after six weeks of his six-month sentence, the wealthy philanthropist Arthur Tappan intervened and William was released. [5]

Now free, he was about to meet one of these contrarian Pennsylvania women. William wanted to start an abolitionist newspaper and was looking for financial support. His former employer pointed him to Lucretia and James Mott, knowing they would share his radical vision.

Eager to help, the Motts arranged a public meeting for William in Philadelphia, but the young man who had so impressed them in private conversation gave a less than stirring public speech, his eyes pointed down at a paper that he read word for word.

Lucretia took William aside and gave him some tips. "William, if thee expects to set forth thy cause by word of mouth, thee must lay aside thy paper and trust to the leading of the spirit."

And thus began a mentorship that would continue for decades. [6]

"It is proper to state that the address of Mrs. Stewart, in our Ladies' Department today, is published at her own request and not by desire of the Society before whom it was delivered," wrote William in his newspaper, the *Liberator*. Maria W. Stewart's words had not been well received by her audience and William felt the need to clarify how to read them. That wasn't necessary for men, who were expected to give fiery speeches. "Mrs. Stewart uses very plain, some may call it severe language but we are satisfied she is actuated by good motives, and that her only aim is to rouse a spirit of virtuous emulation in the breasts of her associates, and to elevate the whole colored population." [7]

Women's writings were siloed into the "Ladies Department" section of the *Liberator*. Perhaps it hadn't occurred to William yet that female wisdom could inhabit the front page. On the other hand, many papers of the day contained virtually no writing by women. Having a Ladies Department made it clear that the *Liberator* expected and wanted women to submit. [8]

"Two capital errors have extensively prevailed greatly to the detriment of the cause of abolition. The first is a proneness on the part of the advocates of immediate and universal emancipation to overlook or depreciate the value of woman in the promotion of this cause; and the other is a similar disposition on the part of the females in our land to undervalue their own power, or through a misconception of duty, to excuse themselves from engaging in the enterprise," William wrote. During the two years since he started working with women like Lucretia and Maria, William's attitude toward the so-called "softer sex" had changed. [9]

"Now I will tell you why I write you and the object is this: I wish to know your opinion respecting changing white scholars for colored ones," a Connecticut school principal, Prudence Crandall, wrote to William.

> I have been for some months past determined if possible during the remaining part of my life to benefit the people of color. I do not dare tell any one of my neighbors anything about the contemplated change in my school and I beg of you, sir, that you will not expose it to any one; for if it was known, I have no reason to expect but it would ruin my present school. Will you be so kind as to write by the next mail and give me your opinion on the subject? [10]

Prudence had reason to be secretive. Just two years before, Arthur Tappan had bought land in New Haven, Connecticut with the intention of starting a college for black men. Protests by local residents, the mayor, and officials of Yale University—to which Arthur was an important donor—killed the project before a single brick could be laid. [11]

Prudence Crandall had been the principal of a secondary school for girls in Canterbury, Connecticut for three years. She resided at the school, along with the school's housekeeper, a black woman named Mariah Davis whose soon-to-be father-in-law was a local agent for the *Liberator*. [12]

Deeply moved by the stories she read in Mariah's copies of the *Liberator*, Prudence felt that she had to do something for the black race. "As wealth was not mine, I saw no other means of benefiting them than by imparting to those of my own sex that were anxious to learn all the instruction I might be able to give, however small the amount," she said. [13]

There was one particular girl that Prudence had in mind. Mariah's fiancé would often stop by with his 17-year-old sister, Sarah Harris. [14] Sarah had attended the same elementary school as most of Prudence's white students, where she had been an intelligent and well-behaved student. [15]

As Prudence explained to her angry neighbors, the idea to enroll Sarah at her school had come about through Sarah's initiative.

"Miss Crandall," said Sarah. "I want to get a little more learning, enough if possible to teach colored children, and if you will admit me to your school, I shall forever be under the greatest obligation to you. If you think it will be the means of injuring you, I will not insist on the favor."

Prudence took some time to think about it, because she thought some of her white students might be upset about racially integrating the school, but Sarah had such a thirst for learning that Prudence couldn't say no.

"If I am injured on your account I will bear it," Prudence eventually told Sarah. "You might enter as one of my pupils."

One of Sarah's friends described the conversation differently. She said that Miss Crandall asked Sarah about her education, and after Sarah admitted she had but little, Miss Crandall urged Sarah to attend her school, assuring her that if she did, in about a year or so she would be qualified to teach school herself. [16]

To Prudence's relief, her students were welcoming when Sarah enrolled. Their parents, on the other hand, were not. [17] Several removed their daughters from the school. [18] A group of neighbors made a formal complaint, led by a lawyer named Andrew Judson, who also happened to be Prudence's next-door neighbor. [19]

"If you continue with that colored girl in your school it will not be sustained," the wife of the local clergyman warned Prudence. [20]

"It might sink then for I shall not turn her out," Prudence replied. [21]

It was sinking. Prudence pivoted. Instead of racially integrating her school, she would teach black girls only. After writing to William Lloyd Garrison, she traveled to Boston to discuss her plan in person. He was impressed. "She is a wonderful woman, as undaunted as if she had the whole world on her side," he told his friends. [22] He introduced her to some black families with daughters and referred her to contacts in Providence and New York who could help her find other students. Within three weeks' time, she had visited those cities as well. [23]

Her neighbors didn't find out about the school's new direction until an advertisement appeared in the *Liberator*.

> Prudence Crandall, Principal of the Canterbury (Connecticut) Female Boarding School, returns her most sincere thanks to those who have patronized her school, and would give information that the first Monday of April next, her school will be opened for the reception of young ladies and little misses of color.

After more details about facilities and courses, the ad was signed by an impressively long list of abolitionists who supported the effort, such as William Lloyd Garrison, James Forten and Arthur Tappan. Some were black, some were white—all were male. Most were from out-of-state, but three were from Connecticut, including Reverend Samuel J. May. [24]

"It hath been publicly announced that a school is to be opened in this town, on the first Monday of April next, using the language of the advertisement, "for young ladies and little misses of color," or in other words for the people of color, the obvious tendency of which would be to collect within the town of Canterbury large numbers of persons from other states whose characters and habits might be various and unknown to us, thereby rendering insecure the persons, property and reputations of our citizens," announced Prudence's neighbors.

> Under such circumstances, our silence might be construed into an approbation of the project: Thereupon, resolved: That the locality of a school for the people of color at any place within the limits of this town, for the admission of persons of foreign jurisdiction, meets with our unqualified disapprobation, and it is to be understood that the inhabitants of Canterbury protest against it in the most earnest manner.

The neighbors appointed a committee of four male residents to call on Prudence and reason with her, but she was difficult. When they asked her what she would do with the girls on Sundays, she couldn't understand why her new students couldn't simply go to church, sitting in the same pews her former students used to occupy. When they shared their concerns about the potential for intermarriage, she replied, "Moses had a black wife." [25]

The committee assured Prudence that they felt a "real regard for the colored people and were perfectly willing they should be educated, provided it could be effected in some other place."

"Although distracted with cares, I must seize my pen to express my admiration of your prompt and generous defense of Miss Crandall from her pitiful assailants," William Lloyd Garrison wrote to his friend, George Benson. George was on his way to Canterbury to speak on behalf of Prudence Crandall's school at their next town meeting.

In view of their outrageous conduct, my indignation kindles intensely. What will be the result? If possible, Miss Crandall must be sustained at all hazards. If we suffer the school to be put down in Canterbury, other places will partake of the panic and also prevent its introduction in their vicinity. ...The New Haven excitement has furnished a bad precedent; a second must not be given. [26]

As a woman, Prudence would not be allowed to testify on her own behalf. In addition to George, Samuel May and Arnold Buffum, an agent of the New England Anti-Slavery Society, offered to speak for her, and Prudence wrote a letter in her own defense, explaining her motivations in pious yet militant terms.

What shall I do? Shall I be inactive and permit prejudice, the mother of abominations, to remain undisturbed? Or should I venture to enlist into the rank of those who with the sword of truth dare hold combat with prevailing iniquity? [27]

Prudence's allies came prepared with a compromise. Prudence was willing to move her school to a less central part of the city, if the town was willing to take her current building off her hands. [28] Living somewhere else would be nicer anyway, because she wouldn't have to live next-door to Andrew Judson any more. [29]

At the meeting, whenever one of Prudence's advocates tried to speak, someone interrupted. As "foreigners" to the town they were refused the floor. [30] When they tried to deliver Prudence's letter, Andrew and some other men sprang to their feet with their fists clenched. After the opponents of the school presented their case, the council abruptly closed the meeting without hearing anyone from Prudence's side. [31]

Samuel tried to get people's attention as they left the hall. "Men of Canterbury, I have a word for you! Hear me!" As they filed past him toward the doors, he tried to tell them that Prudence was willing to move out of the house.

"Mr. May," said Andrew. "We are not merely opposed to the establishment of that school in Canterbury; we mean there shall not be such a school set up anywhere in our state." [32]

William printed scathing coverage of the meeting in the Liberator, prompting a concerned letter from Prudence. What he said about her neighbors was true, but she was the one who needed to live among them, and soon, she would be responsible for protecting a house full of minors.

Permit me to entreat you to handle the prejudices of the people of Canterbury with all the mildness possible, as everything severe tends merely to heighten the flame of malignity amongst them. "Soft words turn away wrath, but grievous words stir up anger." Mr. May and many others of your warmhearted friends feel very much on this subject, and it is our opinion that you and the cause will gain many friends in this town and vicinity if you treat the matter with perfect mildness. [33]

On the first day of the new semester, about 20 black teenage girls arrived from four different states. [34] Canterbury town people welcomed them by filling their well with manure. Shopkeepers refused to serve Prudence or her students. Stagecoach drivers wouldn't allow them to ride. Once, Prudence summoned a doctor to see a sick student. The doctor came, but warned her that he would not respond to calls going forward. The pharmacist would not sell her medicine. Vandals broke windows and started fires. With the well out of service, Prudence's father had to send in water daily from his farm outside of town, and townspeople started threatening him, too.

Oddly, William Lloyd Garrison's response was to urge black families to send more minor girls into this situation. He was determined to keep the school in business "until the heathenish opposers repent of their barbarity."

Looking for some legal ground to stand on, town officials fined students under an archaic vagrancy law, arguing that the young people didn't have homes in town, technically. The punishment for nonpayment was a whipping on the naked body not to exceed ten stripes. Town officials issued a warrant against 17-year-old Eliza Ann Hammond and threatened to follow through with the whipping, but Samuel May raised funds from members of his parish to pay the fines. [35]

The school's opponents didn't have to rely on the vagrancy law for long. Canterbury citizens successfully lobbied the Connecticut Legislature for a new law aimed directly at Prudence Crandall. The "Black Law" forbade anyone from establishing "any school, academy or literary institution for the instruction or education of colored persons who are not inhabitants of this state" without written approval from the local government. [36]

Prudence was arrested. The sheriff contacted George Benson and Samuel May, hoping that the abolitionists would fund her bail. They did, but not until after she had spent a night in jail, allowing the *Liberator* to print this headline:

> Savage Barbarity! Miss Crandall Imprisoned!!! The persecutors of Miss Crandall have placed an indelible seal upon their infamy! They have cast her into prison! Yes, into the very cell occupied by WATKINS the MURDERER!! [37]

As Prudence awaited trial, the *Liberator* published an influx of letters and articles from Prudence's young students.

"The Canterburians are savage—they will not sell Crandall an article at their shops," wrote one student.

> My ride from Hartford to Brooklyn was very unpleasant, being made up of blackguards. I came on foot here from Brooklyn. But the happiness here pays me for all. The place is delightful; all that is wanting to complete the scene is civilized men. Last evening the news reached us that the new law had passed. The bell rang; cannon was fired for half an hour. Where is justice? In all of this Miss Crandall is unmoved. When we walk out, horns are blown and pistols fired. [38]

In the midst of the publicity, Samuel May received a letter from Arthur Tappan in New York.

> I am aware, Sir, that you can ill afford to bear the expense of the contest you have dared. In this respect I am happily able to help you, and shall consider it a duty and a privilege to do so. I wish you to consider me your banker, assured that I will honor promptly your drafts. Keep your accounts carefully and let me know whenever you need any money. Spare no necessary expense; employ the best legal counsel; and let this legal question be fully tried, not doubting that under the good providence of a righteous God, the truth and right will ultimately prevail.

"Oh, that I could only leave Brooklyn long enough to visit you!" wrote Samuel in one of his letters to Arthur about the progress of the case. "For I could tell you in an hour more things that I wish you to know, than I can write in a week."

To Samuel's surprise, Arthur Tappan himself was at his door a few days later, expecting a verbal report.

After speaking with Samuel, Arthur went to Canterbury to meet Prudence and see the school his dollars were defending.[39]

Things had been rough since the arrest. Someone had thrown a stone through a window, shattering glass into the front parlor. The next morning, a hard object hit the other side of the building. Showers of rotten eggs had become an ongoing menace. [40]

"The cause of the whole oppressed, despised colored population of our country is to be much affected by the decision of this question," Arthur realized.

Arthur decided they needed more than a legal defense; they needed a public relations campaign. "You must issue a newspaper, publish it largely, send it to all persons whom you know in the country and state and to all the principal newspapers throughout the country. Many will subscribe to it and contribute otherwise to its support, and I will pay whatever more it costs," he told Samuel. Before Arthur left town, he set up Samuel with a printing office. [41]

Samuel hired a young local man named Charles Burleigh as a writer. One of the few sympathetic neighbors, he had already been writing articles in support of Prudence and her school and sending them to other local papers. [42]

Not satisfied to prosecute only Prudence, Canterbury citizens sued William Lloyd Garrison for libel and tried to secure a warrant for the arrest of Prudence's younger sister, Almira, who had substituted at the school when Prudence was ill. Since Almira was a minor, they wanted her mother brought in too.

Prudence's legal battle was long, with the first trial yielding a hung jury and the second a conviction that was appealed. At last, the case was thrown out for lack of evidence. [43]

At midnight one September night, shortly after the appeal, Prudence and her students awoke to a crash. Windows all around the house were smashed in at once by a large group of men carrying clubs and iron bars. After discussion with Samuel May, Prudence sent the girls home. [44] After closing the Canterbury Female Boarding School, Prudence left Connecticut with her new husband and never came back.

"I felt ashamed of Connecticut, ashamed of my state, ashamed of my country, ashamed of my color," said Samuel May. [45]

Five of Prudence's students went on to become teachers. [46] Sarah Harris, Prudence's first black student, became an abolitionist. [47]

More than 50 years after the school closed, Andrew Clark, the nephew and namesake of Prudence's former neighbor and adversary, Andrew Judson, lobbied the Connecticut Legislature to provide restitution to 82-year-old Prudence Crandall Philleo for her lost school. The Legislature voted to provide Prudence with an annuity for the remainder of her life. [48]

A year after Prudence closed her school, William received another letter from a female stranger, Angelina Grimké. He published the letter in the *Liberator* along with a disclaimer: "Whether it was sent for our private consolation and encouragement exclusively or whether it is meekly committed to the disposal of our judgment either for general or individual perusal we are not certain." [49]

It was the former. While it had occurred to Angelina that she could be quoted anonymously, she hadn't expected William to publish her letter in full with her name on it. At the time, she had not yet entered the activist arena. The reactions of Angelina's friends brought her "to the brink of despair." [50]

The many lines William dedicated to justifying his decision to print the letter without permission made it clear he was aware that he had crossed a line. Aware, but not sorry.

"We cannot, we dare not, suppress it nor the name of her who indited it," wrote William. "We hope if we startle the diffidence of her who wrote it, that we shall not be guilty of a personal wrong. Surely, if the exigencies of our time require this public testimony, she will most joyfully bear it."

Angelina couldn't argue with that, not after what she had written in that letter. "If persecution is the means which God has ordained for the accomplishment of this great end, emancipation, then in dependence upon him for strength to bear it, I feel as if I could say, 'Let it come,' for it is my deep, solemn, deliberate conviction that this is a cause worth dying for." [51]

Angelina's letter proved prescient. Soon after, William's life was threatened during a meeting of the Boston Female Anti-Slavery Society, where controversial English abolitionist George Thompson was scheduled to give an address. When William arrived, there were about 100 protesters outside, mostly young men. He pushed his way through and took a seat inside with the women. Before the meeting could begin, protesters pushed open the doors, screaming, "Thompson! Thompson!"

He had not arrived. William appointed himself to crowd control.

"Gentlemen, perhaps you are not aware that this is a meeting of the Boston Female Anti-Slavery Society, called and intended exclusively for ladies, and those only who have been invited to address them. Understanding this fact, you will not be so rude and indecorous as to thrust your presence upon this meeting. If, gentlemen, any of you are ladies in disguise, why, only apprise me of the fact, give me your names, and I will introduce you to the rest of your sex and you can take seats among them accordingly," he told them.

With no George Thompson to attack, the crowd redirected their fury toward William. Deferring to the authority of the woman presiding, William asked Mary Parker if he shouldn't retire from the hall—unless she desired him to remain?

Mary desired no such thing. "Go at once, not only for the peace of the meeting but for your own safety."

He soon realized there was no way out. The small group of protesters he had seen before the meeting had grown to thousands, completely surrounding the building, so William locked himself in the anti-slavery office along with Charles Burleigh and sat down to write a letter.

Mary continued with the meeting, opening with prayer for "forgiveness of enemies and revilers."

"If this is the last bulwark of freedom, we may as well die here as anywhere," said Maria Weston Chapman.

Outside, someone near the window screamed, "There he is! That's Garrison! Out with the scoundrel!" The mob pounded the door and boards started to splinter and break.

"You may as well open the door and let them come in and do their worst," William told Charles.

"Out with him! Lynch him!" came another voice.

Charles told William to go through a window in back, but the protesters caught him soon after he opened it and dragged him through the streets by a rope until the authorities wrestled him away from the mob and put him in jail for his own safety.

Always eager to attract publicity for the cause, William got Charles to write up an account of the harrowing ordeal for publication. [52] He also ordered reprints of Angelina's letter, retitled, *Slavery and the Boston Riot*, as if Angelina had written the letter about the riot, not before it happened.

One of the thousands of people who read Angelina's private letter to William was Theodore Weld, as William fondly recalled on Angelina and Theodore's wedding day a few years later, where he claimed credit as a matchmaker. His jovial comments were an unexpected surprise because just days before, William had sat Angelina down for a talk and advised her not to marry someone who was so religious. [53] William was becoming frustrated with evangelical Christian abolitionists, particularly Theodore's friends Arthur and Lewis Tappan.

The Tappan brothers' quest to abolish slavery was fueled by their faith. [54]

"It appears to me that one hundred men even, well-educated, honest, thorough, determined, filled with love and faith, spirited with zeal, could, with the blessing of God, revolutionize a continent," said Lewis Tappan. [55]

William, on the other hand, doubted that patriarchal institutions like churches could ever be mobilized to support the abolition movement. Moreover, when Lewis said one hundred men, he literally meant men, to the exclusion of women. [56]

"Garrison and others have grown lukewarm on the anti-slavery subject and have loaded the cause with their no government/woman's rights/non-resistant and etc.," complained Lewis, after a particularly contentious convention where William had led a campaign to integrate women into the meeting. [57] "Garrison told me two and a half years ago that there were subjects he considered paramount to the anti-slavery cause, to which he meant to devote his attention chiefly. It is a sad mistake to make it instrumental in carrying on other matters." [58]

In Lewis's opinion, William was becoming "grossly intemperate and vituperative," qualities that could only harm the movement.

"Abolitionists! You are now feared and respected by all political parties, not because of the number of votes you can throw, so much as in view of the moral integrity and sacred regard to principle which you have exhibited to the country," William said in a speech, ranting about another patriarchal institution William had lost faith in: the government. "If you shall now array yourselves as a political party, and hold out mercenary rewards to induce men to rally under your standard, there is reason to fear that you will be regarded as those who have made the anti-slavery cause a hobby to ride into office, however plausible or sound may be your pretexts for such a course. You cannot, you ought not, to expect that the political action of the state will move faster than the religious action of the church in favor of the abolition of slavery." [59]

At the convention, Society delegates voted to admit women and take political action. To modern ears, it sounds like the majority made the most rational choices, but both William and Lewis walked away unhappy, each having lost one of the battles they waged.

By the next annual convention, opposing factions came prepared for war. Lewis campaigned in New Jersey, circulating fliers urging supporters to attend the convention and support his platform. Garrisonians, as William's supporters started calling themselves, chartered a steamship that brought in almost 500 delegates from Massachusetts alone, numbers certainly high enough to carry a vote. [60]

Arthur Tappan, the president of the Anti-Slavery Society, didn't arrive at the meeting. He sent a letter.

> Dear Sir:
>
> Apprehending a recurrence of the scenes witnessed last year at our business meetings, and also resolved not to be found contending with my abolition brethren, I shall not be present with you and request that you will communicate to the Society that I do not wish to be considered

a candidate for the office I have hitherto occupied. That God may over rule the machinations of disorganizers among us and save us from the disgrace I apprehend, is the prayer of your friend. [61]

Arthur's absence made vice president Francis Jackson the presiding officer— good news for the Garrisonians. [62] Francis was such a fervent supporter of women's rights that he had written a trust fund for the cause into his will. [63] He nominated Lydia Maria Child to the all-male business committee. As Lydia wasn't present (and was female), Lewis suggested Lydia's husband instead. [64] The nomination went to Abby Kelley, who had become an agent of the American Anti-Slavery Society shortly after giving her first speech in Pennsylvania Hall. [65] Several clergymen protested the nomination of a woman to this leadership position, but 55% of the thousand delegates voted in her favor. [66]

Lewis and two other officers of the Association resigned in protest, leaving the convention and taking several supporters with them. By the next day, they had formed a new organization called the American and Foreign Anti-Slavery Society, with 300 members. Arthur Tappan would be president. [67]

Soon after the Anti-Slavery Society divided, abolitionists in England invited American anti-slavery societies to send delegates to London for a World Anti-Slavery Convention. [68]

When the Englishmen heard that the American Anti-Slavery Society had selected female delegates, they sent clarification: they were seeking "gentlemen" delegates. The women came anyway. [69]

"The 'woman question' will inevitably be brought up," said William, as he traveled to England with other delegates. "It is perhaps quite probable that we shall be foiled in our purpose, but the subject cannot be agitated without doing good." [70]

When Lucretia Mott and other delegates from Pennsylvania arrived in London, Joseph Sturge, the convention organizer, met with the women and begged them not to make a scene about being barred from the proceedings. When they were unable to convince him to change his policy, Sarah Pugh wrote a formal protest on behalf of herself and the other female delegates. [71]

On the first day of the convention, the organizers directed the women to a balcony and seated them behind a bar and a curtain. [72]

One of the rejected delegates, Ann Phillips, passed her husband a note, "Wendell, please do maintain the floor. No matter what they do don't give up your right to." [73]

Wendell Phillips stood and announced that some rightful delegates had been denied their seats. Like the lawyer he was, Wendell laid out his case. The call had invited "friends of the slave" which should "include women as well as men." The delegates in question had made a 4,000 mile journey and it would not be just to exclude them after such a sacrifice. He may have exaggerated a bit with his next argument, that "Massachusetts has for several years acted on the principle of admitting women to an equal seat with men," but it was a lovely aspiration.

"I will only add, if the ladies who have come from America are not deemed entitled, in consequence of the credentials they bear to a place in this assembly, I feel for one that I am not entitled to occupy such a position," said Harvard professor William Adam after Wendell had finished. "My credentials proceed from the same persons, and from the same societies, and bear the same names as theirs."

One delegate, while not wishing to in "the least degree to imply an unfavorable opinion of the conduct, exertions, influence, or power of our female friends in this cause," regretted to inform Wendell that English customs were different than those he had described as commonplace in Massachusetts. Another had "the highest possible regard for the ladies of America and England," but simply hadn't planned on accommodating them and didn't intend to now.

"The reception of my respected female friends as a part of this Convention, would…be not only a violation of your customs, and of the customs of other countries, but of the ordinance of Almighty God," said Henry Grew of Pennsylvania. His words must have grated on the ears of his daughter, Mary Grew, who was one of the female delegates listening to the debate from behind the curtain.

"The American delegation is represented as being one on this subject. It is not so. That brother," said Nathaniel Colver, indicating Wendell, "and others are from a Society which allows of ladies sitting in its meetings; but a large portion of the delegates are from another branch who have resisted this attempt to change the customs of the country and but for the assurance that the Convention would be composed as it now is, a large number of us would not have been here today," said Nathaniel Colver. [74]

The debate lasted most of the day before the men agreed to vote on the question. Ninety percent voted against seating the women.[75]

"I hope that as the question is now decided it will never be again brought forward, and I trust that Mr. Phillips will give us the assurance that we shall proceed with one heart and one mind," said George Thompson.

"I have no doubt of it," replied Wendell. "There is no unpleasant feeling in our minds. I have no doubt that the women will sit with as much interest behind the bar as though the original proposition had been carried in the affirmative. All we asked was an expression of opinion, and having obtained it, we shall now act with the utmost cordiality." [76]

At least one of the women behind the bar, Elizabeth Cady Stanton, would not forgive that last remark. [77]

William Lloyd Garrison and a few other delegates arrived late because of bad weather at sea. [78] At least one of the latecomers, Charles Lenox Remond, was there thanks to women; female anti-slavery societies in Rhode Island and

Maine had funded his voyage. [79] Too late to participate in the debate, they made their point by refusing to join the male delegates in the main hall. They sat in the galleries with the ladies. [80]

Elizabeth was moved by this "silent testimony." [81] Lucretia was exasperated. She urged the men to join the delegation. Trapped as she was behind that stupid curtain, she needed her male allies to defend her agenda. [82]

One of her top priorities, a boycott on goods made by slave labor, failed to win support. Henry Grew wanted the boycott, too, and back in the states, he found himself under fire by other Pennsylvania advocates for costing them critical votes; he should have supported their female representatives. [83]

On principle, Lucretia opposed any action that would enable slaveholders to profit from slavery. No one should buy their goods—nor should they buy the people slaveholders claimed to own. Lucretia protested when British abolitionists purchased the freedom of Frederick Douglass. Awkwardly, shortly after the controversy, Lucretia and Frederick ended up traveling together for a week because of anti-slavery meetings in Ohio but they seemed to get along. [84]

Eight years after Lucretia and Elizabeth met at the World Anti-Slavery Convention in London, the two women, along with Lucretia's sister, Martha Coffin Wright, and Elizabeth's neighbor, Mary Ann McClintock, gathered in Mary Ann's parlor to discuss a radical list of demands for women's rights drafted by Elizabeth. [85]

"Why Lizzie, thee will make us ridiculous," Lucretia Mott told Elizabeth Cady Stanton. [86]

The document, titled the *Declaration of Sentiments*, followed the pattern of the *Declaration of Independence*, with a twist: "We hold these truths to be self-evident; that all men and women are created equal."

The part that offended Lucretia read: "Resolved, that it is the duty of the women of this country to secure to themselves their sacred right to the elective franchise." [87]

The idea that women should vote was new. Most of the feminists Lucretia knew were Garrisonian abolitionists who shared with William his aversion to political action—including voting. [88] Not Elizabeth. She had appreciated William's silent protest during the World Anti-Slavery Convention, but after it ended, she noted, "He opened his mouth and forth came, in my opinion, much folly." [89]

Elizabeth presented her declaration a few days later at the Seneca Falls Convention, the first gathering of its kind devoted solely to women's rights. Most of her resolutions passed unanimously, the demand for suffrage excepted. That resolution may not have passed, had it not been for the support of Frederick Douglass. [90]

After achieving consensus, the group debated about whether the declaration should be signed by women only. As a compromise, men and women signed separate sheets of paper. [91]

In Frederick's coverage of the event in the *North Star*, he hearkened back to when so many men left the American Anti-Slavery Society in protest of Abby Kelley's election.

> Many who have at last made the discovery that the negroes have some rights as well as other members of the human family, have yet to be convinced that women are entitled to any. Eight years ago, a number of persons of this description actually abandoned the anti-slavery cause, lest by giving their influence in that direction they might possibly be giving countenance to the dangerous heresy that woman, in respect to rights, stands on an equal footing with man.
>
> …We hold woman to be justly entitled to all we claim for man. We go further, and express our conviction that all political rights which it is expedient for man to exercise, it is equally so for woman. All that distinguishes man as an intelligent and accountable being, is equally true of woman; and if that government only is just which governs by the free consent of the governed, there can be no reason in the world for denying to woman the exercise of the elective franchise, or a hand in making and administering the laws of the land. Our doctrine is that right is of no sex. [92]

Mobilized by the Seneca Falls convention, women in nearby Rochester, New York held their own convention two weeks later and invited the organizers of the Seneca Falls convention to attend. Amy Post opened the meeting by announcing the officers. To the confusion of the Seneca Falls women, Abigail Bush was named president. [93] It had not even occurred to Lucretia and Elizabeth that women might preside over conventions they planned, at least, not with men in the room. In Seneca Falls, the honor of presiding had gone to Lucretia's husband, James. [94]

Some of the Rochester women were confused, too. One of the elected officers declined to accept the position because she was "unprepared to have a woman the presiding officer." Lest anyone think they approved of Abigail's controversial appointment, Lucretia and Elizabeth refused to take their seats on the platform. [95]

By the time the first session adjourned, they had overcome the shock and accepted Abigail's presidency. Lucretia approached Abigail, hugged her, and thanked her for presiding. [96]

"I have so often regretted my foolish conduct in regard to the president of the convention at Rochester," Elizabeth later told Amy Post.

> The result proved that your judgment was good and Mrs. Bush discharged her duty so well that I was really quite delighted that we were able, through her, to do up our business so well without depending on any man. My only excuse is that woman has been so little accustomed to act in a public capacity that she does not always know what is due to those around her. [97]

As black men, Frederick Douglass and Charles Remond had a unique role to play in promoting the advancement of black women within black organizations. They advocated for Mary Ann Shadd to be admitted to the Colored National Convention, when other men wanted to keep the meeting male only. [98] Charles Remond declined a nomination to the business committee of the New England Colored Citizens' Convention because he felt it was time to put women into leadership positions in the organization. Two women were elected instead: Ruth Rice Remond and Eliza Logan Lawton. [99]

It was easier for Frederick to support these educated women than Sojourner Truth, who had little respect for education, or, at times, for Frederick personally. At least, she didn't dote on him like his many fans. Like Frederick, Sojourner had been raised in slavery, but unlike him, she never learned to read and didn't seem to mind that fact. After all, as she liked to say, most people with an education "had all of it in their feet and none of it in their heads." [100] Frederick Douglass met Sojourner Truth at the Northampton Association, a utopian commune whose members sought enlightenment by inviting famous reformers like himself to lecture. He described Sojourner this way: [101]

> I met here for the first time that strange compound of wit and wisdom, of wild enthusiasm and flint-like common sense, who seemed to feel it her duty to trip me up in my speeches and to ridicule my efforts to speak and act like a person of cultivation and refinement. I allude to Sojourner Truth. She was a genuine specimen of the uncultured negro. She cared very little for elegance of speech or refinement of manners. She seemed to please herself and others best when she put her ideas in the oddest forms. She was much respected at Florence for she was honest, industrious and amiable. Her quaint speeches easily gave her an audience and she was one of the most useful members of the community in its day of small things. [102]

Another frequent visitor at Northampton, William Lloyd Garrison, was one of the many people who appreciated Sojourner's "quaint speeches," so much so that he tried to persuade her to lecture with him.

"I am going with George Thompson on a lecturing tour. Come with us and you will have a good chance to dispose of your book," William Lloyd Garrison told Sojourner Truth, shortly after she published her memoir.

William had helped Sojourner find a publisher who was willing to print her self-published book on credit. Sojourner was anxious to pay off her debt. A book tour would help, but she had no means to finance it. After Sojourner explained why she couldn't come, William offered to pay traveling expenses.

Sojourner arrived at the first city on the tour on the appointed day but William was not there to meet her. He had become sick and canceled, failing to notify Sojourner. He would not be picking up the tab.

She found George at the hotel. He intended to carry on the tour without William and encouraged Sojourner to come as planned.

Once again, Sojourner found herself in the awkward position of having to explain that she could not afford the traveling expenses.

"I'll bear your expenses Sojourner. Leave with us."

That decided, George picked up Sojourner's bags and carried them to the train for her. Sojourner was pleased to report of George, "At the hotel tables, he seated me beside himself and never seemed to know that I was poor and a black woman." [103]

Two years after the Seneca Falls convention, Paulina Wright Davis invited several activists to a planning meeting for the First National Woman's Rights Convention. The convention would share the radical vision of Seneca Falls but would take place on a larger scale, with delegates from across the nation.

William Lloyd Garrison, who abstained from voting because of his anti-political convictions, made a surprising announcement at the meeting. "I want the women to have the right to vote."

He warned his female colleagues that they could not depend upon men to help them.

> I say to the women of America, you are not to rely upon those who have taken away your rights in order to obtain them, but you must rely on yourselves, and in that case, the victory is certain at no distant day.

Then William, who rarely had anything nice to say about government, became wistful as he imagined the kind of government he could support.

> I wish I could see one half of the members of Congress women. I wish I could see one half of the members of our legislature women. They are entitled to this. I am quite sure—I think I hazard nothing in saying—that the legislation of our country would be far different from what it is. [104]

The Nevada Legislature would be the first to achieve William Lloyd Garrison's vision, 169 years later. Until 2019, neither Congress nor any of the 50 state legislatures had ever achieved proportional representation of women. Not even once. [105]

By definition, patriarchy puts power in the hands of men, not women. Sexist policies are often governed by men, putting women at a critical disadvantage to enact change. The benefits men enjoy in positions of power leave many without motivation to challenge the status quo. Fortunately, throughout history and still today, some men have used their privileged position as males to promote feminist causes with selfless heroism (and occasional sexist missteps).

Decades after the Seneca Falls Convention, Frederick Douglass would remember his participation with pride. "When I ran away from slavery, it was for myself," he said. "When I advocated emancipation, it was for my people, but when I stood up for the rights of woman, self was out of the question, and I found a little nobility in the act."

But like William Lloyd Garrison, he would warn women not to rely on men. "Woman knows and feels her wrongs as man cannot know and feel them, and she also knows as well as he can know, what measures are needed to redress them. ... She is her own best representative." [106]

A lack of direct experience with sexism can lead to blind spots for men, leading some feminists to raise the question, "Should men limit themselves to an ally role in the feminist movement?" Some men are willing to help women but not to listen to them. Efforts to raise awareness can cross over into sensationalizing women's adversities; protecting women can cross over into paternalism. Even the feminist act of treating women as equals can backfire if men fail to accommodate the unique needs of women or recognize that our sexist society puts women at a vulnerable position, not on a level playing field.

Many of the great feminists of history were men who walked these fine lines. The critical support of men like William Lloyd Garrison, Frederick Douglass, Samuel May and even the problematic Arthur Tappan made feminist milestones possible that could not have been achieved with women working alone.

I maintain that feminism knows no gender. Until we root out patriarchy, we need all of us.

CHAPTER THREE
Can we balance family life and activism?

"Why should not woman seek to be a reformer? ... These duties are not to be limited by man. Nor will woman fulfill less her domestic relations as the faithful companion of her chosen husband and the fitting mother of her children because she has a right estimate of her position and her responsibilities. Her self-respect will be increased. Preserving the dignity of her being, she will not suffer herself to be degraded into a mere dependent." [1]
–Lucretia Mott, 1849

"I do long to be free from housekeeping and children, so as to have some time to think, read and write. But it may be well for me to understand all the trials of woman's lot, that I may more eloquently proclaim them when the time comes." [2]
–Elizabeth Cady Stanton, 1852

"Not another baby is my peremptory command. Two will solve the problem—whether a woman can be anything more than a wife and mother—better than a half dozen or ten even." [3]
–Susan B. Anthony, 1858

The first time Henry Blackwell surprised Lucy Stone at the back door, she was dressed in bloomers—the revolutionary but unflattering uniform of women's rights activists of her time. Of all the awkward positions to be in while meeting one's soul mate, she was standing on the kitchen table, painting the ceiling.

Henry, who went by the nickname Harry, came armed with a letter of introduction from Lucy's abolitionist mentor, William Lloyd Garrison, who wrote it only after warning Harry that courting Lucy would be futile. [4]

Lucy declined Harry's offer to help paint but let him peel the potatoes, a task he performed poorly. In her distraction, Lucy did no better with the carrots, forgetting to peel them before she chopped them up.[5]

Harry had dazzling white teeth—which may have been a natural reward for abstention from slave-produced tobacco.[6] The Blackwells were an abolitionist family.[7] Harry had five sisters who were all trailblazers, particularly Elizabeth, the first American woman to earn a medical degree.

The pair went for a walk outside. Harry beguiled Lucy with sweet nothings about how women should be allowed to "preach; edit newspapers; practice medicine, law and surgery; carry on business and do every other human thing."[8] Caught off guard by the effect this eloquent stranger had on her, and not fully in touch with her own hormones, Lucy accused Harry of hypnotizing her. It was the only explanation she could come up with for that strange, giddy feeling she had in his presence.[9]

This romantic interlude came to an abrupt stop when Harry proposed marriage—a move that may have been a bit too forward for a first date.

Harry left Lucy with a gift: a book by Plato. Personally, he thought Plato was "prosy and dull" but he was excited for a lively philosophy discussion with Lucy. "Let me be your friend and write to you occasionally," he pleaded.[10]

Lucy welcomed him as a friend—and only as a friend. "After our very frank conversation, you will not misunderstand me here, nor give to this ready welcome of your friendship and your letters any other than their true value," she added sternly.[11]

But Harry didn't even pretend to resign himself to mere friendship. He had noticed Lucy's attraction to him and was confident that Lucy's views on "certain subjects" would change.[12]

Harry was a man looking for a cause. And also, cash. Why couldn't he channel his search for a wife toward addressing all of his priorities?

"I see but one way to get into a position to do something, and that is to find some intelligent, go-ahead lady with a fortune to back her go-ahead-ativeness," he had told his sister, Emily.[13] He listed his specifications: "a lady with a purpose, a character and a fortune."[14]

Lucy was hardly in possession of a fortune, but she was becoming quite famous and living comfortably off of her lecture fees.[15] She was certainly go-ahead-a-whatever, and Harry could imagine himself as the other half of a power couple with Lucy by his side.

"I quite envy your position as lecturer, engaged in the advocacy of great though unpopular ideas," Harry told Lucy. "Well, perhaps you will ask me, how can you reconcile it to your views? Instead of going and doing likewise and spending your few and fleeting years as a preacher of the great church of humanity, to see month follow month and the irrevocable years go by, and you still engaged, like everyone else, in a selfish struggle for material riches?"[16]

"I surely should not dare advise if I thought you would be influenced by it. Questions of duty should always be settled by one's own convictions," Lucy responded with practiced neutrality, but she couldn't resist adding: "Allow me, however, to say that I regard moral independence as more needful than pecuniary independence." [17]

"I want wisdom," Harry explained. "I find in every question, even in this of slavery, wheels within wheels, difficulty beneath difficulty. The more I consider it the more complex it becomes. It is easy to say it is wrong, foolish, inhuman, inexcusable. Of course it is and we must and will say so. But how to take the system as it is and do it away?" [18]

Lucy could not resist an opportunity to mentor a potential activist recruit. "We do indeed need time to think before we speak," she told him, "but if we wait until all the difficulties connected with any important movement are solved, we shall die and leave our errand unfulfilled." [19]

Harry peppered Lucy with questions—many of which skillfully led the conversation in a certain direction. Didn't her itinerant reformer lifestyle get lonely, he wondered? [20]

Lucy didn't deny it. "One can well afford to purchase isolation if the price is a life rendered full and intense by a worthy purpose," she said. [21]

Lucy was 34-years-old at the time—seven years older than Harry. Years before, she had told her best friend, Antoinette Brown, that she intended to stay permanently single.

"I am glad of it for so do I, too," replied Nette. "Let us stand alone in the great moral battlefield with none but God for supporter... Let them see that woman can take care of herself and act independently without the encouragement and sympathy of her 'lord and master.'...Oh no, don't let us get married." [22]

But as the years wore on, Lucy's enthusiasm for the single life waned. "It is a wretchedly unnatural way of living," she admitted to Nette once, before catching herself. "But nothing is so bad as to be made a thing, as every married woman now is, in the eye of the law," she rebounded. [23]

There were a number of marriage laws that Lucy wanted to change before she would submit herself to the institution. Husbands had the right to their wives' property, their wages and even custody of their children. [24] But Lucy's biggest legal question was also the most personal:

"Has woman, as wife, a right to herself?" wondered Lucy. "It is very little to me to have the right to vote, to own property, etc. if I may not keep my body and its uses in my absolute right. Not one wife in a thousand can do that now, and so long as she suffers this bondage, all other rights will not help her." [25]

"Nette, let us get down these laws and then marry if we can," suggested Lucy. "We could do so much more good, in a natural, than in an unnatural position." [26]

By the time Lucy met Harry, she had been trying to "get down" those sexist laws for years and had lost hope of achieving success in time to enjoy a relationship under a more egalitarian set of rules.

"For myself, I see no choice but constant conflict—all unnatural—made necessary by the horrid wrongs of society, by circumstances which it will be impossible to change until long after the grave has laid its cold honors over all those who now live," she told Harry.

Notwithstanding this ominous talk about cold graves, Lucy insisted that she was "willing and happy" to stay single. Unattached, she could fully devote herself to reform. "Millions of slaves sighing for freedom; the great soul of womanhood crushed and degraded; outcast children and drunken parents should not be left to suffer on because the development of a few weighed more than that of all of these." [27]

It was a resolute speech, very different from the secret she had once shared with Nette: "My heart aches to love somebody that shall be all its own," Lucy had confessed. [28]

Lucy had reason to worry that marriage would end her activist career; Angelina Grimké had all but disappeared since she got married. Lucy must have mentioned her disappointment about Angelina during that first romantic walk with Harry, because as soon as he left Lucy's home in Massachusetts, he traveled directly to Angelina and Theodore Weld's home in New Jersey to investigate for himself.

"I don't think it was marriage which is to blame for their withdrawal from public life as so many suppose," he wrote back to Lucy, which was certainly the conclusion he had intended to draw when he set out on the trip, whatever the evidence to the contrary—and there was quite a bit of that.

Harry grilled Angelina and her husband about why they had retired from activism. They told him that the "fighting era" of their lives had concluded. [29]

To be fair, spending their honeymoon escaping arsonists must have been traumatizing, but Theodore, at least, had a celebrated history of surviving mortal peril—staring down violent mobs, nursing the sick during epidemics—and a brush with danger had never slowed him down before. [30]

Although it appeared that Angelina—and her sister, Sarah, too—had quit the reform movement immediately after the wedding, the transition had actually been slower than that. Shortly after her wedding, Angelina had been clear that Theodore was not standing in the way of her work. "My dear Theodore entertains the noblest views of the rights and responsibilities of woman and will never lay a straw in the way of my lecturing," she had said. [31] Only ten days after their engagement, Angelina had given a speech at the Massachusetts Legislature, attracting such a crowd that one representative wryly suggested that a "committee be appointed to examine the foundations of the State House of Massachusetts to see whether it will bear another lecture from Miss Grimké."

During the first year of the Welds' marriage, the newlyweds and Sarah put themselves to work writing a book: *American Slavery As It Is: Testimony of a Thousand Witnesses*. The book sold more copies than any anti-slavery tract ever written and served as the primary source of background material for Harriet Beecher Stowe's even more influential work of fiction, *Uncle Tom's Cabin*. [32]

The Grimké sisters had spent about six hours every day for months in their attic, searching more than 20,000 Southern newspapers for anecdotes for the book. Since they were hidden away researching a book instead of out giving speeches, it is understandable that their peers did not realize that they were still at work. Once the book was published, it should have been obvious what the sisters had been up to, if it hadn't been for the fact that Theodore was credited as the only author.

It wasn't until Angelina became pregnant that she experienced what the family euphemistically referred to as a series of "accidents" that effectively ended her reform work for the remainder of her childbearing years. [33] These accidents were actually gynecological problems: a prolapsed uterus, mastitis, a miscarriage. Quality women's healthcare scarcely existed at the time, and now that health problems precluded both Angelina and Theodore from lecturing—Theodore's voice had been damaged—they lacked the income to pay for medical care anyway. [34]

During Harry's visit with Theodore and Angelina, they had not mentioned the sisters' role in authoring the book, and gynecological health was certainly too delicate a topic for polite Victorian society, so Harry left their home feeling quite befuddled. "This all seemed very strange to me," he wrote to Lucy, concluding that "though I can't understand the position of the Welds, I see plainly that in their case they have acted rightly." He underlined the words "their case" to make sure Lucy knew that he was not advocating such a course of action for her. [35]

"I would not have my wife drudge, as Mrs. Weld has had to do in the house," Harry assured Lucy. "If both parties cannot study more, think more, feel more, talk more and work more than they could alone, I will remain an old bachelor and adopt a Newfoundland dog or a terrier as an object of affection." [36]

Most of Lucy's activist friends were married men—who have always had the good fortune to be relatively unfettered in their careers by their family responsibilities—or single women like Antoinette Brown and Susan B. Anthony. The exception was Elizabeth Cady Stanton, the doting mother of an ever-growing family who was ever apologizing to other activists with family-related excuses:

"I can neither meet you at the depot nor attend your meeting in consequence of a kind of biennial clumsiness to which I have been subject many years," wrote Elizabeth, while pregnant with her fourth child. [37]

"I am bound hand and foot with two undeveloped Hibernians in my kitchen, a baby in my arms and four boys all revolving around me as a common center," she wrote, after her fifth child was born the next year. [38]

Sometimes, Elizabeth couldn't even find the time to write the apologies herself. "She wants to write you," wrote Susan, after relaying a message to Lucy from Elizabeth about an upcoming temperance meeting. "But oh dear, Lucy, what can she do with five children and two raw Irish girls?" [39]

Elizabeth's problem was that she was "unsuitably married" to Henry Stanton, opined Harry. [40] Between Elizabeth and Henry Stanton's letters, dappled with innuendo, and the births of their seven children, there is ample evidence that the couple was quite compatible in at least one way. [41] But unlike Lucy, Elizabeth was already married when she helped spearhead the beginning of the suffrage movement. Her husband hadn't anticipated that she would become a suffragist and he vacillated between ardent support, begrudged tolerance, and outright protest of his wife's efforts.

When Elizabeth married Henry, he was already an activist in his own right—a well-known abolitionist. Ten years younger, Elizabeth had yet to find her calling.

Elizabeth and Henry married shortly after American abolitionists had divided in a quarrel over women's rights. Henry had sided with faction that chose to exclude women—not a good omen for the husband of a future women's rights activist.

But it was more complicated than that. William Lloyd Garrison's faction welcomed women as equals but also refused to participate in a political system corrupted by slavery. [42] Henry, and Elizabeth too, saw politics as the road to abolition. [43]

Still, Henry's determination to work through politics may have contributed to his acquiescence to excluding women. Everyone knew that there was no place for women in politics.

Almost everyone.

"Because it is a political subject, it has often been tauntingly said, that Woman has nothing to do with it," Henry had heard Angelina Grimké say, as she testified to the Massachusetts Legislature about the evils of slavery. "Are we aliens because we are women? Are we bereft of citizenship because we are the mothers, wives and daughters of a mighty people? Have women no country, no interests staked in public weal, no liabilities in common peril, no partnership in a nation's guilt and shame?" [44]

It was Henry who had suggested that Angelina give that speech, but he was startled when Angelina agreed.

He had only been kidding. [45]

For Angelina and Sarah, the "family feud" among abolitionists about female roles was just another barrier to their involvement in the cause. They couldn't side against women's rights and there simply wasn't a place yet for those who thought women should be involved in politics. [46]

Elizabeth Cady Stanton would eventually change that, and it was her honeymoon with Henry that put her on that path. After the wedding, Henry brought his new bride to stay with Angelina, Sarah and Theodore. [47] No one could spend time in the Grimké-Weld home without learning a thing or two about feminism. Elizabeth was an eager pupil. [48]

Next, the newlyweds boarded a ship to London, where Elizabeth would tag along while Henry served as a delegate at the World Anti-Slavery Convention. In London, Elizabeth shifted into fangirl mode when she met feminist celebrity Lucretia Mott, who took a liking to Elizabeth—more so than Henry, whom she found wanting in "moral power"—and graciously answered Elizabeth's onslaught of questions about the women's rights movement. [49]

"Lucretia Mott has just given me a long message for you," Elizabeth wrote to Sarah and Angelina from London. "She thinks you have both been in a state of retiracy long enough and that it is not right for you to be still longer, that you should either write for the public or speak out for oppressed woman. Sarah in particular, she thinks, should appear in public again as she has no duty to prevent her." [50]

What was going on with Sarah?

Sarah saw her own efforts as only ancillary to Angelina's. Sarah had planted her ideas about abolition and feminism into the mind of her younger sister, but Angelina had always led the way in transferring these great thoughts into action, dragging Sarah along with her. Their public speaking career had been Angelina's idea. Sarah often seemed embarrassed to be on stage. [51]

Sometimes, she even questioned whether her services were helpful. Even so, she confessed, she didn't want to be "laid aside." [52] Although Sarah began lecturing begrudgingly, to her surprise, she had found that she enjoyed reform work. It gave a "new spring to [her] existence." [53]

But with Angelina tied up with health problems, babies and poverty, Sarah lost her primary motivator. Moreover, she gained a live-in brother-in-law who was a powerful influence in the opposite direction. [54]

While Theodore and Angelina were engaged, Theodore started urging Sarah to quit. It started when he overheard a conversation among strangers during a stagecoach ride. They had attended one of Sarah's lectures in Boston and weren't impressed. Ever tactless, Theodore relayed the conversation to Sarah and urged her to quit public speaking for the sake of the cause; she had such a lack of talent, he told her, that she was doing more harm than good.

Regardless of the opinions of a couple of hecklers in a stagecoach, the Boston abolitionists who had hosted Sarah's speech were actually quite pleased with her performance. But Theodore did not check with them before he confronted Sarah, perhaps because what he overheard confirmed his own opinion. He had been Sarah's trainer and had seen her at her worst, before she had any opportunity to improve with practice.

Unfortunately, Theodore's words also rang true to Sarah, reinforcing her sense of inadequacy. And Sarah valued Theodore's opinion—perhaps too much. When Theodore disparaged her, she said, "It seemed as if God mocked me." [55]

Theodore's criticism triggered an episode of despair in Sarah, but it wasn't her first. Sarah had always been sad, so much so that her colleagues regularly scolded her for her gloominess, as if that would cheer her up. [56] That one person in a community who notices injustice while everyone else chants, "All is well," will never be regarded as the perkiest, but was there more to it than that? Her diaries reflect patterns typical of clinical depression. [57]

When Angelina and Theodore's children grew old enough to need an education, the couple found a new use for the mentoring, organizing, and public speaking skills they had honed in the Anti-Slavery Society. They took in children as borders and educated them alongside their own kids. It was a source of desperately needed income for their impoverished family. Their school gradually grew to 20 pupils, most of whom were the children of progressive parents, such as the Stanton children. [58]

Theodore and Angelina enjoyed teaching school; Sarah hated it. But Sarah found that Angelina and Theodore's children, and later, their students, gave her something she desperately needed in the absence of antidepressants.

"Surrounded by all these dear young people, and drinking in from their exuberance, and scarcely living my own life, I cannot but be cheerful," mused Sarah. Cheer she needed, even if scarcely living her own life was the price.

At one point, she considered going out on her own to pursue her own ambitions. She couldn't do it. "A separation from the darling children who have brightened a few years of my lonely and sorrowful life overwhelms me when I think of it as the probable result of any change," she said. "They seem to be the links that bind me to life, the stars that shed light on my path, the beings in whom past, present, and future enjoyments are centered, without whom existence would have no charms." [59]

Lucretia eventually quit trying to reactivate Sarah and Angelina. "As to the Grimkés, I have little hope of them, after such a flash and such an effectual extinguishment," she told Elizabeth. "We must not depend upon them, nor upon any who have been apostles before us." [60]

When Lucretia made the 4,000-mile journey to the World Anti-Slavery Convention in London, she was fully aware that opponents of women's rights might refuse to seat her when she arrived. As a seasoned activist, she was ready for a fight and prepared for the outcome. [61]

Elizabeth, on the other hand, was shocked by how Lucretia and the other female delegates were treated. Her accidental inclusion in this historic moment filled her soul with a "burning indignation" that would become a springboard for a lifetime of feminist advocacy. [62]

After they left the convention, Elizabeth and Lucretia made plans that would come to fruition years later when they hosted the first American Woman's Rights Convention in Elizabeth's hometown of Seneca Falls, New York. [63]

And what about her beloved Henry?

"He voted to seat the women," said Elizabeth.

"No, he didn't," said everyone else. [64]

Elizabeth was less confused about where Henry stood during the Seneca Falls Woman's Rights Convention, because he wasn't standing in Seneca Falls. He left town to avoid his wife's spectacle. [65]

Absence also became Henry's usual approach to parenting.

"How sad it makes me feel when I see Henry going about just where and when he pleases. He can walk all through the wide world or shut himself up alone within four walls," Elizabeth complained to Susan B. Anthony. "As I contrast his freedom with my bondage and feel that because of the contracted position of woman I have been compelled to hold all my noblest aspirations in abeyance in order to be a wife, a mother, a nurse, a cook, a household drudge, I am fired anew to open my mouth and pour forth from my own experience the whole long story of woman's wrongs." [66]

And she did, channeling these frustrations into women's rights speeches. But since she couldn't leave the children alone, she usually had to send her written speeches with friends who would read them aloud on her behalf.

"One common objection to this movement is that if the principles of freedom and equality which we advocate were put to practice, it would destroy all harmony in the domestic circle. Here let me ask, how many truly harmonious households have we now?" asked Elizabeth in one such speech, reminding her audience that a "thoroughly subdued wife" with "no freedom of thought or action" is in no state of harmony. [67]

Such philosophies found a devoted convert in Henry Blackwell, who wanted a marriage of "perfect equality" with "no sacrifice of individuality" and "no limitation of the career of one or both."

"I would not even consent that my wife should stay at home to rock the baby when she ought to be off addressing a meeting or organizing a society," Harry told Lucy.

But what if a mother actually wants to rock the baby?

"Perhaps you may write more and speak less," suggested Harry. [68]

Harry wasn't the only childless person who thought writing instead of speaking would be a handy way for a busy mother to get involved.

Lucy and Nette told Susan that if they could only get Elizabeth a nice, long-term writing project (editing a suffrage newspaper, perhaps?) they could better involve their perennially pregnant friend. [69]

Elizabeth, on the other hand, knew better than her childless friends about the trials of finding time to write while surrounded by children.

"While I am about the house, surrounded by my children, washing dishes, baking, sewing, I can think up many points but I cannot search books, for my hands, as well as my brains, would be necessary for that work," Elizabeth explained. "I seldom have one hour to sit down and write undisturbed." [70]

Even Henry was complaining about Elizabeth's lack of writing time, although his repeated business trips were contributing to the problem.

"Tell your mother that I have seen a throng of handsome ladies," Henry wrote to their five-year-old. "I had rather see her than the whole of them, but I intend to cut her acquaintance unless she writes me a letter." [71]

Even so, Elizabeth did manage to write more often than she showed up at conventions or gave speeches, publishing her feminist philosophies in progressive women's magazines such as *the Lily*. [72]

But she wanted to do more than write. "Men and angels, give me patience! I am at the boiling point!" announced Elizabeth. "If I do not find someday the use of my tongue on this question, I shall die of an intellectual repression, a woman's rights convulsion!" [73]

Lucy tried to comfort her. "When your children are a little more grown, you will surely be heard, for it cannot be possible to repress what is in you," she told Elizabeth, although she may have been making a mental note to avoid getting herself into the same predicament. [74]

If Lucy's circle of friends had been more diverse, she might have had more role models of working motherhood. Unlike most upper class white women, most black women worked to support their families, as did those Irish house servants Elizabeth kept complaining about. They weren't able to seek rewarding reform work; they were stuck dealing with those "iron pots and kettles" Maria W. Stewart mentioned. [75] Still, these working class women were living evidence that women could perform paid labor and simultaneously raise children.

Harry tried to persuade Lucy that marriage could be an asset to her advocacy career. "A woman who unites herself with a fellow worker with sufficient means and position to prevent the necessity of her drudging, free to be at home when she pleases and to leave it when she thinks it best, with a home of her own for rest and study and with friends to relieve her many responsibilities—is this a position necessarily less influential than your present one?" [76]

"If it is true that a woman cannot be a wife and mother consistently with the exercise of a profession, it justifies to a great extent the argument of our antagonists who say that very thing," pointed out Harry. [77] Besides, couldn't she more persuasively advocate egalitarian marriage if she were living it out in practice? [78]

"To say that one who is not married is not competent to speak in regard to it is about as absurd as it would be to require a physician to have personally the small pox and fever and every other disease," countered Lucy. [79]

"There is no analogy in the cases. Marriage is not a disease, but celibacy is," retorted Harry. [80] "Marriage is the normal state of mature human beings and brings with it experiences, insights which cannot be attained without it." [81]

To Lucy, those "experiences" Harry was hinting about were part of the problem. The thought of having sex revolted her. [82]

As an advocate for women's rights, women regularly approached Lucy for help, exposing her to a wide array of worst-case scenarios that reinforced her dread. One of the women she met had fled her rapist husband by joining a Shaker community where sexual relations were prohibited. Her husband complained to the legislature and the law was "so modified that the man and others like him may sooner be enabled under cover of a legal marriage to claim a 'husband's rights,'" Lucy told Elizabeth.

Lucy and Elizabeth were strategizing about whether to broach the taboo topic of divorce during an upcoming Woman's Rights Convention in Cleveland, Ohio. Or rather, Elizabeth was trying to talk Lucy into doing it. As usual, Elizabeth couldn't attend for family reasons. [83]

When Harry heard that Lucy would stop in Niagara Falls en route to the Cleveland convention, he boldly asked if he could join her. [84] Lucy reminded Harry that she was not interested in him but contradicted herself by consenting to the romantic get-away. [85]

Not surprisingly, a weekend together at Niagara Falls did nothing to dissuade Harry's advances. From there, Harry followed Lucy to the Woman's Rights Convention, where he impressed her by spontaneously rising to his feet to give his first women's rights speech. [86]

Others were less impressed. The *Cleveland Plain Dealer* reported, "Mr. Blackwell spoke too long. He forgot it was a woman's convention." [87]

Conveniently, Harry was able to secure accommodations for Lucy to continue giving speeches in Ohio after the convention ended—at his family home. [88] At last, he could prove that "he could make himself useful" to her, by arranging for—and accompanying her—on a lecture tour throughout Ohio and neighboring states. [89]

During their travels together, Harry finally saw the "striking difference of tone and feeling on certain subjects" that he had been hoping for from Lucy. [90]

"It would be as foolish as it would be untrue for me to pretend that I feel an ordinary friendship for you," Lucy admitted to Harry. She had only one regret: "that the manifestation of the affection which I really feel for you lures you to hopes which can never be realized." [91]

While Lucy was flirting—er, campaigning—with Harry in Ohio, Susan B. Anthony was plotting to make Elizabeth give a speech to the New York Legislature. She assembled a team of prominent reformers to volunteer their services to Elizabeth with research and editing, as well as coax her with good old-fashioned flattery. "There is not a man of us who could tell a story of woman's wrongs as strongly, clearly, tersely, eloquently as yourself," wrote William H. Channing, at Susan's prompting. [92]

"I find there is no use saying no to you," Elizabeth told Susan at last, but she made some stipulations. "I want the exact wording of the most atrocious laws. I can generalize and philosophize by myself, but I have not time to look up statistics." [93]

And thus began a pattern of work that would continue for years. Susan's writing skills were fine, but Susan wouldn't risk so important a cause to merely adequate text, and Elizabeth could produce brilliant text, as long as Susan prodded her, and did the research, and cooked the food and carried the baby. [94]

"Courage, Susan," Elizabeth said after her sixth child was born. "This is my last baby." [95]

But to Elizabeth's surprise, there was another baby yet to come. There weren't enough exclamation points in the world for Susan to express her horror about the news.

"Ah me!! Ah me!!! Alas!! Alas!!!! Mrs. Stanton!! is embarked on the rolling sea," Susan wrote to Nette. "Three long months of terrible nausea are behind and what the future has in store the deep only knows."

Susan continued, ranting about the villain who had impregnated Elizabeth. "Her husband, you know, does not help to make it easy for her to engage in such work… Mr. Stanton will be gone most of the autumn… He was gone seven months last winter. The whole burden of home and children therefore falls to her. If she leaves the post, all is afloat."

Susan was certain that Elizabeth had ruined their chances of winning a woman's suffrage amendment during the next legislative session. And she had done it just "for a moment's pleasure to herself or her husband!" [96]

Susan grew even more peeved during Elizabeth's second trimester, when she canceled a lecture in Boston after her luggage was stolen. [97]

"To lose such a golden moment to say the word which Mrs. Stanton professes she so longs to utter is wholly unaccountable to me. When she wrote me, she had accepted the invitation. She said Mr. Stanton was delighted with the idea. My vision finds no mountain in the way, but the individual women." [98]

Elizabeth hadn't told Susan or the lecture organizers the real reason she didn't make it.

After six easy pregnancies, it hadn't even occurred to Elizabeth that she might be too sick to travel. [99] She prepared her speech, but instead of recovering from first trimester morning sickness, she found herself growing sicker every day. She couldn't read one page aloud without running out of breath.

"As the maternal difficulty has always been one of the arguments against woman entering public life, I did not like the idea that I, who had a hundred times declared that difficulty to be absurd, should illustrate in my own person the contrary thesis. It was all too humiliating to be disclosed," Elizabeth confided to a less judgmental friend than Susan.

When her trunk was stolen, that was the last straw—and the excuse she needed. [100]

It didn't get any easier when the seventh little Stanton was born. Elizabeth, who had often bragged about her quick recoveries after childbirth, found that this time around she could "scarcely walk across the room" for weeks. [101]

"Dear Susan," she wrote. "You need expect nothing from me for some time. I have no vitality of body or soul. All I had and was has gone into the development of that boy." [102]

I hope that during this trying time Elizabeth was able to remember what she had once told impatient Susan: "You and I have a prospect of a good long life. We shall not be in our prime before fifty and after that, we shall be good for twenty years at least." [103]

She would have time to agitate for women's rights later.

"Now let me interpret your real feelings towards me to yourself, as I believe they are," Harry said to Lucy after their Ohio tour.

> You love me as you will never love anybody else in this world. I feel it and know it and am happy in that belief.
>
> But you see in me intellectual differences which in some respects you have been accustomed to associate in your own mind with moral inferiority and which you do not coincide with. You see probably in my character many faults and immaturities and inconsistencies which sometimes pain you.
>
> Above all, you feel unwilling to marry. There is an idea of independence sacrificed. You are not willing to risk any compromise of your efficiency in influencing public opinion and not able to see how you can avoid doing so in marriage. Having made up your mind against matrimony for years, you find it impossible to change it—and yet, at times and when you are with me, you would almost wish that it could be changed. [104]

Lucy didn't know what to think, at least in part because her head hurt too much to think at all. Lucy had always been prone to headaches, but as her relationship with Harry progressed, the headaches grew more frequent and severe. She had to cancel her speaking engagements. [105]

"I am so sorry you are ill and cannot come. I will not urge you, for you must take care of your own health," Susan wrote to Lucy, but somehow, despite Susan's determination not to urge Lucy, the letter continued: "Lucy, if you are able to come here, do so. We will not ask you to make but just one speech and that may be as short as you please, but we do all feel very anxious to have you." [106]

In her own anxiety, Lucy was coming up with new objections to her relationship with Harry at a dizzying rate. She was too old for him, and any children they had would probably have birth defects, and she wasn't cultured enough to hang out with Harry's fancy friends. [107]

Harry's reactions were sometimes wistful: "In spite of all your warnings and rejections and resentments I cannot help loving [you] as my own soul and thinking of [you] as my wife that is and is to be." [108] On other occasions, he was simply exasperated: "Lucy dear, if I could express to you properly my view of matters and things you would see that as to marrying I am right and you are wrong and you would marry me." [109]

Harry was growing despondent. Lucy loved him—he was sure of it, but he suspected that she was about to dump him anyway. "You will go on through life laboring for the good of others and therefore happy but with the consciousness at times of a want never satisfied," he wrote to Lucy forebodingly.

> And yet I could wish things were otherwise. I read the book of life somewhat differently than yourself. I should like a home of my own, a wife whom I could entirely trust and love, a child to carry down my life through posterity, to fight its way up into that better future in which we all believe.
>
> I do not think that either you or I should be less efficient together than separate. I don't think all work and no play is the best mode of getting even the most work out of life. Above all, I do not believe that we were created only for results ulterior to ourselves. I think sufficiently well of myself and of all human beings to believe that we were created as positive ends as well as means. We have a right to be happy in and for ourselves. If not, what a stupid thing to try to make other people happy. [110]

Harry needed backup. First he tried his sister, Elizabeth. Lucy was a big fan of America's first female doctor, but she was an inconsistent ally, as indifferent toward the prospect of having radical Lucy Stone for a sister-in-law as she was toward the suffrage cause itself. [111]

So he tried Lucy's sister, Sarah. He told her about the first time he had seen Lucy, when she had stopped in his store years earlier. From that very moment, he was "strangely attracted" to her. [112] The attraction had been strange indeed, because at the time, he had tried to get his brother Sam to hit on her. [113]

After years of well-concealed inner longing, so much so that some might suspect that he had forgotten about the encounter altogether, he "went East on purpose to see her."

Actually, he had gone to Boston with the intention of courting another woman. [114] While there, he had heard Lucy testify to the Massachusetts Legislature and decided that he preferred her to any lady he had ever met, although he hadn't, technically, met her. [115]

After hearing Harry's creative rewrite of the love story, Sarah exhorted patience and warned Harry that Lucy would never marry him unless he would "leave all and follow her."

"My experience is that the ladies usually manage to carry their husband where they will," said Harry. [116] As for patience: "Jacob, you know, waited patiently fourteen years for Rachel, and if so mean a man could wait so long for a woman who does not seem to have had much to recommend her, I certainly ought to be able to do as much for a better woman." [117]

Harry saved his best strategy for Lucy's best friend. He introduced Nette to his brother Sam. Such a good man, mused Nette, who began to feel friendlier toward the marriage institution in Sam's company. [118]

"How many children has Lucretia Mott?" Nette asked Lucy. "Are her children intelligent, respectable and well-trained? How did she manage to bring them all up and still speak so much in public?" [119]

"She has four children," Lucy responded inaccurately. Lucretia had six children, five of whom survived to adulthood. But Lucy got the next part right: "All of them intelligent, respectable and proud of their mother. She is a Quaker and Quaker men and women preach as the Spirit moves. She preached while she was bringing up her family, being in perfect unity with her husband, who aided in the care of children." [120]

Perfect unity made it possible for Lucretia and her husband James to incorporate reform into nearly every aspect of their lives. They made their home a stop on the underground railroad; involved the whole family, including the children, as volunteers at fundraising bazaars; and endured multiple threats on their home and persons without either partner calling it quits on their marriage or their activism. [121]

They were leaders of the free produce movement: a boycott on goods produced by slave labor. Together, they risked their livelihood for the cause, giving up a profitable cotton business for riskier but slave labor-free wool. [122] The Mott household was among very few that managed long-term tolerance for the expensive yet itchy clothing and inedible foods that had to be substituted for slave-produced merchandise. They didn't falter even when the grandkids complained that their free produce candy was yucky. [123]

How did Lucretia find herself such a supportive partner? She was probably just lucky. She married at the wee age of eighteen, long before she had developed an interest in activism. [124] More important was how Lucretia and James nurtured their marriage over the several decades that followed. Lucretia set a goal early on to make home "comfortable" while "appropriating a portion of time and means" to the causes she believed in. Fortunately, her husband James believed in those causes, too, and unlike Henry Stanton, was flexible and cooperative with his wife in balancing home life and outside pursuits. [125] While Henry was fleeing that first Woman's Rights Convention, James was serving as convention president. [126]

Lucy wrote to Lucretia and James for advice. James wrote back: "I am in favor of matrimony and wish to see all in whom I feel interested made happy that way, which includes thy little self." [127]

But Harry was not such a saint as James Mott was. Take Harry's Wisconsin land speculation scheme, for example, which angered the locals so much that they threatened to tar and feather him and ride him out of town on a rail before Harry managed to talk his way out of the predicament.

"I spoke for nearly an hour explaining my position and views, showing the absurdity of condemning an individual for doing what they would all gladly do if they were able," Harry wrote to Lucy afterward. "I endeavored to say nothing but what was strictly true and wise, though I confess the logic whereby I proved to my own satisfaction at the time that I was not a land monopolist looks rather one-sided to me at present."

While the merits of his defense may have been dubious, Harry "produced a very good effect" on the townspeople, who left "in great good humor."

"Altogether the affair was quite an amusing episode," Harry concluded. Then he stopped laughing and became more reflective. "Lucy, it seems as though in the present constitution of society, do what we will, we cannot advance our own interests without doing a certain injustice for others. If I am able to keep these lands a few years they will make me rich, but meantime I am certainly impeding the settlement and prosperity of the country 'round me." [128]

Lucy wrote back, "Believe me, dear Harry, we do not belong together as husband and wife." [129]

Lucy began to fear that Harry was "constitutionally defective" of "the ability to sacrifice" and "accept the consequences of the carrying out of his real ideas at whatever cost." [130] If she ever married—and Harry had begun to persuade her that she might—she wanted a husband who would work with her in the "great moral movements of the age." After all, "there are plenty of people who can make money—not so many who can bring the world a high thought." [131]

Lucy and Harry's relationship reached a turning point when, in a spontaneous moment of bravado, Harry rescued—or kidnapped, depending on your point of view—a slave girl riding through Ohio on a train.

A crowd of over a thousand people watched from outside as Harry and four other men entered a train and found a black girl who appeared to be about eight-years-old, sitting with a white woman who was holding a baby.

"Whose child are you?" asked a black man who was leading the team.

The child didn't respond, so he asked the white woman beside her.

"None of your business," she said, but when the white men in the group interrogated her, she told them that the child was her slave and that they were headed to Tennessee.

The little girl finally spoke when one of the men asked her if she wished to be free. She said, "Yes."

That was the magic word, or at least, the legally necessary one in Harry's opinion. "The child is now legally free under our laws and must go with us," announced Harry, lifting up the girl only to drop her when the woman screamed, "Murder!" and another Ohio man charged at him. Harry fought with angry train passengers while the other abolitionists recovered the child and tossed her to a black man outside the train. A witness said that Harry attacked the slaveholder, causing her to drop the baby on the floor. Harry denied that part. [132]

"What an exciting scene it must have been! How much of intense thought, feeling and action were crowded in that little space of time!" Lucy gushed, dropping her usual reserve. [133] After such an act of heroism, an act that she imagined would be celebrated in history books, she felt closer to dear Harry than ever before. [134]

Not everyone shared Lucy's enthusiasm. Harry's sisters questioned whether the use of force had been justified. Elizabeth Blackwell was sure that Harry was "acting on his morbid craving for distinction" and "ruining himself through injurious influences."

The injurious influence in question was Lucy. [135]

A reward of $10,000 was offered for Henry Blackwell's capture dead or alive in Tennessee. Harry was indicted for kidnapping in Ohio but the case never came to trial, thanks to a sympathetic prosecutor. His store became crowded with Kentucky slaveholders, threatening to attack him if he ever dared to cross the river. [136] Meanwhile, paying customers dwindled and Harry's business partners bailed. [137] Harry began to wonder if he had done the right thing. [138]

Lucy had no patience for regrets. "Do not defend the deed," she scolded. "It is possible your enemies may try to make this matter interfere with your business. But even then, you will be richer with your self-respect, even though you may have less in dollars." [139]

Lucy's words were hardly comforting to Harry, whatever amount of self-respect poverty might yield, and Harry sent Lucy anxious letters, fretting about his "indiscretion" and "needless loss of influence."

"In regard to the Salem rescue: I can scarcely tell you how the radiance of the halo I had thrown around your action there has been dimmed by your last letters," Lucy replied.

Such an extreme turnaround from the "tenderness" and "trust" Lucy had expressed only a few weeks earlier called for some urgent redirection. [140]

Harry was equal to the challenge, uttering the most romantic words he had ever spoken to the activist he loved: "Lucy dear," he said, "I want to make a protest." [141]

Harry had a plan. They could replace their wedding vows with a protest of marriage law, generating a whirlwind of publicity around women's rights while simultaneously getting hitched. [142]

At last, he had made an offer Lucy couldn't refuse.

Lucy's headaches only worsened after the couple became engaged. With her health deteriorating, they delayed the wedding.

"For my sake, dear Lucy, watch over yourself, keep warm, make people give you fire in your bedroom, get regular meals and wrap up well, also take regular exercise. I want to keep you well," Harry wrote. "And above all dearest, do not let any doubts or forebodings about our future cause you pain or anxiety. Be sure that I have but one desire: your happiness and prosperity. I will try to so act towards you that your love and trust will grow daily more perfect and to so live that I shall be more worthy of your love every day. Surely if I am true to you and to myself I cannot do you harm." [143]

Lucy wasn't so sure about that. When she wasn't suffering too much from the headaches, she was looking for information about just how dreadful sex might be, and how to discourage her husband's advances, and how she might prevent pregnancy. At least on that last point, her concerns were quite justified. Family planning options were virtually nonexistent at the time.

Her fiancé understood the vague, Victorian euphemisms Lucy used to explain her worries, but not the sentiment. [144]

"I think that you underrate the force and virtue of instinct when guided by affection and love," he told her. [145]

When Lucy's headaches eased to the point that she had only "scarcely a fear of insanity" they set a date, although Harry was growing suspicious that Lucy's headaches were a symptom of cold feet. [146]

"Dearest little Lucy, keep up your courage! Don't let evil forebodings and fears find any hold on you," he begged her. "Trust in God, in yourself and in me." [147]

Whatever Lucy's worries, her guests were delighted to see her "beaming" on her wedding day and crying in the right kind of way, "like any village bride." [148]

"We understand that Mr. Blackwell, who last fall assaulted a Southern lady and stole her slave, has lately married Lucy Stone. Justice, though sometimes tardy, never fails to overtake her victim," reported the *Washington Union*. [149]

The wedding included a scripted protest speech that was published in several papers across the nation. It announced their objections "to such of the present laws of marriage as refuse to recognize the wife as an independent, rational being, while they confer upon the husband an injurious and unnatural superiority, investing him with legal powers which no honorable man would exercise and which no man should possess." [150]

On their wedding night, Lucy went to bed alone with a severe headache. [151]

During their engagement, Lucy had gloomily referred to her upcoming nuptials as "putting Lucy Stone to death," in spite of Harry's insistence that she would be "the same Lucy that was and always will be." [152]

It wasn't until after the wedding that Lucy thought of a way to make that literally the case. She became the first known American woman to keep her maiden name after marriage: a palpable symbol of her determination to maintain her independence, as well as a source of confusion to almost everyone she met. [153]

Soon after Harry and Lucy married, Nette married Harry's brother Sam, to the joy of almost everyone.

There was one notable exception.

"Those of you who have the talent to do honor to poor—oh how poor—womanhood, have all given yourselves over to baby-making, and left poor brainless me to battle alone." Susan lamented to Elizabeth. "It is a shame; such a body as I might be spared to rock cradles, but it is a crime for you and Lucy and Nette. I have just engaged to attend a progressive meeting in Erie County the 1st of September just because there is no other woman to be had, not because I feel in the least competent. Oh dear, dear." [154]

Elizabeth tried to soothe her. "Come here and I will do what I can to help you with your address, if you will hold the baby and make the puddings," she wrote.

Send love to Antoinette and Lucy when you write them. Womankind owes them a debt of gratitude for their faithful labors in the past. Let them rest in peace and quietness thinking great thoughts. It is not well to be in the excitement of public life all the time, so do not keep stirring them up or mourning over their repose.

You too, must rest, Susan; let the world alone awhile. We cannot bring about a moral revolution in a day or a year.

Now that I have two daughters, I feel fresh strength to work for women. It is not in vain that in myself I feel all the wearisome care to which woman even in her best estate is subject.

Good night.

Yours in love,

E.C. Stanton [155]

As a modern eavesdropper following Lucy Stone and Harry Blackwell's intimate conversations, I found myself rooting for Harry, whatever his faults. His assertion that those of us seeking to make the world a better place have "a right to be happy in and for ourselves" rings true to my feminist sensibilities. [156] If we value womankind, we must value ourselves.

Valuing ourselves might mean taking a break from activism for self-care every now and then. It might mean making life choices that make us happy, even if they don't leave us with as much time for the causes that we support. After all, respect for women's choices is what feminism is all about.

Elizabeth Cady Stanton complained frequently (incessantly?) about the demands of motherhood on her time, yet she insisted that she would not have chosen to have fewer children and encouraged Lucy and Nette to have as many children as they wanted." [157] Honoring her choice was difficult for her partner in the cause, Susan B. Anthony, but Susan applied her exasperation in the most preferable way possible to a busy mom, taking it upon herself to take over some of Elizabeth's household duties to free her up to write speeches and petitions. We could all take a cue from Susan—an offer of help goes further than a guilt trip.

Susan's life choices were different, leaving her with more time to devote to the cause than her friends who were balancing activism with family life. In a world that still too often equates womanhood with motherhood, Susan B. Anthony's legacy is one of many that remind us that women's contributions don't have to be maternal.

While feminists celebrate choice, how much a woman can contribute to a cause she believes in isn't always about that. Too many women find their choices limited after they have children because of a lack of family-friendly policy. For several decades, the voices of Angelina and Sarah Grimké were missing because of poverty and lack of healthcare, problems that continue to plague American women today, especially women with families. While medical knowledge has advanced, access to healthcare in not universal in this country. Family planning services are often threatened by politicians, in spite of their power to preserve health and prevent poverty. The risks of fertility continue to rest primarily on women in this country, with single mothers facing the highest risk of poverty. [158] We have a lot of work to do to before women will be free from obstacles that limit our choices.

I have about a zillion children myself (four, to be exact) and juggling time between my family, my career and my activism is always challenging. I love my kids, but not the housework they create. Fortunately, modern fathers do more housework and childcare than their forebears—but, on average, still less than their wives. [159] The load varies greatly across households. More than a third of American mothers are single. [160] Among those with spouses, some are married to someone like James Mott, while others have a less helpful Henry Stanton to deal with.

And then there's Theodore Weld. Ah, Theodore. By all accounts, he was a selfless hero and a feminist ally. Angelina liked him, so he must have been alright, even if I happen to want to wring his throat whenever I read one of his letters. Activists need allies, even imperfect ones. As a feminist activist, I have found that a man who has a passion for the feminist cause is a rare bird to be treasured, even if he won't shut his beak. Sometimes, the same strategies we use to cope with the patriarchy must also apply to our friends.

Above all, never mistake a man like Theodore for God. Being a know-it-all is not the same as being omniscient.

CHAPTER FOUR
Is religion compatible with a feminist movement?

"It is that holy religion which is held in derision and contempt by many whose precepts will raise and elevate us above our present condition, and cause our aspirations to ascend up in unison…and become the final means of bursting the bands of oppression." [1]
–Maria W. Stewart, 1832

"The clergy and the church don't recognize your right, my sisters, to speak publicly or in the church. Speak then not in their favor. …What could the church and clergy do without woman? I call upon you then, as you venerate truth and reason, as you love yourself, your children and the race, never to enter a church again. Countenance them not. They oppress you. They prevent progression. They are opposed to reason." [2]
–Ernestine Rose, 1844

"**D**at woman is in de quality of de slave, and man is de tyrant; and dat when de distinction of rights between de sexes ceases, then, and not till then, will woman get her just deserts," Ernestine Rose told the crowd at the first National Woman's Rights Convention. [3]

At least, that is how a rather hostile reporter mockingly rendered it. Other reporters were more friendly but equally inaccurate, referring to Ernestine's accent as sonorous and German or charming and French. [4]

At a subsequent convention, other suffragists would try to clear up the confusion by introducing Ernestine as "a Polish lady of the Jewish faith." It was an odd way to describe someone who had lived in America for over a dozen years and been an outspoken atheist that entire time, but Ernestine ran with it. [5]

"I am an example of the universality of our claims," she said. "For not American women only, but a daughter of poor, crushed Poland, and the downtrodden and persecuted people called the Jews, a child of Israel, pleads for the equal rights of her sex." [6]

The women's rights movement was certainly spreading, at least in the United States. Only two years after the Seneca Falls Convention, which had been groundbreaking but mostly limited to residents of one town in New York, 89 of the most prominent feminist reformers in the United States had called for people from across the nation to join them in Worcester, Massachusetts for the first National Woman's Rights Convention. [7]

Ernestine hadn't signed the call to convention, perhaps because it had credited "the inspiration of the Almighty" for inspiring their movement—unappealing wording to an unbeliever like herself. In her convention speech, Ernestine framed her call for women's rights "in the name of common sense" instead of invoking the name of God. [8] She was the only person at the convention so far who had not made any religious references in her speech, and the next two speakers wouldn't change that. [9] Both Sojourner Truth and Antoinette Brown were preachers.

Sojourner gave an animated rendition of the Adam and Eve story from the Bible, flipping the common interpretation that it justified subordination of women on its head. "There was nothing in Adam's fall to tolerate his rule, and certainly nothing in his general conduct that said he was fit to rule himself—let alone others. If people would only think, they would see that man was only one half of himself, and the other half very well used up," Sojourner told them, to hearty applause. [10]

The next speaker, Antoinette Brown, had just finished postgraduate theology studies. [11] Her best friend, Lucy Stone, one of the primary organizers of the event, had persuaded Nette to come in spite of her reservations.

"I do not believe exactly with your party even on the subject of women's rights," Nette had told Lucy. "I should be a stranger in a strange land." [12]

As Lucretia Mott closed the session, she offered Nette a mixed compliment that was unlikely to put her more at ease. She "was glad their young friend from Oberlin had stated so clearly a part of the scriptural argument on the subject" but she had long ago concluded that "it would not be profitable to consume too much time with the Bible argument" because, although she was a religious woman, she agreed with Ernestine that "the true ground to take is to address themselves to the justice, the humanity and the common sense of those who hear," not that she would have had their "young friend, who had spoken on this subject, say one word less than she did."

Lucretia was more flattering toward Sojourner, quoting her favorite words from her speech: "Goodness is from everlasting and will never die, while evil had a beginning and must come to an end." [13]

Two and a half decades before that first National Woman's Rights Convention, Sojourner had asked God, "How can I get away?" She was living in slavery in New York, before slavery had been abolished there, and she wasn't actually called Sojourner Truth at the time. For the first several years of her life, her first name was Isabella and her last name came from whomever enslaved her. This answered prayer, leading her to safety and freedom, was the first of many spiritual experiences that helped her became Sojourner Truth, the name she eventually chose for herself as a preacher and a human rights activist. [14]

Since Sojourner's five-year-old son, Peter, was enslaved in a different household, he was not with Sojourner at the time she escaped slavery with her youngest baby. Slavery ended gradually in New York, with emancipation laws mandating that enslaved children would be freed during their adulthood. By law, Peter would be enslaved until age 28. The law forbade New York slaveholders from selling slaves South to cash in on them before they could become free, but that did not stop the people who enslaved Peter from selling him to relatives in Alabama. [15]

When Sojourner heard that Peter was in the South, she confronted the woman who had previously enslaved them.

"Ugh! A fine fuss to make about a little nigger!" Sally Dumont exclaimed. "Why, haven't you as many of them left as you can see to and take care of? A pity it is, the niggers are not all in Guinea! Making such a halloo-balloo about the neighborhood and all for a paltry nigger!"

"I'll have my child again," Sojourner told her.

"Have your child again?" repeated Sally incredulously. "How can you get him? And what have you to support him with, if you could? Have you any money?"

"No, I have no money, but God has enough, or what's better!" Sojourner added, more slowly this time, "And I'll have my child again."

Sojourner eventually coaxed the information she needed out of Sally. The Dumonts had sold her son to the Gedney family, who had in turn sent him South with their newlywed daughter Eliza Fowler. Sojourner approached the Gedney family matriarch next, who laughed in her face.

"Dear me!" said Mrs. Gedney. "What a disturbance to make about your child! What? Is your child better than my child? My child is gone out there, and yours is gone to live with her, to have enough of everything and be treated like a gentleman!'

Sojourner had to remind Mrs. Gedney that her child happened to be an adult who had gone South of her own volition, so this was hardly the same kind of situation.

Mrs. Gedney didn't stop laughing.

As practical as she was spiritual, Sojourner quickly realized that reasoning with such people was a futile exercise and found herself a lawyer. Attempting to seek justice through the courts was intimidating; slavery, illiteracy and the as-yet nonexistence of Perry Mason reruns combined to ill-prepare her for the experience. Her repeated missteps—not understanding how to swear in, for example, or even how to tell time, provided a lot of amusement at her expense to the white men who worked in the legal system.

But her perseverance paid off. With the threat of a fourteen-year prison sentence, the Gedneys' own lawyers advised them to get that child out of Alabama posthaste. But there was no such thing as quick travel in that day and it would be another six months before Mrs. Gedney's son, Solomon, returned to New York with Peter.

After such a close call, Sojourner was not willing to risk waiting for Peter to grow up before he became free. Her lawyer thought he could help her; it would just take time—several more months of Peter's childhood.

"What? Wait another court? Wait months?" cried Sojourner. "Why, long before that time, he can go clear off and take my child with him no one knows where. I cannot wait; I must have him now, whilst he is to be had."

"Lord, give my son into my hands, and that speedily!" was her new prayer, accompanied by her next lawsuit. She found a different lawyer who got her into court within 24 hours of taking the case.

Solomon brought Peter with him to court, but instead of running into Sojourner's arms, Peter screamed when he saw her, insisted that he didn't know her and begged the judge to let him stay with the slaveholder.

But even as Peter continued his tantrum, Sojourner won the case, with the judge ruling that the Gedneys had lost ownership of Peter when they broke the law by sending him away from New York.

Peter was placed in Sojourner's arms, still screaming that this was not his mother. Sojourner, her lawyer and the clerks all attempted to soothe Peter. Someone produced bonbons—those helped—and at last he calmed down enough to admit, "Well, you do look like my mother used to."

After Solomon left, Sojourner examined Peter and found his body covered in scars.

"Heavens! What is all this?" she asked.

Now that Solomon was no longer present, Peter didn't hesitate to tell her that Mr. Fowler, the husband of Solomon's sister, Eliza, had beaten him in Alabama.

"Oh, Lord Jesus, look! See my poor child! Oh, Lord, render unto them double!" Sojourner prayed, but she would go on to regret this particular prayer soon after when the same violent man who had abused her son, murdered his wife, Eliza.

Because Sojourner grew up in slavery, she never had the opportunity to learn to read, yet she developed an extensive mastery of scripture. She would study by asking children to read the Bible to her. Children were the best readers because they would follow her instructions and read the same passages to her over and over, just as they were written, so she could commit them to memory. Adults had no patience with this process; they had the annoying habit of interjecting their own interpretations instead of simply repeating the written words as requested. [16]

When Sojourner met Sarah and Elijah Pierson, they recognized Sojourner's spiritual gifts and offered her a housekeeping position in their home, where she became a key player in religious meetings they held there daily with a small group of fervent followers.

When Sarah Pierson was on her deathbed, elders of this religious community gathered to anoint and bless her. Sojourner was one of these elders and took a principal part in this religious ceremony, to the shock of onlooking neighbors. [17]

While still grieving Sarah's death, a self-proclaimed prophet called Matthias arrived at the Piersons' door, dressed like the Jesus of European paintings. Sojourner answered the door and asked, "Art thou the Christ?"

"I am," said Matthias.

Sojourner fell to her knees and burst into tears.

Elijah Pierson was equally impressed with the new stranger and soon abdicated leadership of his little congregation to Matthias. It wasn't long before Matthias convinced Elijah to invest his considerable estate in setting up a commune for Matthias's followers. [18] In turn, Elijah convinced Sojourner to contribute her much less considerable life savings to the same project. [19]

Under new management, the small religious community retained its fanaticism but dropped its charity work and egalitarian sensibilities. Sojourner lost the spiritual leadership roles she had enjoyed in Elijah's household. Her new situation was more like her previous state of slavery, with Sojourner, the only person of color in the community, ordered to cook and clean without pay for all of the other co-religionists. A white woman named Ann Folger, who had joined the commune with her husband Benjamin, was nominally also responsible for household work, but she carried out her responsibility mostly by giving Sojourner orders or feigning incompetence.

The community believed in "match spirits," their term for eternal soul mates or, as more often proved to be the case, short-term flings that tended to swap out every few weeks.

Sojourner was the only adult in the community who never had a match spirit, but she was frank in admitting that it wasn't due to any moral superiority, but rather because she was old (almost 40!), unattractive, and black.

Ann Folger and Matthias convinced Ann's husband Benjamin to make a trade—Ann would be Matthias's match spirit, and in return, Matthias would give Benjamin his daughter, Isabella, as a replacement bride. The daughter in question had no say in the matter.

No one in the commune had ever met Matthias's daughter. None of Matthias's children lived there because Matthias had abandoned his family long before. But Benjamin knew that she was only twenty years old, and according to Matthias's description, quite pretty, so the trade was settled. In preparation for their wedding, a thrilled Ann ordered Sojourner to clean the house and wash the wedding clothes, not that Sojourner knew they were wedding clothes. Sojourner was neither invited to nor informed of the holy event until after it transpired.

Soon after the wedding, Benjamin set off to claim his promised compensation prize. He found Matthias's wife and children living in poverty, under the assumption that Matthias was dead. Relieved to have fewer mouths to feed, Matthias's wife eagerly sent Isabella away with Benjamin, along with four sons as a bonus. Unbeknownst to her deadbeat dad, Isabella was already married—her wedding had transpired about a month previous—but this didn't bother Benjamin too much because the rest of Matthias's description had been accurate; she certainly was young and pretty.

When they arrived back at the commune, Benjamin, in keeping with their ecclesiastical customs, confessed a sin—he had already raped Isabella en route, without waiting for Matthias to conduct a wedding ceremony. Matthias whipped his daughter for the offense, a beating so severe that he was indicted for assault. (But only because Isabella was a married woman at the time—the right to assault her now belonged to her husband, not her father.) The rape gave Matthias a convenient resolution to his mistake in promising his married daughter to another man; he pronounced Isabella's marriage "virtually annulled by the act of hers and Folger's on the road." [20]

About two years after meeting Matthias, Elijah Pierson became violently ill, possibly due to food poisoning—or was he intentionally poisoned? Matthias forbade commune residents from summoning a doctor or even nursing Elijah themselves, asserting that administering medical care showed lack of faith in divine healing power. Elijah died and as Elijah's heirs tried to get their inheritances out of Matthias's hands, they became increasingly suspicious that Elijah's death had been caused by foul play. [21]

Ann moved out of Matthias's room and into Sojourner's. "I am come to you for protection," she explained. The protection sought was not from the suspected murderer, but the victim. "For Father has gone off, laying on the sofa or somewhere or other, and left me alone in the bed and Pierson's devilish spirit haunts me."

Hauntings did not scare Sojourner. "I wish to God he would appear to me," she said. "I would ask him what be wanted."

Benjamin and Ann soon reconciled, left the commune and reported Matthias to the police for theft. With their leader's arrest becoming increasingly more likely, other commune members started to flee as well.

They warned Sojourner, but she remained Matthias's last faithful follower. And much following was required, because he took all the remaining money and left town without her. She eventually found him, but to no avail; he was arrested a few minutes later.

The Folgers accused Sojourner of poisoning their coffee, a character attack that they hoped would cripple her effectiveness as a witness for Matthias's defense. [22] In the midst of the scandal, Ann got a book deal. The book described Sojourner as "the most wicked of the wicked" and attributed Elijah's death to poisoned blackberries, naming Matthias, who picked the berries, and Sojourner, who sprinkled them with sugar and served them to the white people, as potential culprits. [23]

Another former commune member told Sojourner about Ann's book project before it was published. "All this blessed winter Mrs. Benjamin Folger has been writing against you and Matthias," she said. "She will overcome you, and Matthias will be hung, and all the Christians have been helping her."

"I have got the truth, and I know it, and I will crush them with the truth," announced Sojourner.

The naiveté that had made her first encounter with the judicial system so trying had since evaporated. Now an experienced litigant, Sojourner acted swiftly to defend herself. She gathered character references from her former "employers," including the Dumonts, who had enslaved her; successfully sued the Folgers for slander; and found an author to write a competing book about the commune, telling her side of the story. Sojourner's account proved to be a more titillating read than Ann's; Ann had somehow forgotten to mention her affair with the prophet Matthias in her version of the history.

Matthias served three months in prison for assault and then went free. [24]

Eight years later, Sojourner was up early on a snowy day. Snow brought the opportunity to shovel neighbors' walkways in exchange for a tiny bit of much-needed cash, but only if she could arrive at their porches first, offering her services before anyone else did.

"You ought to have let me have the job," complained another would-be snow shoveler when he saw that she had beaten him to the task. "I'm poor and need the pay for my family."

"I am poor too and I need it for mine," Sojourner called back, but her terse response disguised the anguish she felt about depriving someone else of the pennies she was earning. [25] Since she had been a slave almost all of her life before joining Matthias's commune, these poverty-laden years since it had dissolved had been her first experience with capitalism. [26] She wasn't impressed.

"The rich rob the poor, and the poor rob one another," she observed. And as she searched her soul for a better way, Sojourner felt a call to the ministry. [27] With this emancipating realization, she finally abandoned the name given to her in slavery and named herself Sojourner Truth, a fitting title for an itinerant preacher. [28]

She didn't tell her employer or her children—now grown-up—about her plans until just before she left.

"What are you going east for?" one of them asked, after she had packed her clothing into a pillowcase and started for the door.

"The Spirit calls me there and I must go," answered Sojourner, and with nothing but that pillowcase, a basket of food, and two shillings, she traveled toward towns she had never been to, where she knew no one. [29]

She eventually came to a Millerite camp meeting. Millerites had gathered to await their Lord Jesus Christ, whom they predicted would manifest himself to them in the very near future. [30] Sojourner had already experienced a supposed second coming of her Lord in the form of Matthias, and after how that had turned out, she was feeling less enthusiasm about that particular theology this time around. When other camp worshippers asked her if she was a believer, she answered diplomatically. "It has not been revealed to me. Perhaps if I could read, I would see it differently."

"Oh, don't you believe the Lord is coming?" asked a dismayed believer.

"I believe the Lord is as near as he can be, and not be it."

On one part of the grounds, she found a group of people who were particularly agitated, panicking about imminent doom.

Sojourner hopped up on a stump and shouted, "'Hear! Hear!'"

When she had their attention, she continued: "Children, why are you making such a to-do? Are you not commanded to watch and pray? You are neither watching nor praying. Retire to your tents, and there watch and pray without noise or tumult, for the Lord will not come to such a scene of confusion. The Lord comes still and quiet. The Lord might come, move all through the camp, and go away again, and you would never know it in this state!"

Her speech did seem to soothe her listeners, many of whom heeded her advice. Sojourner became a camp meeting favorite, her speeches punctuated by humor and singing.

At another meeting, camp leaders tried to quiet a group of young men who had come to heckle the proceedings, but the situation only escalated. The hecklers brought in about a hundred allies and threatened to set fire to the tents. Camp leadership was at an impasse; some wanted to call the police, but others fervently opposed police intervention because of their pacifist convictions. Sojourner was hiding from the mob with other worshippers, but unlike them, she had extra cause for fear. "I am the only colored person here," she thought. "And on me, probably, their wicked mischief will fall first, and perhaps fatally."

But she did not approve of hiding. She tried to reason with herself: "Shall I run away and hide from the Devil? Me? A servant of the living God? Have I not faith enough to go out and quell that mob, when I know it is written: 'One shall chase a thousand, and two put ten thousand to flight'? I know there are not a thousand here and I know I am a servant of the living God. I'll go to the rescue, and the Lord shall go with and protect me."

Sojourner described the feeling that came over her like this: "I felt as if I had three hearts! And that they were so large, my body could hardly hold them!" She urged the others to help her confront the would-be arsonists, but finding no willing volunteers, she came out of hiding alone and started to sing. Her powerful voice quickly attracted a dense crowd of rioters. They carried weapons but didn't threaten her, and after listening to a few more hymns and talking with Sojourner, left without causing any other disturbances. [31]

Sojourner eventually found herself a home within another commune called the Northampton Association, where she had a more uplifting experience than she had with Matthias. Northampton was a great place for enriching the mind, regularly inviting famous reformers such as William Lloyd Garrison and Frederick Douglass to lecture. The primitive living conditions were less accommodating to the body. [32] When Sojourner first arrived, she "did not fall in love at first sight" but she was won over as she witnessed "accomplished, literary and refined persons" living so simply. Unlike her previous commune experience, here she found "equality of feeling, a liberty of thought and speech, and a largeness of soul." [33]

Like most communal experiments, in the end, Northampton would be a financial failure, but through it, Sojourner found her way out of poverty. When the Northampton Association dissolved, Sojourner dictated her autobiography to another former Northampton resident. [34] Now, in spite of her illiteracy, she had been key to the authorship of two books. *The Narrative of Sojourner Truth* propelled her to fame and provided her with a small income for the rest of her life.

At age 17, a Polish girl named Ernestine Potowska hired a sleigh driver to take her 65 miles to court. Her father, a Jewish rabbi, had arranged a marriage for her, as was the custom in her community. [35] The intended husband was an older man and Ernestine knew that he would rule over her like her father. She told her father that she would only marry for love, and only to someone who would treat her as an equal partner. [36] When he did not relent, she cried at her fiancé's feet, begging him to release her. Not only did he refuse, but he tried to confiscate the inheritance Ernestine's mother had left her, claiming he had a right to her property as her betrothed, whether she went through with the wedding or not. [37]

As she traveled to court to defend her inheritance, the sleigh broke down. The driver wanted to wait until the morning to fix it, but Ernestine persuaded him to go for help immediately because her case would be heard in the morning. She waited alone in the snow until 4:00 AM, listening to the howling wolves that surrounded her. She must have been exhausted, yet she argued her case personally the next morning. (Lawyers were rarely used in these proceedings.)

She won the case but soon afterward left Poland, leaving most of the inheritance she had defended behind, as well as the faith of her youth. [38]

While she may have abandoned the religion, Ernestine continued to vigorously defend the Jewish community against anti-Semitic criticism.

When her friend Horace Seaver described Jewish people as "bigoted, narrow, exclusive, and totally unfit for a progressive people like the Americans" in an editorial in his newspaper, Ernestine sprang to the defense of her people—whom she obviously saw as her people, even if she hadn't worshipped among them for decades. [39]

I imagine her Jewish peers nodding vigorously as they read these words in Ernestine's letter to the editor: "In spite of the barbarous treatment and deadly persecution they suffered, they have lived and spread and outlived much of the poisonous rancor and prejudice against them."

But they probably stopped nodding when she continued. "For a Jew, there is but one step between his religion and atheism." From an atheist like Ernestine, this was a high compliment, but I doubt that a devout Jew would appreciate it as such. [40]

Although Horace published Ernestine's rebuke of him in his paper, instead of apologizing, he followed it with a rebuttal of his "too sensitive sister." And more anti-Semitism.

Clearly, Ernestine had inherited the long-suffering diligence of her Jewish forebears, for she wrote back again, and thus, a written debate ensued that would go on for months. [41] As the debate continued, any precept of civility melted away. Ernestine called Horace "mean and cowardly" and he made fun of her for "scolding." [42]

"Perhaps if you had received a little more scolding from women, the right kind I mean, you might deserve it less now," wrote Ernestine. [43]

While living in England, Ernestine became a fervent supporter of Robert Owen's social reform movement. Owenites advocated that children should receive schooling instead of factory jobs and that social problems like crime should be addressed at the community level instead of by punishing individuals. They also had a more progressive view of the role of women in society. Owenite women organized conventions, gave speeches, and, um, did the dishes. [44] (Hey, it was the 1830s—and while women have come a long way, modern women still do most of the dishes. [45])

With a group of Owenites and her new husband, William Rose, Ernestine immigrated to the United States to start a commune—a popular experiment among religious and secular groups alike at the time. [46]

The boat ride from England to the United States was about six weeks long, and after that much time in close quarters, the newlyweds realized they'd rather not have their travel companions as permanent neighbors. [47] Instead, they became businesspeople, opening a shop in New York where Ernestine sold perfume and William sold jewelry. [48] There, the Roses met regularly with freethinkers, agnostics, atheists and others who worked together to promote ethics without theology—a sort of church congregation for nonreligious people. But even without biblical sanctions against women at these secular gatherings, female speakers were not the norm. Ernestine had to get creative to get floor time, scripting her addresses to seem like spontaneous responses to the scheduled, male speakers. [49]

Within only a few months of arriving in America, she had learned enough about her new country to know that under American law, everything she owned was considered the property of her husband. She had fought to retain her property from her betrothed in Poland, and she was ready and willing to fight such injustice again, even if her new legal steward was someone she liked as much as William.

She didn't know the city very well, her English was poor, and she had no allies to help her, yet she traveled door-to-door with a petition supporting a long-shot bill to give married women property rights. Most people she spoke with had trouble catching the vision. Women told her that they had enough rights already and men told her that women had too many rights. Some women expressed worries that the menfolk would laugh at them if they signed. [50] After five months of work, she had only managed to get five signatures on her petition. [51]

After years of petitioning alone for property rights for married women, Ernestine met two other New Yorkers with the same goal, Paulina Wright Davis and Elizabeth Cady Stanton, and the three joined forces. [52] Twelve years after Ernestine started her first petition, the state of New York finally changed the law to allow married women to keep the deeds to their real estate but not their wages—a concession that was more likely to benefit heiresses than housekeepers. While critiquing the law as "only for the favored few and not for the suffering many" Ernestine saw this change as "a beginning and an important step, for it proved that a law had to be altered." [53]

And only two years later, Elizabeth announced further progress: "So this winter it seems a bill sprung up in the lower House to this effect, that a married woman might work hard and put, for instance, $1000 in the bank, and then she should have a perfect right to draw out $250. The remainder should be the disposal of her husband, whoever or whatever he might chance to be. This was magnanimous!! $250 is a great sum for a woman to have at her disposal, particularly if she has the skills to make more and providence to save what she earns. This bill passed the Assembly and went to the Senate; and what do you think that august body said to this outburst of chivalry from the lower House? In their amendment they surpassed their co-adjutors, and themselves even, in generosity. They said a married woman might not only deposit money in a savings bank, but she might also draw it *all* out again *herself*. The length, the breadth, the height and depth of this act of mercy and justice is only equaled by the fact that our legislature has been but fifty short years in arriving at its truth." [54]

When Antoinette Brown met women's rights activist Lucy Stone at Oberlin, she thought she had found someone who would support her goal to become the first woman ordained as a Protestant minister, but Lucy's reaction was less than encouraging.

"You will never be allowed to do this," said Lucy. "You will never be allowed to stand in a pulpit, nor to preach in a church, and certainly you will never be ordained." [55]

Lucy hadn't always been so cynical. Five years earlier, she had tried to effect change at her own hometown church congregation. A local deacon had been placed in a church disciplinary trial for sharing his pulpit with abolitionist Abby

Kelley. When the minister called for a vote, Lucy raised her hand to vote against punishing him—a bold and unwelcome move from a woman.

"Don't you count her," said the minister. "She is a member, but she is not a voting member."

Lucy held firm, so much so that the vote had to be taken seven times because of her protests. But her efforts had not yielded fruit, and Lucy had gradually become disenchanted with religious patriarchy. Their Oberlin clergyman, the renowned Charles Grandison Finney, inspired Nette but gave Lucy headaches. [56]

When Nette applied for postgraduate theology studies, Oberlin officials balked; their charter called for men and women to have equal access to courses, but it had never occurred to them that a woman would want to study for the ministry. In the end, Oberlin officials allowed Nette to attend, and of course, pay them for the education, but with the knowledge that she would never receive a diploma. [57]

Nette was almost universally scorned for her decision to attend divinity school, both by those who wanted to maintain the male-only status quo and by other women's rights advocates, who criticized her for agreeing to such an unfair arrangement. Lucy was particularly unimpressed by this rather lopsided compromise.

"Nette, I am so sorry you are at Oberlin on terms which to me seem dishonorable. They trampled your womanhood and you did not spurn it. I do believe that even they would have thought better of you if you had stayed away," Lucy told her. [58]

"You think I have come back to Oberlin upon dishonorable terms? Then you don't know me. I never did a dishonorable public act that could make me blush to look anybody in the face, never!" insisted Nette. "I came back to study theology and get knowledge. I do get it." [59]

"I wonder if you have any idea how dreadfully I feel about your studying that old musty theology, which already has its grave clothes on and is about to be buried in so deep a grave that no resurrection trump can call it into being," Lucy began one particularly macabre rant. She followed up that metaphor with others, invoking images of starvation, darkness, pollution, stench, bloodstains and decaying corpses before getting to the point: "You have honesty and candor now, more than most others. I dread to see these noble qualities trimmed and your generous soul belittled to the defense of an outgrown creed. Oh Nette, it is intolerable and I can think of it with allowance only when I think that the loss of what is invaluable in you will purchase apparatus to batter down that wall of Bible, brimstone, church and corruption which has hitherto hemmed women into nothingness. The fact that you have entered a field forbidden to women will be a good to the sex, but I half fear it will be purchased at too dear a rate." [60]

"Lucy, if I believed I should one day throw away the Bible, should one day come to believe that prayer to God was impious, that the Sabbath was an ordinance of man, that the church was the great reservoir of iniquity and that the present system of theology was composed of blasphemous dogmas, still I firmly believe that I should continue to be thankful that I had spent three years in the theological investigations at Oberlin, merely for the sake of the mental discipline I have acquired and which I believe could be obtained in no other way." [61]

"Why, Nette, you would get as much discipline in a thousand ways, with far less danger to yourself, and you would learn more of the world in one month by actual conflict with it then you possibly can in the three years you will spend there." [62]

As women, the Oberlin Ladies Board had no say in the decision to admit Nette to divinity school, so they had to resort to passive-aggressive means to make their (strongly opposed) feelings known. They forced Nette out of her paid Oberlin job just as Nette's family decided to discontinue financial support of her education. [63]

Lydia Finney, a member of the Ladies Board and wife of Reverend Finney, tried to reason with Nette. "You will never feel yourself wise enough to go directly against the opinions of all the great men of the past," she said.

"That is exactly what Professor Finney is doing and we all feel that he is making a great advance of thought," answered Nette. [64]

Nette tried to support herself independently instead by teaching art classes, and when her classes proved popular, she sent Lucy a triumphant letter: "I decided to stay here and as I told you, trust Providence for assistance, and Lucy, Providence has assisted me. I learned then to cast myself on the Lord as I had never done before and I learned to pray to him as I had never prayed before. Perhaps you will think me superstitious, but I have learned to talk with God as I would talk with a friend and I feel that to have His sympathy is all I need. You know, we used to wish sometimes that we could live on and feel no need of sympathy of anyone? And I have learned to feel so. I do not mean that I do not wish for sympathy, but I can feel perfectly happy without it and when anything troubles me I can tell it all to God and He certainly does comfort me even in the most trifling griefs. And see how He has helped me in pecuniary matters?" [65]

When Nette would tell new acquaintances that she was attending divinity school, they would pepper her with questions about her plans. Was she hoping to write sermons for a brother or a future husband, perhaps? Some assumed she was joking, some stared in amazement and some startled in horror. Nette found no distinction between men's and women's reactions, reporting that both seemed to "have their eyes opened and their tongues loosed to about the same extent." [66]

Even the professors didn't seem to understand her purpose there. Early in the term, Nette's hero, Reverend Finney, called on each theology student to stand up one at a time and talk about their decision to become clergymen. When another student reminded him that Nette hadn't had a turn, a startled Finney said, "Oh! The women—we don't ask them to speak now."

But after some discussion about how Nette was studying for the ministry, just like the other students, he said, "Oh, of course then, she must tell us why she wishes to become a minister."

When it was Nette's turn to open studies with prayer, Reverend Finney passed her and asked the next male student, causing Nette to burst into tears and flee the room. He followed her out, and finding her far ahead of him on the street, yelled, "Antoinette, you must pray! You shall pray! I did not know you wanted to pray." [67]

"I am no more conservative, creed-loving, time-serving or bigoted than I was three years since—am no less of a freethinker or independent actor," Nette proudly wrote to Lucy upon completion of her coursework. "But I have more settled and consistent views and more self-reliance, or rather more implicit reliance upon an arm that will never fail me and will hold me up in opposition to our mistaken world if need be. In short, I have a great deal more individuality." [68]

Oberlin officials had not relented in their decision to withhold Nette's diploma. When she left Oberlin, it appeared that in addition to being no more conservative, creed-loving and bigoted, she was also no closer to being ordained.

As Nette tried to network with ministers, she could "hardly find anyone to talk with." Those who did agree to speak to her seemed to be trapped in an epidemic of not-quite-readiness. Some weren't "quite ready to get a new standing point" on their position against female ordination. Others were more persuadable yet "not quite ready to advocate" on her behalf. [69]

Her beloved Professor Finney "expressed a world of sympathy" and called her "his dear child, daughter, dearest sister," but proved better at being nice than being helpful. [70]

A less nice but equally unhelpful minister urged her to "become a missionary in some foreign land rather than a helplessly handicapped woman minister in a civilized community." [71]

"Am I following a chimera and depending upon a bubble?" Nette asked Lucy. "I think not, but there is not a friend in the wide world, so far as I know, that can feel that I am acting wisely and at the call of God…Oh dear! Well, I must stand alone."

Nette was feeling "a vague sensation of dread or apprehension" about "the dim, unknown future." [72] The future carried fewer unknowns from the perspective of the men she was approaching. One prophesied to her, "Whatever you may think ought to be, the place and position of woman will never be greatly different from what it is now."

With no prospects for a job in the ministry, Nette accepted a job with a women's charity. [73] She intended to start work immediately following the first National Woman's Rights Convention, but her new employer didn't want her anymore after learning that she had participated in such a shocking event. [74]

"What hard work it is to stand alone! I am forever wanting to lean over onto somebody but nobody will support me and I think seriously of swallowing the yardstick or putting on a buckram corset, so as to get a little assistance somehow, for I am determined to maintain the perpendicular position," she told Lucy. [75] "Oh dear! Lucy, I do wish we believed alike. I wish somebody believed as I do." [76]

Seeking allies in her quest for ordination, Nette introduced a resolution to her fellow suffragists: "Resolved, that the Bible recognizes the rights, duties and privileges of woman as a public teacher, as every way equal with those of man; that it enjoins upon her no subjection that is not enjoined upon him; and that it truly and practically recognizes neither male nor female in Christ Jesus."

Ernestine Rose was the first to object. "I see no need to appeal to any written authority, particularly when it is so obscure and indefinite as to admit of different interpretations," she said, before submitting a counter-resolution declaring the need for women's rights in more secular terms.

Ernestine's resolution was adopted and Nette's was tabled.

Nette had more success with her next venture. She passed along a message to Lucretia, who was presiding, telling her that she felt called to offer a prayer. [77] A news account of the first National Convention had scoffed at Nette's attempt to support women's rights with scripture at a meeting that didn't even follow the common custom of opening with prayer. [78] Afterwards, Nette had confided in Lucy that she wished they would open with prayer, but "most of the members, I suppose, do not approve of anything of this kind." [79]

Lucretia responded that she would not require prayer, but had no objections to spontaneous prayers by attendees. Nette stood and prayed.

Toward the end of the meeting, Nette's resolution came up for debate again.

"I cannot have any objection to any one's interpreting the Bible as he or she thinks best but I object that such interpretation go forth as the doctrine of this Convention," Ernestine stated.

"We have met here for nobler purposes than to discuss theology," complained Ernestine, as if forgetting that Nette had chosen theology as her life work. "Our claims are on the broad basis of human rights, irrespective of what Moses, Paul or Peter may say. Those who have nothing better to do may dispute about these authorities." [80]

Nette's resolution did not pass, but she learned some things from Ernestine during that debate, or at least, from the part that came before the personal digs.

"I'm very sensitive about fastening theological questions upon the woman movement," Nette told Elizabeth Cady Stanton after a subsequent meeting, as if borrowing Ernestine's script. "It is not that I am horrified at your calling St. Paul's writings human parchments; but because I think when it is done officially that it is really unjust to the cause. It is compelling it to endorse something which does not belong to it. When you write for yourself, say exactly what you please, but if you write as chairwoman of the Woman's Rights Convention, do not compel us to endorse anything foreign to the movement." [81]

Nette eventually found a congregation willing to hire her, in part because they could not find a male minister willing to accept their low wages. [82] Because she wanted to be ordained within her own faith, Nette refused an offer of $1000 per year to preach at an interdenominational chapel for a $300 per year ministerial post. [83]

Regardless of the pay, Nette was enthusiastic about her "little parish" and the opportunity to practice her pastoral skills in "a miniature world in good and evil."

Nette's ordination took place several months after she began work; it took that long to find ordained ministers willing to participate in the ceremony, which was a "very solemn thing" to Nette and, in spite of the humble venue, a wild spectacle to the press that immediately made her famous, or infamous, throughout the country.

Shortly after her ordination, Nette performed a wedding, the first officiated by a woman to her knowledge. Susan B. Anthony was so excited about this milestone that she tried to introduce a women's rights speech into the proceedings, but other wedding guests intercepted.

Not all of Nette's friends shared Susan's enthusiasm. "Some of my old intimates of my own age look at me with a kind of curious incredulity, and utterly unable to comprehend the kind of motive which could lead me to take so peculiar position in life," said Nette. She speculated that "it must have been more or less difficult for any young minister to meet his familiar friends with exactly the same freedom as he did before you take a ministerial duty. For a woman minister, the situation was even more estranging. " [84]

"You are the biggest little goose and granny fuss that I ever did see. So you will not go to South Butler! Then you want to be giffarooned or gibbeted or something of that sort!" Nette told Lucy, when she backed out of her promise to give a woman's rights speech at Nette's church.

Lucy worried that her presence would injure Nette's reputation within the church, a concern that Nette dismissed as "nonsense."

"They are all expecting you there and they know besides that you wear bloomers and are an infidel." [85]

A few months after the first National Woman's Rights Convention, Lucy had received a letter from the deacon of her local Congregational church, informing her that they were excommunicating her because she had "engaged in a course of life evidently inconsistent with her covenant engagement to this church."

"My course of life is not only not inconsistent with, but demanded by my covenant engagements," Lucy had written back, but to no avail. [86]

"I never will have a friend who is ashamed of me or I ashamed of her or one that must keep away from me to preserve my reputation or ensure my success. I'm still much more of a woman than a minister." Nette told her, adding that "any congregation I may preach to will not be scared over much by anything you will say. They believe in free speech!" And anyhow, "everybody there knows you and your reputation as well almost now as they will after seeing you, for your fame is abroad in the land. They think you of course worse than you are." [87]

Even Ernestine spoke at churches regularly—and she was an atheist. [88] Nette suspected that Lucy had other motives for staying away; maybe she didn't care to waste her time in such a "wee village" or worse, maybe Lucy didn't want to see her.

"I have still need of you whether you have of me or not," she admitted. "Unless you wish me to become as bigoted as you think the church is, don't stay away to make me so." [89]

Not long into Nette's service at South Butler, one of the most conservative members of her congregation approached her and begged her to visit her dying son. In seeking Nette's help, she was extending an olive branch, because until then she had been one of the least accepting of female clergy, but Nette was dismayed to find that she expected Nette to compel the boy to a deathbed conversion by threatening him with eternal damnation.

After holding vigil with another dying child, Nette found herself pressured to preach a funeral sermon chastising the mother for giving birth out of wedlock.

These experiences led Nette to question her denomination's doctrines around death and the afterlife, and as she studied, only parts of the Bible seemed inspired to her "but other parts definitely not and discrepancies began to make themselves evident."

When members of her congregation asked her doctrinal questions, she found that she was having trouble giving the "right" answers, according to Congregational church theology, without troubling her own conscience.

"Suddenly, I found that the whole groundwork of my faith had dropped away from me," wrote Nette. "I found myself absolutely believing nothing, not even in my own continuous personal existence" and yet, "I had so lately received ordination as a sincerely orthodox believer that I felt as though my sincerity at that time might even be called in question." [90]

In the midst of this cognitive dissonance, Nette started having nightmares. Sleep disruptions left her physically exhausted and prone to illness.

As an advocate for women's ordination, I would love to report that the triumph of Nette's ordination led to a long career in the ministry and many other women following in her footsteps. Instead, less than a year after the triumph of her ordination, Nette made the heartrending decision to resign her ministerial post. [91] It would be another decade before Olympia Brown became the next Protestant woman to be ordained. [92]

Susan B. Anthony tried to recruit Nette to campaign for women's rights with her, but Nette declined. "I have the blues and feel horribly. That's the whole of the matter," she said. [93]

Ernestine was game, but the chaplain at the United States capitol would not allow Ernestine to speak. [94] He was one of many ministers boycotting Ernestine after a recent, well-publicized clash between her and a rowdy group of male theology students at a Bible convention. [95]

Unlike Nette, Ernestine could find nothing favorable to the cause of women's rights in that book, which she credited as the cause of "war, slavery, rapine, murder, and all the vices and crimes that blind selfishness and corruption could suggest." Shouting to be heard over the screaming male students, she told the women in the room: "The Bible has enslaved you; the churches have been built upon your subjugated necks. Do you wish to be free? Then you must trample the Bible, the church, and the priests under your feet." [96]

Susan attempted to pacify the chaplain with an appeal to freedom of religion. "Ours is a country professing religious as well as civil liberty. To not allow any and every faith to be declared in the capitol of the nation makes the profession to religious freedom a perfect mockery," she said.

"That's true," agreed the chaplain, before repeating that he could not allow an atheist to speak at the Capitol. [97]

During their speaking tour, Ernestine startled Susan by criticizing their own allies, Lucy Stone and Wendell Phillips. [98] Lucy and Wendell had both given speeches complaining that male immigrants could vote while American-born women could not. Wendell had blamed Jewish people for opposition to women's rights, even going so far as to paradoxically call the Christian saint Paul—whose words had given women's rights activists so much trouble—a Jew instead of a Christian. [99]

"I've heard them both express themselves in terms of prejudice against granting to foreigners the right to citizenship," Ernestine told Susan.

"I don't believe either of them could have that narrow, mean prejudice in their souls," objected Susan.

"You are blinded. You cannot see nor hear anything wrong in that clique of abolitionists. I'm not connected with any society or association, either in religion or reform, so I can judge all impartially." [100]

Susan wasn't convinced that Ernestine's lack of religious and political affiliations really did make her less biased. After all, hadn't she praised a Hungarian leader for his stance against European oppression, ignoring his apparent tolerance for American slavery? [101]

"I could see reasons why he pursued the course he did," insisted Ernestine.

"Yes!" Susan gloated, confident that she had won her point. "You excuse him because you can see the causes why he acted and spoke thus, while you will not allow me to bring forward the probable causes of Lucy's seeming fault."

But the argument was not won. As the clash continued, Susan cried out in frustration: "Mrs. Rose, there is not one in the reform ranks whom you think is true, not one but who panders to the popular feeling!"

"I can't help it," said Ernestine. "I take them by the words of their own mouths. I trust all until their own words or acts declare them false to truth and right. No one can tell the hours of anguish I have suffered as one after another I have seen those whom I trusted betray falsity of motive, as I have been compelled to place one after another on the list of panderers to public favor."

"Do you know Mrs. Rose, that I can but feel that you place me too on that list," whispered a horrified Susan.

But Susan was yet safe. "I will tell you," said Ernestine, "when I see you untrue."

They became silent. Susan transcribed a verse from a church hymnal and offered it to Ernestine. She may have meant it as a peace offering, but it was a poor choice of gift for an unbeliever. Ernestine started to cry.

"Mrs. Rose, have I been wicked and hurt your feelings?" asked Susan.

"No," she answered, "but I expect never to be understood while I live."

Ernestine was at least somewhat right; Susan confessed to her diary that night that she, for one, didn't understand Ernestine at all. Trying to sort out the meaning of the conversation, she concluded that "Mrs. Rose is not appreciated nor cannot be by this age." Ernestine was even more radical than the most extreme reformers. Associating themselves with someone whose views were even further from the mainstream than their own, Susan thought, would bring on even more persecution than these weary reformers already endured. [102]

When Lucretia suggested that Nette serve as president of the next Woman's Rights Convention, Nette demurred. [103] "Everything seems uncertain in these days, since I have taken to idleness. So please choose some better material for a president." [104] The honor fell to Ernestine.

After several months of recuperation, Nette did join Susan and Ernestine on their speaking tour. Even with their religious differences, Ernestine and Nette proved they could work together as amicable and effective partners. [105] Ernestine would tell religious people, "Whatever good you would do out of fear of punishment, or hope of reward hereafter, the atheist would do simply because it is good." [106] This was a sentiment Nette could respect, especially now, when her faith felt shaky but she was finding it possible to go on lecturing "on the basis of belief in the law of love" and "in practical service, in justice, and a few moral principles."

Gradually, Nette felt faith again, but it was of a different sort. She had new ideas about theology; views that she believed would disqualify her as a Congregational minister. She reached out to Horace Greeley about revisiting his offer of a position as a nondenominational preacher. [107]

"Of course I can never again be the pastor of a church," she told him. "But I must be a preacher for the people." [108]

Never say, "never." Nette would return to organized religion again in her later years. But she was right about one thing: "I shall not fail!" she said. "There is that within me that gives me the assurance of success!"

More than two decades after giving up her ministry at the Congregational church in South Butler, Nette wrote to a Unitarian minister about joining their ranks. "Having grown up in the midst of those who shared common beliefs, sins, sympathies and work religiously, I have greatly missed the moral support which that kind of association can give," she explained in her letter. She did have misgivings. "I do not know, nor could I well judge, unsided, whether my present views, my past orthodox beliefs or my womanhood would tempt the cold shoulder rather than the warm one from the average Unitarian today."

They accepted her application, but with a warning; she might have difficulty finding work. "You are, of course, aware of the feeling that exists in many of our established churches in regard to the propriety of women appearing in the pulpit," they wrote. [109] Their warning proved accurate; Nette was unsuccessful at finding a permanent post, but she did go on to preach often as a special guest. [110]

Almost three decades after Nette finished theology studies at Oberlin, the school got proud of her and offered her an honorary Masters degree for the work she had actually completed.

Looking back, Nette explained the barriers to her quest for ordination this way: "The American clergyman of the 30s and 40s was an oracle and a political and social arbiter as well as the head of his church and he feared the growth of a new power—in the hands of women."

Unfortunately, her words hold true in many patriarchal religions today. Religious institutions remain among the last bastions of overt sexism in American society. Many communities of faith have outright bans on women in positions of authority and bar women from participating in religious rituals.

Sexism in religion is particularly difficult to address because religious patriarchy has been established through centuries of tradition, many people believe that religious sexism is mandated by God and religious institutions are largely exempt from discrimination laws that govern other sectors of society.

Although I am a person of faith, I can't fault Ernestine Rose for saying, "All the progress I can see in religion is the getting out of it, not in it." [111] But I respectfully question Ernestine's assumption that abstaining from patriarchy is a more feminist act than combating it from within.

Nette's efforts to change sexist policy and theology from within her own religion benefited everyone, even Ernestine, because sexism in religion doesn't only affect religious people. It spills over into all areas of society, affecting the way people vote, work, and even how they think about the women that surround them on a day-to-day basis. Feminists who focus on sexism in politics and workplaces need the help of religious feminists because one of their greatest barriers to success is the sexism people learn to tolerate at their places of worship.

It is within the context of religious faith that Nette and Sojourner developed the keen sense of right and wrong, compassion for others and thirst for social justice that led them to work as activists. A combination of edifying spiritual experiences and less positive encounters with religious patriarchy instilled in them the passion, eloquence and optimism that made them the powerful activists they became.

CHAPTER FIVE
How do we break the glass ceiling?

"Don't be discouraged. There is no doubt about our losing many opportunities because of our sex, but you must also bear in mind the disadvantages all students labor under, unless in exceptional cases. Crowded together in masses, they only see at a distance the most interesting cases. ...Now I say this because I don't want you to over-estimate the worth of pantaloons. Disguise in France or elsewhere would by no means give you all you need; if the disguise were complete you would just be reduced to the level of the common poor student, and would be, I think, quite disappointed. It needs also that influential men should take an interest in you, and give you chances quite beyond the ordinary run." [1]
–Elizabeth Blackwell, 1854

"With few talents, and very moderate means for developing them, I have accomplished more than many women of genius and education would have done in my place, for the reason that confidence and faith in their own powers were wanting." [2]
–Marie Zakrzewska, 1857

When Harriot Hunt's sister, Sarah, became ill, Harriot sought the best medical care available to save her, bringing in a stream of doctors who administered a variety of leeches and poisons.

"All these remedies, no benefit!" observed Harriot.

Twenty-five-year-old Harriot was paying for her sister's healthcare on the meager salary of a schoolteacher. She had supported the family since her father became too sick to work three years earlier.

Entering a profession made her something of an "enigma" among her married female friends, who liked to boast to her they had "nothing to do" as if that were something to be proud of. [3] And yet, over a century before Betty Friedan noticed the "problem that had no name" haunting unfulfilled American housewives in the 1950s, Harriot diagnosed the same problem in her friends. [4] She saw them sinking into a "monotonous half-life" that was "poisoning womanhood." Not so for Harriot, who basked in "the magic of usefulness." At least, she did at first.

"The miserable remuneration commonly given to female teachers, sadly cripples their usefulness," noted Harriot. "It weakens their own estimation of the worth of their services by showing them at what a low market value those services are held."

The pay certainly was inadequate to cover the growing mountain of doctors' bills that accumulated until her father's death, and now again with Sarah.

Sarah spent her time propped up in her bed, reading medical books in an attempt to find the cure the doctors had missed. After nearly a year, Sarah evolved into an astute healthcare consumer, demanding a second opinion before she would accept any new treatments. Her doctor dutifully called in another for a consultation.

"We will talk the matter over, then I will give you an opinion," the doctor told Harriot, when she tried to join the meeting taking place in her own parlor.

"Is not this an outrage on common sense and propriety?" said Harriot. She "had watched the case day and night" and felt that she had "some observations about symptoms" and "some suggestions to offer at the consultation."

The Hunt family turned to a pair of married homeopaths, Dr. and Mrs. Mott, who were willing to openly discuss the case with them. They treated Sarah with water treatments, herbs, exercise and good hygiene. With this healthy lifestyle, and freedom from doctors' dangerous treatments, Sarah's condition improved.

"Here was my first thought of woman as a physician," recalled Harriot. After Sarah recovered, both sisters began working for the Motts as apprentices. [5] In the 1830s, many doctors learned medicine through apprenticeship, instead of medical school, but women were usually precluded from such training because of social mores against men and women working together. Because the Motts were a married team, Harriot and Sarah could evade scandal. [6]

Their apprenticeship came to an abrupt stop when Dr. Mott died and Mrs. Mott returned to her home country of England. Ready or not, it was time for Harriot and Sarah to start their own medical practice.

A medical journal mockingly suggested that this new female medical team probably couldn't differentiate between the sternum and the spinal column. Harriot did not let this "skeleton of a joke" get to her, but she did feel inadequate. As Harriot put it, a typical physician "studied before he practiced. We studied and practiced at the same time, for our knowledge seemed very trifling when we commenced."

Patients trickled in slowly, and yet Harriot and Sarah refused some of the few who arrived because they did not feel qualified to treat them. Each night, they stayed up late studying medical texts and investigating options for the patients they had seen that day.

"My mind was greedy of knowledge. The more I investigated, the more I was delighted, wonder-struck," said Harriot. However, the more she learned, the more she realized how much she needed a formal education. [7]

When Sarah married, she quit medicine. Since male doctors avoided Harriot more than "cholera, hydrophobia, smallpox, or any malignant disease," she was forced to carry on alone, but she found a friend in Mary Gove. Like Harriot, Mary advocated hydropathy—healing by bathing and drinking water. (The modern exhortation to drink eight glasses of water a day originated with hydropaths like Harriot and Mary Gove. [8]) Harriot disagreed with most of Mary's other ideas— Harriot thought the trendy Graham diet Mary loved was excessive and that Mary's advocacy of free love was an outright abomination. Even so, Harriot was inspired by Mary's public lectures to women about their own anatomy.

Following Mary's lead, Harriot formed the Charlestown Physiological Society, a group of about a dozen women, soon growing to fifty, that met twice a month. While the ladies knit stockings for charity, Harriot led discussions about female anatomy and women's health. Eventually, she expanded the effort, forming groups across the country.

"It is not fitting for women to know about themselves. It makes them nervous," male physicians told Harriot.

When Harriot's mother died, Harriot's sister Sarah, now a mother of six, invited Harriot to move in with her, but Harriot refused because moving would mean giving up her clinic. "My profession seemed hallowed to me. My patients were my family and a new purpose to labor more effectively for woman seized my soul." [9]

But her clinic was in peril. Adding to the disadvantage she already sustained as an anomalous female doctor, public opinion was shifting toward a preference for doctors with medical degrees. [10]

"Why do you not apply to Harvard College for permission to attend the lectures there?" asked one of Harriot's patients. "You have been in practice so many years in Boston, that such a request could not be refused."

"I have no doubt Harvard would open its doors to you," agreed another. "Your age and your birthright as a Bostonian must have weight with them." [11]

When Harriot inquired, Harvard officials were less encouraging. There was no such thing as a female medical student and they saw no reason to change that. [12]

Like Harriot, Elizabeth Blackwell's decision to become a doctor was rooted in a loved one's illness.

"You are fond of study, have health and leisure. Why not study medicine?" asked Elizabeth's friend. She considered her treatments to be as distressing as the disease itself. "If I could have been treated by a lady doctor, my worst sufferings would have been spared me," she told Elizabeth.

Weeks later, the suggestion was still occupying Elizabeth's thoughts, but it wasn't the only thing distracting her. Elizabeth was suffering from "an acute attack" of a "common malady: falling in love." It wasn't the first time she'd experienced such symptoms, but it proved to be as painful and disappointing as all the previous.

"I must have something to engross my thoughts, some object in life which will fill this vacuum and prevent this sad wearing away of the heart," she scribbled into her diary.

Elizabeth began asking around. What did the physicians she knew think of the idea of Elizabeth becoming a doctor? They were unanimous: "the idea was a good one" but "impossible."

Elizabeth applied to medical school anyway. She traveled to Philadelphia, where she secured an interview with a school official named Dr. Jackson.

"Well, what is it? What do you want?" he began abruptly.

"I want to study medicine."

Dr. Jackson laughed, then asked her why.

Elizabeth maintained her composure and detailed her plans. By the time she finished, Dr. Jackson had become more serious.

"I cannot give you an answer now," he told Elizabeth. "There are great difficulties, but I don't know that they are insurmountable. I'll let you know on Monday."

Elizabeth was pleased with the interview and felt hopeful, but on Monday Dr. Jackson told her the other professors were all opposed to admitting a woman to the school. He suggested some other schools she might apply to instead, and their officers referred her to still others.

At one school, she met with a man named Dr. Darrach, who stared at her silently for five straight minutes.

"Can you give me any encouragement?" Elizabeth finally asked.

"The subject is a novel one, madam, I have nothing to say either for or against it," he responded at last. "You have awakened trains of thought upon which my mind is taking action, but I cannot express my opinion to you either one way or another."

"Your opinion, I fear, is unfavorable," said Elizabeth.

"I did not say so. I beg you, madam, distinctly to understand that I express no opinion one way or another. The way in which my mind acts in this matter I do not feel at liberty to unfold."

"Shall I call on the other professors of your college?"

"I cannot take the responsibility of advising you to pursue such a course."

"Can you not grant me admittance to your lectures, as you do not feel unfavorable to my scheme?"

"I have said no such thing, whether favorable or unfavorable. I have not expressed any opinion and I beg leave to state clearly that the operation of my mind in regard to this matter I do not feel at liberty to unfold."

Not everyone was so guarded. "You cannot expect us to furnish you with a stick to break our heads with," said one dean, who was certain that if women were welcomed into the profession, they would steal all business from male doctors.

The professor of surgery at the largest college in Philadelphia, proposed an elaborate plan. She could disguise herself as a man and he would choose one or two trusted male students to spy on their classmates. If they heard rumors that anyone suspected her true identity, she could immediately drop out and flee the state.

Elizabeth vetoed the scheme.

"It was to my mind a moral crusade on which I had entered, a course of justice and common sense," she said. "And it must be pursued in the light of day, and with public sanction, in order to accomplish its end."

"Elizabeth, it is of no use trying. Thee cannot gain admission to these schools," one Quaker doctor told her. "Thee must go to Paris and don masculine attire to gain the necessary knowledge."

With interviews going this well in the United States, Elizabeth did consider studying in France. She had heard that in Paris, the French government sponsored free medical lectures open to anyone who wished to attend.

"If one country rejects me, I will go to another," she wrote to her family.

But the only woman Elizabeth knew of who had been educated in France had been disguised as a man. As rejections accumulated, even her most supportive friends urged her to give up.

"But a strong idea, long cherished 'til it has taken deep root in the soul and become an all-absorbing duty, cannot thus be laid aside," Elizabeth wrote home.

After being rejected by every major medical school in Philadelphia and New York, Elizabeth researched the less prestigious country schools and sent applications to a dozen at once. [13]

One of these was Geneva Medical College, now called Hobart and William Smith Colleges. The school had about 150 students, mostly young men from neighboring towns. The Geneva student body had a reputation for unruliness. Their wild behavior disrupted classes and more than once, residents of the neighborhood had reported Geneva students for causing a public nuisance.

Elizabeth sent Geneva officials a letter written by a doctor in Philadelphia who empathized with her plight. The letter explained that Elizabeth had been refused admission by several medical schools, but flattered Geneva faculty with the expectation that they would be freer from prejudice than those stuffy city doctors.

The faculty was not as unprejudiced as the letter presumed, but they were also hesitant to admit such with a refusal. Instead, they found an indirect way to accomplish the same end.

The dean called for a student meeting. Holding the letter in his hand, he announced that it contained "the most extraordinary request which had ever been made to the faculty." Then he turned the decision over to the students, informing them that they would only admit this woman if every student unanimously voted in her favor (like that would happen). [14]

Several of the students suspected that the letter had been planted by a rival school as a hoax. [15] Chaos ensued. Students vigorously campaigned for the nutty proposition with extravagant speeches and enthusiastic cheers. When the vote was taken, one person did vote "No," but the other students quickly identified the dissenter and rushed to the corner of the room where they helped him change his mind. [16]

A few days later, Elizabeth had an acceptance letter in her hand.

"Your plan is capital!" exclaimed Dr. James Webster, Elizabeth's new professor of anatomy, as he shook her hand on her first day of class. "What branches of medicine have you studied?"

"All but surgery," answered Elizabeth.

"Well, do you mean to practice surgery?" asked the dean, Dr. Charles Lee.

"Why, of course she does," Dr. Webster answered for her. "Think of the cases of femoral hernia. Only think what a well-educated woman would do in a city like New York. Why, my dear sir, she'd have her hands full in no time. Her success would be immense. Yes, yes, you'll go through the course, and get your diploma with great éclat too. We'll give you the opportunities. You'll make a stir, I can tell you."

He asked Elizabeth to wait in the lobby while he announced her arrival to the other students. After she heard them clap, she walked into the room. Unlike the townspeople, who had had stared at her like "a curious animal" as she walked to school that morning, the students seemed friendly.

After the lecture, Dr. Webster approached Elizabeth laughing.

"You attract too much attention, Miss Blackwell," he told her. "There was a very large number of strangers present this afternoon. I shall guard against this in the future."

"Yes. We were saying today that this step might prove quite a good advertisement for the college. If there were no other advantage to be gained, it will attract so much notice," said Dr. Lee. "I shall bring the matter into the medical journals. Why, I'll venture to say in ten years' time one-third of the classes in our colleges will consist of women. After the precedent you will have established, people's eyes will be opened."

"The little fat professor of anatomy is a capital fellow," Elizabeth wrote in her diary that night. "Certainly I shall love fat men more than lean ones henceforth."

After such a warm welcome, Elizabeth was taken by surprise a few days later when Dr. Webster barred her from his classroom. [17] Certain lectures, he explained, were only for men. It would be too indelicate with a woman present, and modifying the lecture to accommodate female sensibilities would be unfair to the rest of a class. He promised to make it up to her with some private instruction later. [18]

Elizabeth wrote Dr. Webster a letter suggesting that discussing human anatomy could only be embarrassing for those with impure thoughts, not to doctors whose minds had been purified by science. She asked him to let the students decide whether she should attend. [19] This strategy had worked well for her the first time around and she hoped to repeat the success.

Dr. Webster did read her letter to the class, but when he finished, instead of calling for a vote, he apologized for his backward thinking. Elizabeth was not barred again.

Elizabeth never witnessed her fellow students' famous rowdiness, since they always behaved when she was present. [20] The magical reformation of the Geneva boys became an oft-repeated case study among reformers advocating for coeducation. [21]

Elizabeth was several years older than most of the other students and for the most part, they treated her like a big sister, not that she allowed them to treat her any other way.

Once, a folded paper note dropped onto Elizabeth's arm during a lecture. She shook her arm and let it fall to the floor, unread. The rejected note passer tried again, and then Elizabeth heard a hiss from the other side of the room, and finally someone came over to her and tapped her from behind, but she continued looking forward as if oblivious.

"I sit quietly in this large assemblage of young men, and they might be women or mummies for aught I care," she told her sister. "I sometimes think I'm much too disciplined, but it is certainly necessary for the position I occupy. I believe the professors don't exactly know in what species of the human family to place me, and the students are a little bewildered."

Two weeks after Elizabeth began courses, the Boston Medical Journal did a feature about America's first female medical student, describing Elizabeth, much to her annoyance, as "a pretty little specimen of the feminine gender." [22]

Harriot Hunt clipped the article and quoted it in a letter to Harvard requesting admission. Only a few months before, Harvard officials had discouraged her on the basis that female medical students did not exist—but clearly, now they did!

The Dean of Harvard Medical College, Oliver Wendell Holmes (father of the Supreme Court Justice of the same name), was impressed with Harriot's application, which emphasized her dozen years of medical experience. [23] "The applicant is of mature age and might be fully trusted so far as appearances go. She is full of zeal for science and may become hereafter the worthy rival of Madame le Docteur Boivin of the Parisian faculty," he told the admissions committee. [24] This was high praise indeed. Marie Boivin, who had passed away six years earlier, had been a prolific medical text author and a biomedical engineer.

Nevertheless, the committee voted no, deeming her admission "inexpedient."

"Expedient for us to enter hospitals as patients, but inexpedient for woman, however well qualified, to be there as a physician?" asked Harriot. "Any kind of a reason might have been accepted, but this 'inexpedient' aroused my risibles." [25]

On Elizabeth Blackwell's graduation day, two messengers failed to produce her for the procession, so Dr. Webster went looking for her himself. People had arrived from across the country to see the first female medical school graduate in America. Where was she?

Elizabeth would be skipping the procession. "It wouldn't be ladylike," she said. As modern as she was for her time, she still maintained seemingly contradictory Victorian ideals of femininity.

Instead, Elizabeth entered the building with her brother, Henry Blackwell. They found the room crowded with women, filling the pews and even the galleries. [26]

Dr. Lee saved Elizabeth's name for last and called her up alone. [27] He proclaimed the experiment of educating a woman in medicine to be a success. Elizabeth had been a leader of her class and had proven that "the strongest intellect and nerve and the most untiring perseverance are compatible with the softest attributes of feminine delicacy and grace."

While this part of the ceremony must have been gratifying to the crowds of women who had come to witness this milestone for their sex, the rest of Dr. Lee's commencement speech may have been less so.

He took the opportunity to scold women generally for supporting homeopaths, hydropaths, and other "quacks" and warned the ladies that they "had better study a little the principles of medicine before attempting to practice what they were so profoundly ignorant about." [28]

In spite of her background in homeopathy and hydropathy, Harriot Hunt actually shared some of Lee's concerns. "I am sorry to say, too, that kind but ignorant women are traveling through the country, advertising to cure all diseases," Harriot said in a speech a short time later. But she had a more nuanced view of the situation. Why would a woman be susceptible to one of these quacks? Because she was "longing to consult one of her own sex" and women were barred from medical educations.

"There is a gap in society here which must be filled," said Harriot. "Must woman go forth unprepared for this work? Or is the truth to be felt and a response given to the demand for equal privileges?" [29]

Harriot's "whole being rejoiced" when she saw the call for the first National Woman's Rights Convention. And it would be held in her home state of Massachusetts!

In Harriot's clinic, she had met widows impoverished because they had no rights to the property their husbands had accumulated during their marriages, women who married and stayed with abusive husbands because they had no options to support themselves on their own, and working women who could not pay their bills with their meager wages.

"Was I to have the privilege of meeting those who have thought, and reasoned, and prayed over this subject?" Harriot asked herself. "Imagine hunger exasperating you, thirst driving to desperation. In a moment as by magic, food and drink appear. That call was bread and water to my soul. It electrified me." [30]

Harriot gave a speech at the convention. "We demand equal freedom of development, equal advantages of education, for both sexes," she said. "Will not there be more completeness in our hospitals when physicians of both sexes meet there to perform their duties?" [31]

During the train ride home afterwards, a fellow passenger recognized her. "I saw you at the convention ma'am," he said.

"Yes, I was there."

He told her that he had learned a few things about women's lack of property rights at the convention and intended to make arrangements for his wife in his will. "Why, dividing what little I have would leave her a mere pittance. She has worked hard and helped me earn it."

The conductor overheard their conversation and offered his two cents. "I have been to your meeting and when I went home I proposed to my wife that we should change work: I take care of the children, etc., and she take my place in the cars."

He was joking, but it wasn't funny to Harriot, who had long advocated for more flexible gender roles. Girls need exercise as much as boys do, she would explain to her patients, and why shouldn't boys enjoy needlework as much as girls?

"Perhaps a change might be well," suggested Harriot. "You might realize the cares and vexations of domesticity, and your wife appreciate better the trials to which you are exposed. You would then sympathize more fully with each other. There is great need of more oneness in marriage."

"Then you wish to be a man?" came the inevitable non sequitur. (Modern women's rights advocates still hear this one on a regular basis.)

"Far from it, I have seen too clearly the need of woman in the medical profession."

"So you are going to take man's place?"

"How vain you men are to suppose that we wish to be like you," cried Harriot. She reached for a pencil and passed it to him. "Please take this pencil and set down the names of the great men you think we would like to imitate." [32]

Two of Elizabeth Blackwell's sisters, Marian and Ellen, were in attendance at the convention but Elizabeth was out of the country. [33] After a brief residency in Philadelphia, Elizabeth had gone to Paris to learn surgery. Things hadn't gone as planned. While treating a baby with an eye infection, her own left eye became contaminated and had to be removed, ending her surgical ambitions. [34]

Elizabeth's absence hadn't prevented convention-goers from voting her onto the Industrial Committee, alongside Harriot Hunt and other well-known professional women. [35] Marian was dispatched to send word to Elizabeth, who was recuperating in London.

"I was touched by the kind remembrance of William H. Channing which placed my name on the Industrial Committee," Elizabeth wrote back to Marian. "And if I were in America and called on to attend I should certainly send them a note full of respect and sympathy, but must keep my energy for what seems to me a deeper movement."

Elizabeth had read the proceedings of the convention and wasn't impressed. "They show great energy, much right feeling, but not, to my judgment, a great amount of strong, clear thought," said Elizabeth. She decided that her role in this movement would be "to respect, to feel sympathy for, to help incidentally, but not—for me—to work with body and soul."

Elizabeth had some serious reservations about the themes of the convention as she interpreted them. "I cannot sympathize fully with an anti-man movement. I have had too much kindness, aid, and just recognition from men to make such attitudes of women otherwise than painful; and I think the true end of freedom may be gained better in another way."

Men had been kind to Elizabeth, but certainly not all of them. During her residency in Philadelphia, whenever she entered a hospital ward, the other residents walked out in protest. They even boycotted filling out patients' charts to prevent Elizabeth from reading them. In London, the professor of midwifery barred her from the maternity ward on the basis that he "entirely disapproved of a lady's studying medicine," assuring her that his decision was "owing to no disrespect to her as a lady." [36]

Anyhow, few if any suffragists (or modern feminists) would characterize their movements as anti-man, but Elizabeth certainly wasn't the first onlooker to do so. Nor would she be the last.

Feeling encouraged by the warm reception to her ideas at the convention, Harriot Hunt applied to Harvard again soon after returning home.

"Your refusal in the city of my birth, education, and life, seemed unjust to me, and I now hope for something better," Harriot wrote to Harvard officials. In her letter, she suggested that educated, female doctors might save troubled women from being sent to insane asylums and stem the trend toward quackery. She pointed out that Elizabeth Blackwell had since graduated from medical school in New York and, according to medical journals, had been well received in Europe.

"And thus will you, as guardians of the public will, open your institution (as in other states) to prepare woman for one of the noblest callings in life?" she asked. [37]

Dean Holmes supported Harriot's application again, arguing that public opinion had shifted in favor of female practitioners. [38] It was a historic meeting;

not only did the Harvard Medical School faculty vote to admit a woman, but they also accepted black men for the first time. [39]

It would be a couple weeks before Harriot could start attending classes. In the meantime, the black students arrived at school, much to the white students' consternation. When word got out that a woman had been accepted as well, the students organized a protest. [40] Graduating women and blacks would tarnish Harvard's reputation and lesson the value of Harvard diplomas, they argued. They were determined "to preserve the dignity of the school" and their "own self-respect." [41]

According to the local news, Harvard faculty met with Harriot for an exceptionally conciliatory exchange. They "treated her with great candor and politeness" and "entirely out of courtesy to them" Harriot decided to wait until the next term to start classes. [42]

But by the next term, all of the black students had been forced to leave. [43] Harriot never did matriculate. Her memoirs hint that she was strong-armed by the faculty to stay out. "Shall I ever forgive the Harvard Medical College for depriving me of a thorough knowledge of that science, a knowledge only to be gained by witnessing dissections in connection with close study and able lectures?" she asked. [44]

Shortly before the first National Woman's Rights Convention, Congress passed the Fugitive Slave Act, prompting a mass migration of black Americans to Canada to avoid being kidnapped and transported to slaveholders in the South. One of them was Henry Bibb, who started a newspaper, the *Voice of the Fugitive*, shortly after arriving in Canada West, now modern-day Ontario. [45]

"Hundreds of children are growing up in ignorance where there are no schools," he wrote in the first edition. "In the township of Windsor we have no school but there is great need of one." [46]

At the Great North American Anti-Slavery Convention in Toronto, he met Mary Ann Shadd, a free black teacher from Pennsylvania. [47]

Mary Ann had attended despite her lack of faith in conventions. "We have been holding conventions for years—have been assembled together and whining over our difficulties and afflictions, passing resolutions on resolutions to any extent but it does really seem that we have made but little progress considering our results," she said. "We should do more and talk less." [48]

Henry knew something Mary Ann could do. Recruiting Mary Ann to teach in Windsor helped Henry meet one of the two top priorities he had identified for black fugitives in Canada. "What they need mostly on their arrival here is homes for themselves and an education for their children; around these cluster all other temporal blessings." [49]

To address his other priority, he began the Refugee Home Society, calling for donors to fund the purchase of 20,000 acres of land to subdivide into lots for immigrants who had escaped slavery. [50]

Since Mary Ann had never been enslaved, she was not eligible for property through the Refugee Home Society, but she settled a short distance from Henry's home. Her school accepted all local children—and some adults—regardless of ability to pay. Many of the town's residents were fugitive slaves living in run-down 40-year-old barracks left over from the War of 1812. Finding enough paying students to cover expenses proved impossible. Acting on Henry's advice, she sought funding from the American Missionary Association. [51]

Somehow, as she struggled to establish her school, the industrious Mary Ann found time to write and publish a short book promoting black immigration to Canada as a solution to American slavery and the Fugitive Slave Act. After encyclopedia-like discussions of Canadian agriculture and commerce, Mary Ann's book included a less than flattering description of Henry's pet project, the Refugee Home Society. Mary Ann accused the Society of paternalism and interference with free market economics and questioned the policy that only escaped slaves were eligible, not free blacks. [52]

Even so, Henry printed a mostly complimentary review of Mary Ann's book in his paper, describing her as an "accomplished and talented authoress" and encouraging people of color in the United States to read it. He made no mention of Mary Ann's criticism of the Refugee Home Society. [53]

That same issue included an article about Mary Ann's school. "There is a very respectable school of colored children taught now in Windsor by Miss Mary Ann Shadd, who is sustained mostly by the American Missionary Association of New York as she receives only 37 ½ cents from each pupil and very little from others in the States who are interested in the support of the school. The above Association has voted to give her $120 annually while she teaches the school." [54]

The tone of the article sounded friendly enough, but it was an unauthorized and erroneous disclosure of Mary Ann's finances. Moreover, referring to Mary Ann's school as a "school of colored children" was a threat to her livelihood because the American Missionary Association had agreed to fund the school on the condition that Mary Ann would teach students of all races. It stung all the more because Mary Ann herself had strong feelings against segregation. When Mary Ann was 10, her family had moved to Pennsylvania because Delaware public schools only admitted white students. [55]

The *Voice of the Fugitive* printed a dismissive response to Mary Ann's complaints about the article: "Miss Shadd has said and written many things which we think will add nothing to her credit as a lady, for there should be no insult taken where there is none intended." [56]

"The vicinity of Henry Bibb and wife will ever be a hindrance to both teachers and preachers stationed here," Mary Ann told George Whipple, her contact at the American Missionary Association. [57]

Like many political conservatives, Mary Ann abhorred welfare, describing the Refugee Home Society's efforts to solicit donations as "begging." As time went on, her critiques went beyond ideology; Mary Ann called the Refugee Home Society an "exceedingly cunning land scheme" and accused its administrators, including Henry Bibb, of embezzlement. [58]

Mary Ann organized public meetings to expose the Refugee Home Society, but since Henry owned the local paper, press coverage was a problem.

"There has been some feeble opposition shown to the Society in Windsor, only by a set of half-cracked, hotheaded individuals," reported the *Voice of the Fugitive*. [59]

"What a vast amount of mischief a man like H. Bibb can do with an organ of his own to nod, insinuate and fling away the reputation of others and how much he has already done to persons who had no means equally extensive at their control to counteract it is appalling," Mary Ann told George Whipple. "I have not a paper of my own and must leave the result with God."

Mary Ann tried to publicize her point of view by writing letters to other newspapers in the United States and Canada. Once, she and her allies bought advertising space. [60]

The *Voice of the Fugitive* reported that "Shadd assembled her corporal guard to reiterate for the hundredth time her abuse of the Refugees Home Society, its constitution and officers," describing one of Mary Ann's allies as a "mere tool and lackey" of Mary Ann, who came armed with resolutions written in Mary Ann's handwriting that he was not literate enough to read. "The substance of these resolutions were to denounce all the papers published in Canada as unworthy of the support of herself and clique in Windsor, none of whom except her takes a newspaper, and to recommend the establishment of a journal of their own of which we suppose the lady in question is to have employment begging and at the same time to have a vent to pour out her vituperation." [61]

Charles Foote, the Refugee Home Society's chief fundraiser, reached out to Horace Hallock, a Society supporter who also happened to be a powerful player within the American Missionary Association.

"Regarding Miss Shadd and the malign influence she is seeking to exert against our Society, I know not what may grow of it, but of this I feel well assured, that she is not only a busybody in other men's matters, but a notorious mischief maker to the extent of her ability, if half of what I hear of her efforts in that line be true," Horace responded. "We propose soon to do something through a committee and if no truce can be declared shall take such action as we trust may at least weaken her power for evil against our society." [62]

George Whipple tried to get Mary Ann to meet with Horace to smooth things over but Mary Ann refused. "I am not personally acquainted with Mr. Hallock, but as himself and others in Detroit have willingly listened to false reports concerning me from Henry Bibb and have given Mr. Bibb instructions on which he has acted, I cannot subject myself to the degradation of an interview with him." [63]

As for Charles Foote, Mary Ann was certain that he was targeting her because she was "a mere woman" while he cautiously avoided offending "able and weighty men whom he knew to be actively opposed to the scheme." [64]

At the next meeting of the American Missionary Association, the committee voted to terminate Mary Ann's contract at the end of the school year. [65]

The day after her school closed, Mary Ann released the first copy of her own newspaper, the *Provincial Freeman*. [66]

Three years after Elizabeth Blackwell graduated from Geneva Medical School, her younger sister Emily applied to the same school, only to find that the door that had opened for Elizabeth had since slammed shut. After several other rejections, she was accepted to Rush Medical College where she studied for a semester before the state medical board forced her out. Eventually, she finished her degree at Western Reserve University in Cleveland, Ohio (now called Case Western Reserve University). [67]

Elizabeth and Emily planned to work together. Since Elizabeth's bad eye precluded her from surgery, Emily would be the surgeon. While Emily was in Europe studying surgery, Elizabeth started practicing medicine solo in New York.

It had been nearly two decades since Harriot Hunt had first opened her clinic, yet Elizabeth found that most male doctors still refused to work with women. Other New Yorkers weren't friendly, either. Hate mail came regularly by post and evening work was complicated by incessant street harassment. Her clinic primarily served Quakers, who had more egalitarian ideals than most of the population, and German immigrants, who had no other options for healthcare.

"This institution was commenced by the subscriptions of a few friends. Its expenses have been kept within its means, but the power of doing good has necessarily been limited by the smallness of its funds," stated the clinic's first annual report. [68]

"Woman must have a purse of her own," declared a frustrated Susan B. Anthony.

She had just finished a tour of New York, visiting about ten towns where women's temperance societies had been organized about a year earlier. She had hoped to follow up with these reform groups but found that most of them had already evaporated due to lack of funding.

"As I passed from town to town, I was made to feel the great evil of women's entire dependency upon man for the necessary means to aid on any and every reform movement," wrote Susan. "It matters not how overflowing with benevolence towards suffering humanity may be the heart of women, it avails nothing so long as she possesses not power to act in accordance with those promptings."

Susan had found a new mission, to advance "the grand idea of pecuniary and personal independence." [69] A teacher by trade, Susan started within her own profession. [70]

A quarter century had passed since Harriot Hunt had been a teacher. When Harriot started teaching in the 1820s, female teachers were rare. By the 1840s, schools had started hiring women in large numbers because women were great teachers, and more importantly, because they could get away with paying them only one third of the salaries men expected. [71] Susan's data showed that in New York, four out of five teachers were women, yet two-thirds of pay went to male educators.

Susan joined the New York State Teachers Association, and at her first meeting, campaigned to diversify the organization's male-only leadership with female officers.

"The majority of the women here would not prepare a report, nor act in the convention, even if voted for," complained one of the men.

A school principal named Mrs. Northrop supported Susan. [72] "A few men came for the purpose of elevating themselves, while the women present are entirely forgotten," she said, adding that she was paid only $250 per year, while male principals made $650. [73]

The convention president, Charles Davies, called her to order.

"It seems women are always out of order," remarked Susan.

President Davies used his closing remarks to compare female teachers to the decorative moldings topping pillars in Greek architecture. "Could I aid in bringing this beautiful entablature from its proud elevation and placing it in the dust and dirt which surrounds the pedestal? Never!" [74]

At the next annual meeting, the women remained securely perched on their pedestals again as only men were named to Association leadership.

"So long as woman be not appointed to fill any of the offices of the Association, or act upon any of its committees, her equality is ignored," said Susan. As such, all claims about women's rights within the Association "are not only meaningless, but insulting to her womanhood."

James McElligott, a powerful member of the Association, objected to Susan's "repulsive" suggestion that excluding women was somehow insulting to them. "Yes, there are no women in our committees and offices, but I cannot concede that this is an insult to the sex. It was not so designed."

Susan wanted the Association to direct the committee to nominate women, too.

"There has been no instruction to select men rather than women," objected James. "The ladies in the Association have all power and could confirm all committees or officers or reject them. They have the right to vote and can fill every office as they please." [75]

He had a point. Many of the women in the Association did not support Susan's efforts on their behalf. She had overheard several gossiping about her. [76]

"I do not desire to make a speech on this occasion," said Susan, who nevertheless embarked on one. "There is something wrong with the management of this Association. There are a majority of women in the Association, but not one says a word or does a thing in managing or carrying on the affairs of the Association. I think it a shame that all the business of such an Association should be transacted by men while so large a number of ladies are present, some of them of long experience as teachers and much more able to instruct in regard to a teacher's duty and suggest and act at a teachers convention than the boys who generally undertake and carry on all the business connected with it."

Someone suggested that the women vote on Susan's proposals and the men could abide by their decision. Susan's support among the women may not have been universal, but it was enough. Henrietta Hughes became the Association's first female vice president. [77]

"I have at last found a student in whom I can take a great deal of interest: Marie Zakrzewska, a German, about twenty-six," Elizabeth Blackwell wrote to her sister, Emily. "There is true stuff in her and I shall do my best to bring it out. She must obtain a medical degree." [78]

Marie had been interested in medicine since she was only 10 years old, when she had an eye operation that required an extended stay at the hospital in Berlin. One of the physicians there, Dr. Müller, would take her with him on his rounds, leading her by the hand because her eyes were bandaged and introducing her as a "little blind doctor." When she could see again, she asked him for some books to read. She liked history, but his library contained only medical books, so he offered her *History of Midwifery* and *History of Surgery*, both of which she read in full during her stay at the hospital.

When Marie was 15, her great-aunt had cancer, and after the tumor was removed, Marie was responsible for dressing the wound and caring for her mentally ill daughter, Marie's aunt. The younger woman was too confused to appreciate Marie's efforts and the older was too nasty. When her great aunt died, Marie put on mourning clothes for the first time, although "certainly not through grief." She came away with skills that would suit a medical career; she had learned "to be cheerful and light-hearted in all circumstances" and to manage the stress of caretaking by escaping regularly to the foyer for "a healthy, hearty laugh."

She applied to midwifery school when she was 18 but was refused on the grounds that she was much too young; men were eligible as soon as they turned 18, but women had to be older or married.

Marie continued to apply annually. After her third refusal, when she was 20 years old, Dr. Joseph Hermann Schmidt, a professor of midwifery at the school, went over the heads of school administrators and petitioned King Frederick William IV of Prussia directly to allow Marie to enroll.

Dr. Schmidt had plans for Marie. He had tuberculosis, and as a women's rights advocate, his dieing wish was that his replacement would be a female professor. On Marie's first day of class, Dr. Schmidt introduced her to the other students as his assistant teacher, much to her surprise. Then he took her to meet the hospital's chief physician, hoping she would make a good impression on this powerful potential ally or foe.

"This is my private pupil and I want you to give her particular attention. Her name is Marie Zakrzewska," he told the doctor.

The doctor ran over to her, took her by hand and cried, "Why, this is my little blind doctor!" That is when Marie recognized Dr. Müller, the doctor who had been so kind to her when she was a child.

On the day of Marie's final verbal exam, Dr. Schmidt invited several of the most prominent doctors in the country to sit in, much to Marie's dismay.

"I want to convince them that you can do better than half of the young men at their examination," he told her.

As soon as Marie had secured her diploma, Dr. Schmidt began lobbying for her to have a faculty position, inciting a debate that reverberated through Berlin's medical community.

"To give this position to Miss M. E. Zakrzewska is dangerous. She is a prepossessing young lady and from coming in contact with so many gentlemen, must necessarily fall in love with some one of them and thus end her career," argued one opponent.

"I am sorry that I could not have found one among them that could have made me follow the suggestion," Marie answered ruefully.

Marie's father had the opposite concern—he was afraid that becoming a professor would prevent Marie from ever getting married. He unexpectedly threw a wrench into the scheme when he told officials considering the question that he would never consent for his daughter to accept the position.

Dr. Schmidt's health was failing fast, and his friends urged Marie's father to reconsider, hoping that Marie's appointment would revitalize him. At last, her father relented.

On the day Marie received the job offer, she went straight to Dr. Schmidt before sharing the news with anyone else.

"There is the victory!" she announced, throwing the memo onto the table.

The next morning, Marie arrived at the hospital early to start her new duties.

"I am astonished to see you so cheerful," said the doorkeeper. "Don't you know that Dr. Schmidt is dead?"

Without Dr. Schmidt's support (and favoritism), Marie was only able to hold on to her new position for six months. She didn't see a future for herself in Berlin, but she had heard exciting reports about the women's rights movement in America. Bringing her younger sister Anna with her, she boarded a ship to the United States.

"I had to show to those men who had opposed me so strongly because I was a woman that in this land of liberty, equality, and fraternity, I could maintain that position which they would not permit to me at home."

Shortly after arriving in New York, Marie went to meet a doctor who was a family friend, hoping he could help her find a job. His close-up view of the status of women in America didn't exactly match the tales of liberty, equality and fraternity she had heard from afar. "Female physicians in this country are of the lowest rank. They don't hold even the position of a good nurse," he told her. He offered to help her out if she was willing to take a nursing position but Marie decided that she "could not condescend to be patronized."

During the next year, Marie survived by pawning her few items of value and investing in yarn. She hired a team of women to knit tassels for local German-speaking merchants. Finding employees was easy; there were plenty of women in New York who needed work; job opportunities for women offering reasonable pay were scarce. Marie observed that Americans composed "a great, free nation who, notwithstanding, let their women starve."

Just as tassels went out of fashion and the market for Marie's start-up dried up, Marie met Elizabeth Blackwell. By then, Marie had reconsidered her stance against taking a nursing job and hoped Dr. Blackwell would offer her one. [79]

Elizabeth saw Marie as a potential partner, not a nurse, but it would take some work. [80] Elizabeth wanted Marie to learn English and get an American medical degree. She helped Marie apply to the same Ohio school where Emily had recently graduated and tutored her in English twice weekly.

Looking back later, when she had enough command of the English language to compose such a metaphor, Marie would describe Elizabeth's English lessons as "raindrops falling upon stone" and confess that she hadn't absorbed anything.

No one could understand Marie when she arrived in Ohio. She showed hotel staff a slate and wrote her name on it, then "Caroline Severance," the name of the woman Elizabeth had arranged for Marie to stay with until she had found permanent boarding.

Caroline was the president of the local physiological society, one of the many throughout the country established by Harriot Hunt. [81] Harriot and Caroline had recently started a student loan fund for women seeking medical degrees and Marie would be one of their first beneficiaries.

Marie next wrote "a carriage tomorrow" on the slate and at last someone correctly interpreted that to mean that Marie needed a room for the night and a carriage to the Severance home in the morning. Marie also tried to ask about dinner, but failed and went to bed hungry.

She woke up the next day determined to eat, rang the bell furiously and tried to order breakfast, but it came out as "beefsteak." The bellhop had a good laugh at her expense but brought her some food.

Getting established in Ohio was a perpetual series of language barrier disasters, so when Marie finally had a routine, she quit trying to communicate at all and went mute for a full semester, silently listening to lectures and studying for six hours a day with the help of four dictionaries at her desk. At the New Year, she resolved to speak again and was delighted to find that now, everyone could understand her. [82]

In Canada West, Mary Ann Shadd recruited Samuel Ringgold Ward to serve as editor for the *Provincial Freeman*. Like Mary Ann, he had criticized the Refugee Home Society for promoting segregation and encouraging "begging."

Black Canadian settlements were no different than the English, Irish, French and Dutch sectors in the states, countered the *Voice of the Fugitive*. [83] With regards to begging, "we agree with Brother Ward in opposing this perpetual begging of old clothing for the refugees in Canada," stated the *Voice of the Fugitive*, "not that we depreciate the motives of those who, from the benevolence of their hearts, have sent boxes upon boxes among missionaries here to be distributed." [84]

Unlike the *Voice of the Fugitive*, the *Provincial Freeman* would not thank anyone for old clothes, especially since the donations kept vanishing. "There are German and Irish and no doubt other classes as poor hereabouts as any fugitives in the community," editorialized the *Freeman*. "And no one thinks of sending secretly for old clothes for them that they will never get." [85]

Samuel was an experienced journalist and Mary Ann hoped that his name would be a draw, but his name was about the only thing he was willing to contribute. A disclaimer in the first edition acknowledged that he lived 350 miles away in Toronto, that most of his attention would be directed elsewhere to his other occupations and that he hadn't made any financial investment in the paper.

In addition to Samuel, several other prominent male leaders of the black Canadian community were listed as board members. Mary Ann's name was mentioned only once and without any title: "Letters must be addressed, postpaid, to Mary A. Shadd, Windsor, Canada West." [86]

After the first issue, it would be another year before the *Provincial Freeman* resumed regular publication. During that time, Mary Ann prepared by fundraising and moving to Toronto, where there was a larger base of black readers. Black-owned newspapers faced an uphill challenge; many black people didn't know how to read because slavery and racism had blocked their educations. [87]

Mary Ann worked on the second issue alone because Samuel was out of the country. "His tour is to be considered the most important ever made by a colored man to England," reported the *Provincial Freeman*. [88] "All letters, whether intended for publication or on business, must, during the absence of the editor, be addressed postpaid to M. A. Shadd, Toronto, Canada West." [89]

Samuel's stay in England dragged on, and meanwhile, Mary Ann served as the sole writer, editor, salesperson and printer of the *Provincial Freeman*. Most readers didn't notice her unilateral efforts because Samuel Ward's name graced the masthead, articles were usually unsigned and Mary Ann used the plural "we" instead of saying "I," as if she were speaking on behalf of a newsroom team. [90]

The shady dealings of the Refugee Home Society and other charities targeting black refugees in Canada were recurring themes in the *Provincial Freeman*. While the *Voice of the Fugitive* had addressed the problem of fraudulent charities with vague warnings, the *Freeman* picked apart hyperbolic speeches that overstated refugee poverty to attract donors, called out charities for fabricating reports about their work, and not infrequently, accused specific employees of fraud and embezzlement. [91]

"We must mind what we say of our friends, for though true, it may sound harsh," some readers told Mary Ann. She had no patience for tone critiques, and wrote a stinging response to all who thought "we ought to be regulated by the thought that we colored people should all think alike, get along together without contention, should go to but one market, and all partake of the same commodities when there."

Mary Ann summed up her philosophy like this: "The fact that somebody is displeased is no evidence that we are wrong." [92]

Samuel stopped communicating with Mary Ann at all after several months away and Mary Ann's strategies for maintaining the illusion of his involvement were backfiring. Donors felt indifferent about fundraising for the *Freeman* because they assumed Samuel was collecting more than enough money in England. [93]

Mary Ann began signing her work—as M.A. Shadd, which allowed just enough clarification that letters to the editor started coming in addressed to "Mr. Shadd" instead of Mr. Ward. When one of these letters expressed astonishment that "a colored man publishes such a paper," Mary Ann decided she was done with the charade. "We do not like the Mr. and Esq. by which we are so often addressed," she wrote, and for the first time, published her full name as editor. [94] Soon after, she removed Samuel Ward's name from the masthead. [95]

After nearly two years of doing the job on the sly, Mary Ann Shadd was acknowledged as "the first colored women on the American continent to establish and edit a weekly newspaper." [96]

Other American suffragists took note. Lucretia Mott sent "generous donations" to the Provincial Freeman and Lucy Stone visited Toronto. [97]

"We must absolutely take the brightest view we can as it seems to be inevitable and if Lucy will soften her heresies it may be a very happy union," Elizabeth Blackwell told Emily when their brother Henry became engaged to the famous suffragist Lucy Stone. [98]

In public, Elizabeth described her future sister-in-law as a "noble-hearted woman," but privately, Lucy's in-your-face style of activism annoyed her. [99] Even as she tried to congratulate dear Harry on his engagement, she couldn't help but insert a dig about Lucy being something of a walking cartoon, wrapped up in all "the eccentricities and accidents of the American phase of this 19th century: in bloomerism, abolitionism, women's rightism." Taking "the brightest view" only became harder for Elizabeth when Harry and Lucy scandalized the nation—and Elizabeth, specifically—by turning their wedding into a protest of marriage law. Protests were not Elizabeth's thing. [100]

"I sometimes reproach myself for my prudence and the calmness with which I answer some outrageous injustice, while I am really raging with indignation," Elizabeth once confessed to her activist siblings. "But it is the only way in which I can hope to do any good, for the slightest display of feeling arms all their prejudices, and I am no orator to convert by a burst of passionate eloquence. So I must even go on in my own quiet manner, knowing that it does not proceed from cowardice."

Elizabeth had a plan to advance women's rights in her own way. The number of women graduating from medical school was growing, but employment opportunities were few. Elizabeth wanted to open the first American hospital administered by women, providing these new graduates a place to work. [101]

When Marie Zakrzewska finished her studies, she joined Elizabeth in New York where both women treated patients in Elizabeth's parlor. Every Thursday evening, a small but fervent group of supporters joined them to make crafts for fairs to raise the $10,000 needed to open a hospital.

"Tomorrow we have our fair meeting. I wonder whether there will be, as usual, two and a half persons present, or three and three-quarters," Marie said to Elizabeth one Wednesday afternoon. Marie had more experience in the knitting industry than Elizabeth and doubted that their slowly growing collection of handmade baby socks would bring in even $100.

Marie pulled out her notebook and started calculating the price of everything they needed, from real estate to hospital beds to spoons and forks. The next day, she presented Elizabeth with a written plan for a scaled-down version of the hospital originally envisioned, which could be paid for within one year with a door-to-door fundraiser.

Elizabeth hated the fundraiser idea but was impressed with Marie's detailed proposal for a miniature hospital they could establish soon and expand later. She was confident that they could find donors to cover that smaller sum. The women set a date and opened the New York Infirmary for Women and Children exactly one year later. [102] By that time, Emily had returned to the states to serve as the hospital's first surgeon, bringing donations from European supporters with her. [103]

"We hear a great deal about woman and wonders expressed as to what use she can possibly make of mathematics and other branches of learning in washing her dishes or her babies. True, but who are to be the lucky ones? All women do not have husbands," Susan B. Anthony repeated to herself as she paced across the orchard in her backyard. [104]

After three years as a member of the New York Teachers Association, she had been invited to present for the first time and she was determined to make the most of the opportunity. [105]

"I must not and will not allow those schoolmasters to say, 'See, these women can't or won't do anything when we do give them a chance,'" said Susan. [106]

Susan wanted to prove the thesis of her speech—that women were just as competent as men and should be allowed to attend the same schools and universities—by giving a speech that would rival any male orator's address. Redeeming all womankind through one brilliant speech was a tall order to fill for a beginner—or anyone—and Susan was failing. After several hours of rehearsal indoors, she still hadn't memorized the darn thing and restlessly moved outside to practice in different scenery. [107]

Two months before the convention, she sent her first draft to Elizabeth Cady Stanton, along with a desperate letter.

"I can't get a decent document, so for the love of me and for the saving of the reputation of womanhood, I beg you with one baby on your knee and another at your feet and four boys whistling, buzzing, hallooing, "Ma, Ma," set yourself about the work." [108]

When Susan delivered the speech Elizabeth had helped her write, she still didn't have it memorized. Even so, the new Association president, Mr. Hazeltine, seemed impressed.

"Madam, that was a splendid production and well-delivered. I could not have asked for a single thing different either in matter or manner," he told her as he shook her hand. That would have been a good place for him to stop talking. "But I would rather have followed my wife or daughter to Green-Wood Cemetery," he continued, "than to have had her stand here before this promiscuous audience and deliver that address." [109]

"Well, my dear, another notice of Susan," said Henry Stanton, as he passed his wife Elizabeth the paper. "You stir up Susan and she stirs the world." [110]

Susan was in the news for proposing radically progressive changes to the New York State Teachers Association platform. First, she demanded an end to racial segregation in schools. [111]

After "considerable uproar" Susan's resolutions were referred to a committee for consideration. Thanks to Susan's efforts in previous years, Association committees now included women and two of Susan's allies were on this one: Mary Booth and Julia Wilbur. The committee announced support for all of Susan's resolutions but they were surprised by an unscheduled "minority report" by a dissenting committee member. [112] In the end, a watered down statement was adopted: "In our opinion, the colored children of the State should enjoy equal advantages of education with the white."

Susan's next resolution should have come as a surprise to no one, after her speech on the subject, but the men reacted as if she had dropped a bomb. "Resolved, that it is the duty of all our schools, colleges and universities to open their doors to woman and to give her equal and identical educational advantages side by side with her brother man."

"Here is an attempt to introduce a vast social evil. I have been trying for four years, that is, ever since Miss Anthony's first appearance at a teachers convention, to escape this question, but if it has to come, let it be boldly met and disposed of," announced the same Charles Davies who had been the Association president at Susan's first Teachers Convention. "These resolutions are the first step in the school which seeks to abolish marriage and behind this picture I see a monster of social deformity."

Several other men followed Charles's lead and raised their own objections. Susan didn't let their speeches worry her. Even if every man voted no, women could pass the resolution without them. The women present outnumbered the men by a large margin.

The resolution lost. It wasn't even close. [113]

When Susan brought up the wage gap, detractors invoked the institution of marriage again. Women didn't need as much money as men because their husbands supported their families, and if women could earn enough money to support a family alone, they would never marry. [114]

"What an infernal set of fools those school marms must be!" Elizabeth Cady Stanton wrote to Susan after reading the article. "Well, if in order to please men, they wish to live on air, let them. The sooner the present generation of women die out the better. We have jackasses enough in the world now without such women propagating any more." [115]

By the next year, Susan's sixth appearance at the New York State Teachers Convention, several members of the Association were anxious to "go on without this eternal jangle about women's rights."

"This question of women's rights, at every meeting of the Association," complained an exasperated man, "has come to be a stench in the nostrils of many prominent educational men." [116]

They would not get their wish just yet. Susan attended the annual Teachers Convention for ten consecutive years before she moved on to other priorities. [117]

"Adieu," Mary Ann titled the editorial in which she announced her resignation as editor of the *Provincial Freeman*. The reaction of her readers to her leadership over the past several months had justified her choice to hide her female identity for so long and she worried that unless she hired a male editor, the paper would not survive. "Taking leave of our readers at this time, we do so for the best interest of the enterprise and with the hope that our absence will be their gain. We want the *Freeman* to prosper and shall labor to that end." [118]

The new editor, William Newman, used his first editorial to make it clear that he had accepted the position begrudgingly. He described Mary Ann as "one of the best editors our province ever had, if such did wear the petticoats instead of the breaches, one that would now be blessing our country in the same capacity but for the folly of adhering to a wrongly developed public sentiment that would crush a woman whenever she attempts to do what has hitherto been assigned to men." [119]

"Be less captious to him than to us," Mary Ann told readers. "Be more considerate, if you will. It is fit that you should deport your ugliest to a woman."

Mary Ann closed her announcement by speaking directly to other ambitious women like herself: "To colored women, we have a word: we have broken the editorial ice, whether willingly or not, for your class in America. So go to editing as many of you as are willing and able." [120]

Mary Ann's "adieu" was largely symbolic, as she still owned the paper and continued to write for it. Even after her own wedding, she was back on the road for a subscription drive within a few days, without her new spouse. Mary Ann and her husband, Thomas Cary, maintained a long-distance relationship, never combining households. After only about five years of marriage, while Mary Ann was pregnant with their second child, Thomas died and Mary Ann closed the *Provincial Freeman*. It had a seven-year run, quite an accomplishment for an antebellum newspaper. [121]

Almost 15 years later, Mary Ann became the first black woman accepted to law school in the United States, joining Howard University's first cohort of law students. She wasn't the first to graduate, though. That honor fell to the next woman to enter Howard, Charlotte Ray. Mary Ann did not graduate with her class. Problems with the State Bar may have had something to do with it; Charlotte may have had an easier time because she submitted her name as C.E. Ray—the same way Mary Ann had disguised her female identity at the *Freeman*.

Since those *Freeman* days, Mary Ann had developed too much name recognition to hide her identity by using initials. The same year she began law school, Mary Ann chaired the Woman's Labor Committee at the Colored National Labor Convention, where she persuaded the mostly male delegation to acknowledge and address "unjust discrimination" against women in the workforce and actively seek to recruit women into the organization, "profiting by the mistakes heretofore made by our white fellow citizens in omitting women as coworkers in such societies." [122]

Mary Ann also faced some of the same difficulties nontraditional students face today; she was a single mother with two children to support, attending evening classes so she could work as a school principal during the day. At the age of 60, Mary Ann returned to Howard and finished her law degree. Now a pioneer for women in two different professions, Mary Ann formed her own organization to support professional opportunity for other black women as well as women's suffrage. [123]

The tone critiques Mary Ann received as she forged a path for women in journalism and law continue to follow outspoken women today. These biased perceptions of women are costly. Unlike men, women who ask for raises are often seen as aggressive or complaining—and their bosses are more likely to answer, "No." [124]

Entrepreneurship is not an easy road for women either. The good news is that female entrepreneurs are more likely to secure venture capital funding than ever before. The bad news is that women collect only 2% of the pot. [125] A recent study found that venture capitalists tend to ask female entrepreneurs questions about risks, while they ask men about opportunities. [126]

Over 150 years after Susan B. Anthony declared that a woman needed a purse of her own, American women are paid only 80¢ to the dollar a man makes, with most women of color earning even less than white and Asian women. [127] The gender gap among educators that Susan noticed in the 1850s persists today; modern male educators are still paid more than their female peers, because men are more likely to advance into better-paid positions such as principal or superintendent. [128] Women are still in the minority within high-paying jobs such as business executive and within many STEM professions. [129]

Change can be exasperatingly slow. Harvard Medical School admitted women for the first time in 1945, almost 100 years after Harriot Hunt was the first woman to apply. [130]

"The new position of women must necessarily be of slow growth. It must be, in fact, a life work," said Elizabeth Blackwell. "The children of the present generation will grow up accustomed to women doctors, respecting and trusting them, but the large majority of the adults will only hold a half-faith, and this will be a gradual growth."

In the microcosm of Elizabeth's home, she was already witnessing the change. "How very odd it is to hear a man called Doctor!" said Kitty Barry, Elizabeth's adopted daughter, when she met a male doctor for the first time. In the small corner of the world Kitty was growing up in, she had only known women with that title. [131]

CHAPTER SIX
Does art inspire change?

Let me make the songs for the people,
Songs for the old and young;
Songs to stir like a battle-cry
Wherever they are sung.

…Our world, so worn and weary,
Needs music, pure and strong,
To hush the jangle and discords
Of sorrow, pain, and wrong.

Music to soothe all its sorrow,
Till war and crime shall cease;
And the hearts of men grown tender
Girdle the world with peace. [1]
–Frances Ellen Watkins Harper, 1895

When women's rights advocate and transcendentalist philosopher Margaret Fuller read poems by a local teenager, she was astonished that a girl who had lived such a pampered and sheltered life could have such deep thoughts. "I can hardly realize that the Julia Ward I have seen has lived this life. It has not yet pervaded her whole being, though I can recall something of it in the steady light of her eye. May she become all attempered and ennobled by this music," she said. [2]

She urged Julia to publish the poems, but she never did.

Five years later, other eminent family friends, author Henry Wadsworth Longfellow and politician Charles Sumner, invited Julia and her sisters to come with them to the Perkins School for the Blind to meet Laura Bridgman, the first deaf and blind child to learn American Sign Language. (Later, Anne Sullivan would also be educated at Perkins, and use the methods she learned there to train her famous student, Helen Keller.)

Watching Laura finger spell was fine, but Laura's teacher, Dr. Samuel Gridley Howe, made more of an impression on Julia. Dr. Howe was "among the champions of human freedom," a star-struck Julia gushed. [3] He had rescued starving children during the Greek revolution, advocated for the mentally ill with Dorothea Dix, and helped Horace Mann reinvent public education. His friends called him "Chev," short for "Chevalier," a title bestowed on him for his heroism by a grateful monarch. [4]

Julia was flattered when 41-year-old Chev, a man who had "acquired the practical knowledge which is rarely attained in the closet or at the desk," took an interest in her. At age 23, Julia considered herself to be a mere "student" and "dreamer." [5] Yet, it wasn't until after Julia had married her favorite local celebrity that it occurred to her, "We are not born alike." [6]

A week after Julia and Chev's wedding, they sailed to Rome for a long honeymoon and to her dismay, Julia became pregnant. Julia's mother had died giving birth to her younger sister and Julia was certain she wouldn't survive childbirth, either. [7]

Chev couldn't or wouldn't empathize with Julia's fears. She wrote poems despairing about her new marriage in her diary.

> Hope died as I was led
> Unto my marriage bed [8]

Julia distracted herself from her pregnancy and her husband by writing. An ancient statue she saw in Rome, *Sleeping Hermaphrodite*, provided some inspiration.

"My pen has been unusually busy during the last year—it has brought me some happy inspirations, and though the golden tide is now at its ebb, I live in the hope that it may rise again in time to float off the stranded wreck of a novel, or rather story, in the which I have been deeply engaged for three months past," she wrote to a friend. "It is not, understand me, a moral and fashionable work, destined to be published in three volumes, but the history of a strange being, written as truly as I knew how to write it. Whether it will ever be published, I cannot tell, but I should like to have had you read it, and to talk with you about it." [9]

Julia wrote that "when, in the spring of 1844, I left Rome in company with my husband, my sisters, and my baby, it seemed like returning to the living world after a long separation from it."

Now that she had survived childbirth, Julia's mood lifted. They traveled to the British Isles, where Chev visited interesting medical cases in workhouses and Julia entertained herself by rewriting his medical notes in rhyme.

> Dear Sir, I went south
> As far as Portsmouth,

And found a most charming old woman,
Delightfully void
Of all that 's enjoyed
By the animal vaguely called human.

She has but one jaw,
Has teeth like a saw,
Her ears and her eyes I delight in:
The one could not hear
Tho' a cannon were near,
The others are holes with no sight in.

Chev was not amused. [10]

In Wales, Julia saw another work of art that intrigued her, an engraving of Eleanor Butler and Sarah Ponsonby. In the 1770s, rather than be forced into arranged heterosexual marriages that neither wanted, they had run away together. The engraving showed them years later, a happy elderly couple "engaged in some friendly game." [11]

"Is it selfish, is it egotistical to wish that others may love us, take an interest in us, sympathize with us?" asked Julia. "Where shall I go to beg some scraps and remnants of affection to feed my hungry heart?" [12]

Julia and Chev returned to Massachusetts and took up residence within the Perkins Institute, where Chev could immerse himself in his work. [13]

"Mr. Emerson somewhere speaks of the romance of some special philanthropy. Dr. Howe's life became an embodiment of this romance," wrote Julia. [14]

Romancing his wife, on the other hand, was not on the agenda—Chev was "grumpy, never fond of kissing"—and her family and friends were two hours away in Boston. [15]

"The change had already been great, from my position as a family idol and 'the superior young lady' of an admiring circle to that of a wife overshadowed for the time by the splendor of her husband's reputation," said Julia. "But the change from my life of easy circumstances and brilliant surroundings to that of the mistress of a suite of rooms in the Institution for the Blind at South Boston was much greater."

One morning, Julia struggled to hold back tears when she found a pail of ice cream sitting in a snow bank outside the door. She had ordered it for one of Chev's dinner parties the night before and apparently hadn't heard the messenger knock. Chev regularly invited his distinguished friends and business associates to weekly dinner parties that he expected Julia to host. [16] This assignment was a source of constant anxiety to Julia. At her father's house, she had never been responsible for cooking (or anything else, actually). [17]

Chev did not want Julia to share his work educating the blind, but he delegated management of housekeeping for the Institute to her. Hoping to embarrass herself less often, Julia bought Catharine Beecher's cookbook and devoted herself to studying it, "with no satisfactory result." [18] Amidst her new responsibilities, she found no energy for poetry. "My fingers are becoming less and less familiar with the pen. My thoughts grow daily more insignificant and commonplace," she told her sister, Louisa. [19]

After Julia survived birthing another baby that she hoped would be her last, Chev hired a housekeeper to do the cooking, and the family moved out of the Perkins Institute and into a house next to it, Julia's writer's block continued. [20]

"My voice is still frozen to silence, my poetry chained down by an icy band of indifference. I begin at last to believe that I am no poet and never was one, save in my imagination." [21]

Perhaps her poetic voice felt cold, but the muse had not abandoned her. She remembered the *Sleeping Hermaphrodite*. An intersex body like that might free someone from the rigid gender roles that trapped her.

Julia took up her pen.

Fictional doctors could not decide if Julia's main character was "either man or woman," but determined "he is rather both than neither." The character's parents named their child Laurence, choosing a masculine name because "the dignity and insignia of manhood…would at least permit [him] to choose [his] own terms in associating with the world." [22]

Julia should have liked such a choice. In Julia's life, "the Doctor was captain, beyond dispute." [23]

At one point in the novel, Julia required Laurence to trade out that masculine identity for a more "odious disguise." When fictional Laurence put on the same clothing that Julia wore every day in real life, the character protested. "I should be released from the ignominious bondage of petticoats, that my legs should be disencumbered of a mass of articles utterly foreign to their use and purpose, and that my diaphragm should be allowed to expand in freedom broader than the lacings of a woman's bodice."

Whether dressed as a man or a woman, "nature" –and Julia–"had endowed [Laurence] with rare beauty." Laurence had romantic relationships with both men and women, the most enduring with a man named Ronald.

Their relationship may have been based on Chev's intimacy with his best friend, Charles Sumner. [24] He was Chev's "alter ego, the brother of his heart." [25] Julia could not compete with that. "I should like to know how it feels to be something better than an object of disgust to one's husband," she said. [26]

Her character understood her feelings of rejection. In the bedroom, Laurence's lovers had melodramatic reactions to Laurence's ambiguously gendered body. [27]

"There are bounds to all things, and no woman is under any obligation to sacrifice the whole of her existence to the mere act of bringing children into the world," Julia decided, after several months of wrestling with gender issues within the pages of her manuscript. "I cannot help considering the excess of this as materializing and degrading to a woman whose spiritual nature has any strength. Men, on the contrary, think it glorification enough for a woman to be a wife and mother in any way and upon any terms." [28]

When Julia was 28 years old, a year older than her mother had been when childbirth killed her, Julia found herself pregnant again. She "cried and raved" before assuring her family that she had "reconciled to the idea." [29] Actually, the "melancholy" persisted. [30]

There was nothing that could ease her anxiety about childbirth for the nine months preceding it, but she could hope for some relief during the dreaded event. Just a few months earlier, Fanny Longfellow, wife of Henry Wadsworth Longfellow, had been the first American woman to use anesthesia during childbirth. Julia was determined to have it, too. [31]

"Depend upon it, it is all wrong and wicked for women to make such delicate things of themselves," argued Chev. "And the pains of childbirth are meant by a beneficent creator to be the means of leading them back to lives of temperance, exercise, and reason." [32]

On the day the baby was born, Julia sent a servant to the pharmacy for chloroform anyway but a precipitous labor precluded its use. The afterpains were severe. [33]

Julia let Laurence voice her complaints about woman's lot:

> Women, the adored of all, but trusted of none; women, the golden treasures, too easily lost or stolen, and therefore to be kept under lock and key; women, who cannot stay at home without surveillance, who cannot walk abroad without being interrogated at every turn by the sentinel of public opinion; women, I say, are very naturally glad now and then to throw off their chains with their petticoats, and to assume for a time the right to go where they please, and the power of doing as they please. [34]

Sometimes Julia felt desperate for Chev to understand her. "I have come to him, have left my poetry, my music, my religion, have walked with him in his cold world of actualities. There I have learned much, but there, I can do nothing. He must come to me, must have ears for my music, must have a soul for my faith." [35]

But at other times, she felt resigned. "I am nearer the attainment of peace than I have been. I will not expect too much from you," she told Chev. "I will enjoy the moments of sunshine which we can enjoy together. I will treasure up every word, every look of yours that is kind and genial, to comfort me in those long, cold wintry days that I feel you do not love me." [36]

"Now Childhood is gone, and Youth and Love have slain each other, and I am here to weep for them, and to wait for the spirit of consolation," said Laurence. [37]

"I have no family around me, my children are babies, and my husband has scarcely half an hour in twenty-four to give me. So, as I think much, in my way, and nobody takes the least interest in what I think, I am freed to make myself an imaginary public, and to tell it the secrets of my poor little ridiculous brain," Julia told her diary. An imaginary public would be the only audience for Julia's novel until almost a century after her death, but Laurence had given Julia what she needed. "While I am employed with fictions, my husband is dealing with facts, but as we both seek truth that lies beyond either, we do not get so very far apart as you would think. At least I know all that is in his mind, if he does not occupy himself much with mine." [38]

"I have a right to do my share of the work," Frances Ellen Watkins told William Still, a conductor on the Underground Railroad. "The humblest and feeblest of us can do something; and though I may be deficient in many of the conventionalisms of city life, and be considered as a person of good impulses but unfinished, yet if there is common rough work to be done, call on me." [39]

Frances had recently moved to Pennsylvania for a teaching position. She moved in with the Still family, a stop on the Underground Railroad, and her notebooks filled up with poetry inspired by the stories of escaped fugitives. [40] She would have liked to devote herself full-time to the cause, instead of supervising "fifty-three untrained little urchins," but her efforts to find a publisher for her abolition poetry in Pennsylvania were proving futile. [41]

"What would you do if you were in my place? Would you give up and go back and work at your trade?" Frances asked a friend.

Teaching was important too, she reassured herself, especially for a black woman teaching black children, as she was doing. "There are no people that need all the benefits resulting from a well-directed education more than we do. The condition of our people, the wants of our children, and the welfare of our race demand the aid of every helping hand, the Godspeed of every Christian heart."

But here was the problem: "It is a work of time, a labor of patience, to become an effective schoolteacher; and it should be a work of love."

For Frances, it wasn't.

Not long after moving to Pennsylvania, Frances heard that that her home state of Maryland had passed a law threatening free black people who entered the state with sale into slavery. She wouldn't be able to go back home—a free black man had already unwittingly violated the new law, been sold into slavery in Georgia and died there after a failed escape. Frances decided that she couldn't wait any longer to become a full-time abolitionist.

She quit teaching, started lecturing freelance, and soon found a position with the Anti-Slavery Society of Maine. In Maine, she was the only black person in a sea of white people but she had "a pleasant time."

"If you could see our Maine ladies, some of them among the noblest types of womanhood you have ever seen!" she told William Still, one of her old colleagues from the Underground Railroad in Pennsylvania. "They are for putting men of anti-slavery principles in office."

(Too bad they couldn't vote.)

Frances had been around white people before. When she was a 13-year-old orphan, Frances had quit school to support herself as a seamstress and nanny for a white family. Fortunately, her employers were booksellers who allowed Frances to borrow from their store, feeding a reading habit that would continue long after she left them. *Twelve Years a Slave* by Solomon Northrup inspired her to support an embargo on goods produced by enslaved people. [42] She amplified Harriet Beecher Stowe's *Uncle Tom's Cabin* with a poem about one of its characters, Eliza Harris. [43]

> Like a fawn from the arrow, startled and wild,
> A woman swept by us, bearing a child;
> In her eye was the night of a settled despair,
> And her brow was o'ershaded with anguish and care.
>
> She was nearing the river—in reaching the brink,
> She heeded no danger, she paused not to think!
> For she is a mother—her child is a slave—
> And she'll give him his freedom, or find him a grave! [44]

At anti-slavery events, Frances would recite her poetry with "her disarmingly dramatic voice and gestures and sighs and tears." Like modern slam poetry, her poetry was written to be performed. [45]

Projecting her voice loudly enough to be heard by her ever-growing audiences was taxing—the microphone wouldn't be invented for another two decades. [46]

"My health is not very strong and I may have to give up before long. I may have to yield on account of my voice which I think has become somewhat affected," she wrote to William. "I might be so glad if it was only so that I could go home among my own kindred and people, but slavery comes up like a dark shadow between me and the home of my childhood."

The Maryland law barring free blacks from entering the state was still in place; returning was out of the question.

"Well, perhaps it is my lot to die away from home and be buried among strangers," she continued—but hopefully not before slavery could be abolished. "Bury me in a free land," she wrote, in one of her most popular poems. [47]

> Make me a grave where'er you will,
> In a lowly plain, or a lofty hill;
> Make it among earth's humblest graves,
> But not in a land where men are slaves.

The poem described each of the horrors that would disturb her eternal rest, "the lash drinking her blood at each fearful gash," "bloodhounds seizing their human prey," or "young girls from their mothers' arms bartered and sold for their youthful charms." [48]

"We need men and women whose hearts are the homes of a high and lofty enthusiasm, and a noble devotion to the cause of emancipation, who are ready and willing to lay time, talent and money on the altar of universal freedom," she told her audiences. "Let us not then defer all our noble opportunities 'til we get rich." [49]

Following her own advice, she sent regular donations to the Underground Railroad, care of William Still, but when he heard that she might be losing her speaking voice, he wondered if he shouldn't stop accepting her donations.

"Now, please do not write back that you are not going to do any such thing," Frances replied. "Let me explain a few matters to you. In the first place, I am able to give something. In the second place, I am willing to do so." [50]

William's concerns were not unfounded. In antebellum America, financial security was precarious for single women; with so many career options closed to women and so few property rights granted to them, a husband was a woman's surest source of income, and Frances didn't have one.

At the age of 34, Frances wrote *the Two Offers*. In the story, a single woman named Laura feels pressure to accept one of two marriage proposals. Neither would be ideal, "but then if I refuse," fretted the character, "there is the risk of being an old maid and that is not to be thought of."

"Is that the most dreadful fate that can befall a woman?" counters Janette, an accomplished, unmarried character bearing a striking resemblance to the real-life Frances. "Is there not more intense wretchedness in an ill-assorted marriage— more utter loneliness in a loveless home, than in the lot of the old maid who accepts her earthly mission as a gift from God, and strives to walk the path of life with earnest and unfaltering steps?"

By story's end, Janette's "genius had won her a position in the literary world, where she shone as one of its bright particular stars. And with her fame came a competence of worldly means, which gave her leisure for improvement, and the riper development of her rare talents." [51]

It was an apt description of how Frances's career had evolved. She sold over fifty thousand copies of her first two books. [52]

The character of Laura married one of her suitors, a drunk who made her miserable. "Intense love is often akin to intense suffering," explained Frances's narrative. "And to trust the whole wealth of a woman's nature on the frail barque of human love, may often be like trusting a cargo of gold and precious gems to a barque that has never battled with the storm or buffeted the waves."

A woman needed more than marriage to "render her happy...Her conscience should be enlightened, her faith in the true and right established, scope given to her heaven-endowed and God-given faculties." [53]

Julia Ward Howe's first published book of poetry had a similar title to Frances's *Forest Leaves*. It was called *Passion-flowers*.

By then, Julia had a fourth baby; she couldn't stop them from coming. She named her Anna-Louisa after her sisters until Chev put his foot down and renamed the baby Laura after his student, Laura Bridgman. [54]

When the baby was only three months old, Julia and Chev set off for another long vacation in Europe. Chev was there for six months before he returned to America to care for their two oldest children, which they had left behind. Julia said goodbye to Chev in Germany and took the two youngest to spend the winter in Rome with her sisters. [55]

At a Christmas party in Rome, Julia met another American tourist, author Horace Wallace. He took her sightseeing and shopping, gave her flowers everyday, and spent many evenings in Julia's parlor, reading Julia's poetry. [56]

"Your life is not worthy of your talent," he told her. She should be more serious about her writing, study more, and above all, stop tossing off "poems here and there, as a child tosses flowers" not bothering about whether "someone picked them up" or they "were left to perish." [57]

When spring came, she couldn't bring herself to go home.

"Pain, amounting almost to anguish, seized me at the thought that I might never again behold those ancient monuments, those stately churches, or take part in the society which had charmed me principally through its unlikeness to any that I had known elsewhere," explained Julia. She didn't mention Horace's name specifically. [58]

Julia's sister Annie wrote an urgent letter to Chev, pleading with him to ask Julia to come back. "Here she must stand alone, and unprotected save by her own virtue and dignity. Indeed I cannot tell you, dear Chevie, how much it would grieve me to leave her in such a position. I do not write at her request, nor shall I even tell her that I have done so. But I know that you will understand the motive which prompts me to trouble you." [59]

Julia came home to Chev. Horace lived for only one more Christmas. When Julia learned of his death by suicide the following December, she decided to stop tossing away her poetry "flowers." She would honor his memory by publishing her work. [60]

When a publisher accepted Julia's manuscript, she told Annie the joyful news, but not Chev. "I have a great mind to keep the whole matter entirely from him, and not let him know anything until the morning the volume comes out. Then he can do nothing to prevent its sale in its proper form," she said. [61]

Henry Wadsworth Longfellow helped her edit her poems, predicting they would "make a sensation." On his advice, Julia published anonymously. [62]

Passion-flowers launched just before Christmas in 1853, a year after Horace's death and three years after the Christmas when Julia and Horace met in Rome. [63]

"Its success became certain at once. Hundreds of copies have already been sold, and every one likes it. Fields foretells a second edition. It is sure to pay for itself," Julia told Annie only a week after the book came out. "The authorship is, of course, no secret now," she added.

If Julia had intended to keep her book anonymous, she probably shouldn't have sent a signed copy to nearly every famous writer in Massachusetts. John

Greenleaf Whittier, Ralph Waldo Emerson and Oliver Wendell Holmes (who was an accomplished poet as well as dean of Harvard Medical School) gave her favorable reviews. [64] Theodore Parker quoted *Passion-flowers* in his Christmas sermon.

Chev was not pleased that Julia had gone behind his back, but it was Christmas, after all, and he couldn't complain about extra income. [65] He remained calm until about a month later, when he read the book.

"Some foolish and impertinent people have hinted to him that the Miller was meant for himself. This has made him almost crazy," Julia told Annie. [66]

Julia's poem, *Mind Versus Mill-stream*, portrayed a miller who wanted the same qualities in his water source that a man might want in a wife: "mild, efficient… beautiful and bland" but found that his stream had a will of her own. [67]

"He has fancied, moreover, that every one despised and neglected him, and indeed it is true that I have left him too much to himself," continued Julia. "I will not expand upon the topic of our miseries. He has been in a very dangerous state, I think, very near insanity." [68]

The first edition of *Passion-flowers* sold out by February. In the second edition, Julia changed the title of *Mind Versus Mill-stream* to simply *The Mill Stream* and cut the last few stanzas, which had made it clear that the poem was a metaphor for marital strife. [69]

Chev was not appeased. The book's commercial success could only mean more people reading poetry that embarrassed him. It wasn't just what the poems may have implied about him. What did the collection reveal about his wife? "There are things in the book…such as a pure minded and sensitive lady should not write," he told Julia. [70]

Chev threatened divorce. He wanted "to marry again—some young girl who would love him supremely," Julia told Louisa. A divorce might have been welcome, but Chev planned to cut off Julia from her oldest daughter and son as part of the break-up. "Before God, Louisa, I thought it my real duty to give up everything that was dear and sacred to me, rather than be forced to leave two of my children, and those two the dearest, Julia and Harry. In this view, I made the greatest sacrifice I can ever be called upon to make. God must accept it, and the bitter suffering of these subsequent months, as some expiation for the errors of my life." [71]

What bitter suffering was she referring to? For one thing, she was pregnant again.

But Julia now saw herself as an author. She made herself a writing studio in the attic, insisted on a few hours of uninterrupted writing time each day, and started publishing regularly—whether Chev liked it or not. [72]

When Chev brought her along on a trip to Cuba, she found herself a gig: writing a monthly column about her voyage for *the Atlantic*. She started the series by poking some fun at her seasick self. [73]

A woman, said to be of a literary turn of mind, in the miserablest condition imaginable. Her clothes, flung at her by the stewardess, seem to have hit in some places and missed in others. Her listless hands occasionally make an attempt to keep her draperies together and to pull her hat on her head but though the intention is evident, she accomplishes little by her motion. She is perpetually being lugged about by a stout steward, who knocks her head against both sides of the vessel, folds her up in the gangway, spreads her out on the deck, and takes her upstairs, downstairs and in my lady's chamber where, report says, he feeds her with a spoon. [74]

Despite the playful tone of the series, "some things in it" made Chev "sad." [75]After mocking herself, Julia quickly moved on to other targets.

You must allow us one heretical whisper, very small and low. The negro of the North is an ideal negro; it is the negro refined by white culture, elevated by white blood, instructed even by white iniquity. The negro among negroes is a coarse, grinning, flat-footed, thick-skulled creature, ugly as Caliban, lazy as the laziest of brutes, chiefly ambitious to be of no use to any in the world. [76]

Chev was horrified, and rightly so. How could Julia "question whether viewing the actual condition of the negro, enforced labor is not best! As if anything would justify the perpetuation of such wrong by the stronger race?" [77]

When abolitionist Wendell Phillips bought a copy of *Passion-flowers* at a bazaar, he said, "She doesn't like me, but I like her poetry."

It was true. "I had supposed the abolitionists to be men and women of rather coarse fiber, abounding in cheap and easy denunciation, and seeking to lay rash hands on the complex machinery of government and of society," Julia admitted later.

Chev introduced Julia to Wendell and other abolitionists, exposing her to worldviews she had never encountered in her youth. At one party, guests gathered around the piano to sing—one of Julia's favorite pastimes. She didn't know the name of the nice man who shared a hymnal with her until later, when Chev expressed surprise at seeing her getting along so well with William Lloyd Garrison.

"From this time forth the imaginary Garrison ceased to exist for me. I learned to respect and honor the real one more and more," said Julia. "It partly amuses, and partly saddens me to recall, at this advanced period of my life, the altogether mistaken views which I once held regarding certain sets of people in Boston, of whom I really knew little or nothing."

"Do you remember that man of whom I spoke to you, the one who wished to be a savior for the negro race?" Chev asked Julia one morning.

"Yes," said Julia, although she didn't.

"That man will call here this afternoon. You will receive him. His name is John Brown."

Julia remembered now. About a year before, Chev had told her John Brown would be famous in the near future, but oddly, he made Julia promise not to tell anyone about the conversation. To make sure she wouldn't, Julia promptly forgot the whole matter.

After his visit that day, Julia only saw John Brown one other time, talking to Chev in his office, before she read in the news that he and a small group of men were raiding the Federal Arsenal at Harper's Ferry, Virginia.

When Julia showed Chev the paper, he seemed unsurprised. "Brown has got to work," he said.

Chev told Julia that John hoped for support from such large numbers of enslaved people at Harper's Ferry that they would overwhelm the slaveholders, perhaps even force them to give in and liberate the slaves without a fight.

"The whole scheme appeared to me wild and chimerical," said Julia. [78]

The peaceful image Chev tried to paint for his wife was a chimera; a victory without a fight would have been entirely out of character for John Brown, who had murdered five people in Pottawatomie Creek, Kansas three years before, kidnapping them from their homes and executing them one at a time.

More news came a few days later: nearly half of the raiders had died in the fight, as had several other people, and John and four of his men were in jail. As disturbing as all of this was, Chev was most upset upon hearing that authorities had confiscated a stash of letters from John's house.

Within a few weeks, newspapers were publishing stories about the contents of those letters, which revealed the names of "the Secret Six" who had financed the raid: Franklin Sanborn, Thomas Wentworth Higginson, Gerrit Smith, George Luther Sterns, Theodore Parker, and the chevalier himself, Samuel Gridley Howe. [79]

"Of course, all the stories about the Northern abolitionists are the merest stuff. No one knew of Brown's intentions but Brown himself and his handful of men," Julia lied to Annie, who was usually her confidant. [80]

Chev repeated the lie to the rest of the world via a letter to the New York Tribune, written from the train station on his way to Canada, where he stayed until after John's execution. [81]

Julia, eight months pregnant with their sixth child, stayed behind in Boston, where she could communicate with Chev about her difficult pregnancy only through letters. [82]

"Do not be so hypochondriacal," he wrote back. [83]

John's wife, Mary Brown, passed through Boston en route to see her husband in jail. Julia met her, gave her a hug and cried. [84]

Mary only made it as far as Baltimore before she received word that John did not want her to come to Virginia. She turned around and went back to Philadelphia where she spent a couple weeks in William Still's home and then a few more with Lucretia Mott. [85] The raiders who had managed to escape were staying at the Still home too, as was Frances Ellen Watkins. [86]

Frances offered all the emotional support she could during the two weeks she spent with Mary, and continued to send her sympathy via post when she had to leave to fulfill Anti-Slavery Society obligations in Ohio.

> In an hour like this the common words of sympathy may seem like idle words, and yet I want to say something to you, the noble wife of the hero of the nineteenth century. Belonging to the race your dear husband reached forth his hand to assist, I need not tell you that my sympathies are with you. I thank you for the brave words you have spoken. A republic that produces such a wife and mother may hope for better days.

Frances enclosed some cash as a token of her "gratitude, reverence and love." [87]

Frances arranged for care packages and letters to be sent to the imprisoned men weekly until they had all been executed, in the hopes of sending "one ray through the night around them." [88]

Shortly before his execution, Frances wrote to John Brown:

> Dear friend: although the hands of slavery throw a barrier between you and me, and it may not be my privilege to see you in your prison-house, Virginia has no bolts or bars through which I dread to send you my sympathy. In the name of the young girl sold from the warm clasp of a mother's arms to the clutches of a libertine or a profligate, in the name of the slave mother, her heart rocked to and fro by the agony of her mournful separations, I thank you, that you have been brave enough to reach out your hands to the crushed and blighted of my race.
>
> ...And, if universal freedom is ever to be the dominant power of the land, your bodies may be only the first stepping stones to dominion. I would prefer to see slavery go down peaceably by men breaking off their sins by righteousness and their inequities by showing justice and mercy to the poor; but we cannot tell what the future may bring forth. God writes national judgments upon national sins, and what may be slumbering in the storehouse of divine justice we do not know. We may earnestly hope that your fate will not be a vain lesson, that it will intensify our hatred of slavery and love of freedom, and that your martyr grave will be a sacred altar upon which men will record their vows of undying hatred to that system which tramples on man and bids defiance to God.[89]

One of the most popular marching songs of the Civil War drew from the same imagery about John Brown's body and his "martyr grave."

> John Brown's body lies a-mouldering in the grave
> John Brown's body lies a-mouldering in the grave
> John Brown's body lies a-mouldering in the grave
> But his soul goes marching on! [90]

Julia Ward Howe and her traveling companions sang *John Brown's Body* as they sat in a carriage in Washington, D.C., delayed by swarms of marching Civil War soldiers. Julia had come along with Chev, who was one of the directors of the Sanitary Commission, tasked with solving the problem of communicable disease outbreaks in army camps.

"Good for you!" called soldiers as they passed. [91] Some of them chimed in on the chorus: [92]

> Glory, glory, hallelujah! Glory, glory, hallelujah!
> Glory, glory, hallelujah! His soul is marching on![93]

"Mrs. Howe, why do you not write some good words for that stirring tune?" asked James Clarke. [94] Improvising new verses for *John Brown's Body* was a popular pastime. [95]

"I have often wished to do so!" Julia replied, but she had never found the right words. [96]

That night, Julia woke up with the song singing in her head and new lyrics forming themselves. [97]

> Mine eyes have seen the glory of the coming of the Lord;
> He is trampling out the vintage where the grapes of wrath are stored;
> He hath loosed the fatal lightning of his terrible swift sword:
> His truth is marching on. [98]

Not moving from her bed, she worked through the lines in her mind, all the way to the last stanza. [99]

> In the beauty of the lilies Christ was born across the sea,
> With a glory in His bosom that transfigures you and me;
> As He died to make men holy, let us die to make men free;
> While God is marching on. [100]

"I must get up and write these verses down, lest I fall asleep again and forget them," she thought.

She sprang out of bed and fumbled around searching for a pen and paper. Once found, she wrote out the verses in the dark, not even looking as she scribbled.

She read through it once, just to make sure it was legible, before going back to bed.

"I like this better than most things that I have written," she thought before she fell asleep again. [101]

Julia sent her lyrics to the editor of the *Atlantic*, who titled the poem *Battle Hymn of the Republic* and published it on the cover of the magazine.[102] Since *Passion-flowers*, nothing Julia had written had made such a sensation. The *Battle Hymn* became an instant favorite among the troops at war and was soon reprinted in other papers and translated into other languages. Julia was besieged with requests for autographs, and even more unexpectedly, for speaking engagements. [103]

"I wish to be heard, to commend my own thoughts with my own voice," Julia had once confessed to her minister, Theodore Parker.

"This is not only natural, but also in accordance with the spirit of the age, which calls for the living presence and the living utterance," he had responded.

Theodore Parker was too progressive to subscribe to the common idea of the time that public speaking was unladylike, but the same was not true for Julia's husband. Julia stayed quiet. [104]

Before the war, Julia had never spoken in public. When an army colonel asked her to speak to his troops, she hid in a tent. When found, she reluctantly managed her first little speech.

Shortly after the war. Julia's uncle died. Julia had hoped for a big inheritance, but he divided his estate among so many beneficiaries that her share was quite small. Most of us don't get big inheritances from rich uncles—nor do we have other funds at our disposal to console ourselves with hired help and world travel—but to Julia, this felt like a blow.

After getting over feeling "dull, sad and perplexed" about the windfall that hadn't come, Julia decided to stop hiding her talent under a bushel (or in a tent). "My uncle not having made me a rich woman, I feel more than ever impelled to make some great effort to realize the value of my mental capacities and acquisitions," she announced, and her speaking career began. [105]

"I am feeling something of novice upon this platform," Frances Ellen Watkins Harper began her speech at the Eleventh National Woman's Rights Convention. She had been an activist for over a decade, but this was the first women's rights meeting she had ever attended. "Born of a race whose inheritance has been outrage and wrong, most of my life has been spent in battling these wrongs. But I did not feel as keenly as others that I had these rights, in common with other women, which are now demanded." [106]

What had changed? The country had, for one thing. This was the first Woman's Rights Convention since the Civil War and the abolition of slavery.

Frances's personal life had changed, too. She had married, become a stepmother to four children, and had a baby of her own. She invested the money she saved from her books and her lecture tours on a house and a farm for her new family, and then, only three years into their marriage, her husband died. [107]

"I tried to keep my children together," said Frances. "But my husband died in debt and before he had been in his grave three months, the administrator had swept the very milk-crocks and wash tubs from my hands. I was a farmer's wife and had made butter for the Columbus market; but what could I do, when they had swept all away? They left me one thing—and that thing was a looking glass!" [108]

Frances was devastated but not surprised. She had been writing about this kind of injustice for years. In her story, the *Two Offers*, the character Janette had a tragic backstory—raised in poverty because creditors had seized her family's estate from her mother when her father died. [109]

"Had I died instead of my husband, how different would have been the result. By this time, he would have another wife, it is likely; and no administrator would have gone into his house, broken up his home, sold his bed, and taken away his means of support," Frances continued. "I say then that justice is not fulfilled so long as woman is unequal before the law. We are all bound up together in one great bundle of humanity, and society cannot trample on the weakest and feeblest of its members without receiving the curse in its own soul."

Here, Frances stopped telling her own story, and spoke directly to her audience, composed mostly of white people.

> You tried that in the case of the negro. You pressed him down
> for two centuries; and in so doing you crippled the moral strength and
> paralyzed the spiritual energies of the white men of the country. [110]

Frances argued that slavery had not only harmed black people, but poor whites, as legislation of the slavery era had favored rich slaveholders over everyone else. [111]

"Society cannot afford to neglect the enlightenment of any class of its members," she told them. "That very class of neglected poor white men" had elected a president who was "the incarnation of meanness." She was talking about Andrew Johnson, but her words will ring familiar to many who witnessed the election of Donald Trump in 2016.

"I do not believe that giving the woman the ballot is immediately going to cure all the ills of life," Frances acknowledged, and then more pointedly added, "I do not believe that white women are dewdrops just exhaled from the skies."

> You white women speak here of rights. I speak of wrongs. I, as a
> colored woman, have had in this country an education which has made
> me feel as if I were in the situation of Ishmael, my hand against every
> man, and every man's hand against me.

Frances schooled her white audience with several examples of discrimination black people like herself experienced everyday. She hoped access to the ballot box would wake up white women to the racism most of them tolerated.

"I tell you that if there is any class of people who need to be lifted out of their airy nothings and selfishness, it is the white women of America," she said, and with that, Frances took her seat. [112]

While Frances was speaking at her first Woman's Rights Convention, Julia Ward Howe expressed her own opinion of the movement through poetry.

> I am not with you, sisters, in your talk…
> In carpet council ye may win the day;
> But keep your limits,—do not rule the world.
> What strife should come, what discord rule the times,
> Could but your pettish will assert its way! [113]

Julia's views began to shift when Caroline Severance moved to Boston from Ohio and founded the New England Woman's Club, organizing women to work together for social justice.

"What did the club life give me?" asked Julia. "Understanding of my own sex; faith in its moral and intellectual growth." [114]

Shortly after joining the New England Woman's Club, Thomas Wentworth Higginson talked Julia into adding her signature to a call for a women's suffrage meeting, promising her "it would be conducted in a very liberal and friendly spirit, without bitterness or extravagance." [115]

Julia sent word to Chev about the event and his reaction was typical.

> Your note of yesterday gives me new pain and sorrow, for it almost crushes the hope I had begun to form that you would yield to my most earnest entreaties and to the consideration of family wishes and interests, and forego further indulgence in your passion for public appearance and display. [116]

At the meeting, Julia tried to maintain a low profile, but the chairperson spotted her and asked her to take a seat on the platform, alongside several men she had come to respect over the years: William Lloyd Garrison, Wendell Phillips, Thomas Wentworth Higginson and James Clarke. The reformers that made the greatest impression on Julia were two she had not met before, Lucy Stone and her husband, Henry B. Blackwell. On Lucy, Julia felt she could see "the light of her good life shining in every feature of her face" and in sharp contrast to her own, Lucy's husband "ably seconded her life work."

Julia found their arguments to be "simple, strong and convincing." More than that, being with suffragists, she felt "relief" from "a sense of isolation and eccentricity."

"For years past I had felt strongly impelled to lend my voice to the convictions of my heart," Julia realized.

> I had done this in a way, from time to time, always with the feeling that my course in so doing was held to call for apology and explanation by the men and women with whose opinions I had hitherto been familiar. I now found a sphere of action in which this mode of expression no longer appeared singular or eccentric, but simple, natural and under the circumstances, inevitable.

And yet, the thoughts collecting in Julia's mind did not make it to her tongue. When someone asked Julia to speak, all she could say was, "I am with you." [117]

Her speechlessness did not prevent her friends from electing her to be the first president of the newly formed New England Woman Suffrage Association. [118]

Chev explained Julia's new project to the children like this: "Mama is in high feather, and is organizing all kinds of clubs and associations, under the guise of advancing the cause of human progress, civilization, women's rights, etc., etc., but with the appearance of good times at picnics, aesthetic teas, lobster salads, clam bakes, etc., which are to be taken inwardly, while the breath of eloquent exhortation is vented outwardly. Vive le suffrage quand même!" [119]

Julia didn't need his validation.

> During the first two thirds of my life I looked to the masculine ideal of character as the only true one. I sought its inspiration, and referred my

merits and demerits to its judicial verdict," she said. "In an unexpected hour a new light came to me, showing me a world of thought and of character quite beyond the limits within which I had hitherto been content to abide. The new domain now made clear to me was that of true womanhood, woman no longer in her ancillary relation to her opposite, man, but in her direct relation to the divine plan and purpose, as a free agent, fully sharing with man every human right and every human responsibility. This discovery was like the addition of a new continent to the map of the world. [120]

Frances observed, "If the fifteenth century discovered America to the Old World, the nineteenth is discovering woman to herself." [121]

In their biography of their mother, Julia's daughters wrote, "She was often unhappy, sometimes suffering. Humanity, her husband's faithful taskmistress, had not yet set her to work, and the long hours of his service left her lonely and—the babies once in bed—at a loss." [122]

Margaret Fuller was the first person to see a glimpse of Julia's yet undiscovered self in her poetry. In the publishing industry, people talk pejoratively about authors who use writing as therapy, but Julia's private therapy through writing was transformational. Fiction provided a medium for Julia to express unorthodox opinions through the voice of a character more bold than she, without committing to whether or not she agreed with the words she was writing. There is no evidence she ever tried to publish the novel she wrote in the 1840s, but it provided her with a way to work through her own questions about gender fluidity within the privacy of her own thoughts. Julia had a genius for changing her mind. As she worked, she adjusted her views with the efficiency of an editor cleaning up a manuscript.

Frances knew herself sooner than Julia. Her writing was designed for the public, and not merely to entertain them but to change them. Rejecting an aesthetic of art for art's sake, Frances's art was a medium for social justice, luring in the masses with entertainment and then motivating them to action. [123] Because she developed her craft, Frances's work not only gave voice to her views, but funded her regular donations to the causes she believed in.

There will always be those who dismiss art with an activist message as propaganda. "Activism never makes for great art," an exasperated film critic complained after the 2018 Cannes Film Festival. In the wake of the Me Too movement, which exposed rampant sexual harassment within the entertainment industry, she believed the Festival was promoting feminist films with questionable artistic value. [124]

I make the bold assertion that even art's ugly little sister, propaganda, has its merits. The Women's March on Washington in January 2017 was the largest protest in American history up until that date, and the visual of tens of thousands of women filling the streets was even more powerful because of the bright pink hats so many were wearing. [125] The hand-knit, cat-ear shaped "pussy hats" were a tongue-in-cheek mockery of recently elected President Donald Trump's infamous comment, "Grab 'em by the pussy." [126]

A few months later, a new statue called *Fearless Girl* appeared in New York, staring down an older statue, *Charging Bull*. This inspirational symbol of women's potential to take down patriarchy integrated itself into the memories of individuals and the conversations of the masses in a way that facts and figures rarely do. [127]

But the very qualities that make art powerful make it inherently risky. Art is vulnerable. When Julia Ward Howe started publishing her work, she revealed both her hidden virtues and her ugliest biases. Art is subjective. Each person will interpret its symbols differently, building new layers of meaning that do not always match the intent of the artist.

While the people who wore pussy hats saw themselves as defying Trump's vulgarity, some who looked on saw the hats themselves as vulgar. Others saw them as noninclusive of women without pink anatomy. Pink was intended to represent womanhood, not the color of anyone's anatomy, the women who popularized the hats responded with surprise. [128] The artist who originally created *Charging Bull* had a similar reaction. His statue was intended to represent prosperity, not patriarchy. Placing *Fearless Girl* next to it changed its meaning without his permission. [129]

Debates will never cease about whether art with a social-political view is "real" art, and in the end, not every attempt at art will prove to have merit—either as art or as effective propaganda. [130] Nevertheless, modern feminists continue to express themselves through media such as filmmaking, blogging and subversive cross stitching. (Yes, that's a thing.) Only the most talented among us will create masterpieces that change the world, but any of us could change ourselves. That is enough.

CHAPTER SEVEN
How do we define our priorities?

"Let us no longer talk of prejudice, until prejudice becomes extinct at home.
Let us no longer talk of opposition, until we cease to oppose our own. For
while these evils exist, to talk is like giving breath to air and labor to the wind." [1]
–Maria W. Stewart, 1833

"There are two lines of action for the true reformer to pursue at the same time.
One is to mitigate as far as possible existing evils; the other and far higher duty
is to prevent their recurrence by removing, if possible, their cause." [2]
–Elizabeth Cady Stanton, 1852

"The question of precedence has no place on an equal rights platform." [3]
–Susan B. Anthony, 1869

It was after hours of yardwork, her long, heavy skirt growing heavier as it collected mud, that Elizabeth Smith Miller cut her skirt short and made a pair of pants to wear under it. Appraising herself in the new outfit, she decided that she looked tolerable while standing, awkward and uncouth when seated. Nevertheless, freedom from gardening in a ball gown compensated for any sacrifice in appearance. [4]

A couple months later, she visited her cousin, women's rights activist Elizabeth Cady Stanton, who thought the new outfit could be useful for more than pulling weeds—perhaps it could help uproot patriarchy itself. Long dresses, corsets and petticoats were tools of oppression. "The comfort and convenience of the woman is never considered. ...No wonder man prescribes her sphere. She needs his aid at every turn. He must help her up stairs and down, in the carriage and out, on the horse, up the hill, over the ditch and fence, and thus teach her the poetry of dependence." [5]

Elizabeth Cady Stanton's 16-year-old housekeeper Amelia Willard copied Elizabeth Miller's sewing pattern and set to work making pants for her boss, and for herself as well. [6]

Their neighbor, Amelia Bloomer, ran a women's paper called the *Lily*, to which Elizabeth Cady Stanton was a regular contributor. Amelia happened to be in the midst of mild war of words with the editor of another local paper, the *Seneca County Courier*. [7]

The editor of the *Courier*, Isaac Fuller, had recently published an article in support of dress reform for women. Amelia reprinted the article in the *Lily* with an endorsement— "We favor such reform for the reason that it would contribute greatly to the comfort, happiness and convenience of the sex" —accompanied by a taunt:

> Really, we are surprised that the cautious editor of the *Seneca County Courier* has so far overcome his opposition to woman's rights as to become himself an advocate of their wearing the pantaloons! ...Had we broached the subject the cry would have been raised on all sides, "She wants to wear the pantaloons," and a pretty hornet's nest we should have got into. But now that our cautious editor of the *Courier* recommends it, we suppose that there will be no harm in our doing so. ...Women should not dare to make a change in their costume 'til they have the consent of men—for they claim the right to prescribe for us in the fashion of our dress as well as in all things else. [8]

Now that Amelia had publicly endorsed dress reform in her paper, she was feeling pressure to practice what she preached. [9]

"A respectable dozen of the women of our village have decided to assume this costume at once," Elizabeth Cady Stanton announced on the pages of the *Lily*. "So prepare yourselves, ye Lords of Seneca, to see the idols of your affections soon flitting about your muddy street with as much ease and freedom as you do yourselves. And you, Mr. *Courier*, please write another stirring article and talk up the fashion as fast as possible." [10]

The first time Amelia Bloomer answered the door wearing her new clothes, her caller startled and backed away, blocking his view of Amelia with both hands.

Amelia and her husband tried to call him back, but he ran off yelling, "Don't speak to me! Oh, don't speak to me!" [11]

Undaunted, Amelia announced that she had changed out her wardrobe for a short skirt with pants in the next issue of the *Lily*. The *New York Tribune*, with a circulation far beyond the mere 500 people reading the *Lily*, saw fit to reprint her announcement, and soon Amelia's clothing was under discussion in papers throughout the country and abroad. [12] Headlines around the world read "Bloomerism" or "Bloomerites" or "Bloomers," despite Amelia's repeated attempts to give proper credit to Elizabeth Miller for designing the outfit. [13]

"I was praised and censured, glorified and ridiculed, until I stood in amazement at the furor I had wrought by my pen while sitting quietly in my little office at home attending to my duties," said Amelia. [14]

The Ladies Temperance Society withdrew support of the *Lily* due to controversy over Amelia's wardrobe, which might have been devastating if it weren't for the fact that circulation was skyrocketing. [15]

"Ladies, unhook your dresses, and let everything hang loosely about you. Now take a long breath, swell out as far as you can, and at that point fasten your clothes. Now please cut off those flowing skirts to your knees, and put on a pair of loose trousers buttoned round your ankle," Elizabeth Cady Stanton instructed readers of the *Lily*, along with a full-proof method to test the results: "To appreciate the great freedom this slight change has made, go down cellar, and bring up a pan of milk, or take yonder lamp and pitcher of water and go upstairs." [16]

Women flooded the office of the *Lily* with letters requesting pictures and patterns for the new outfit. Amelia obliged. [17]

"Heretofore rags have been primary, and woman secondary. We propose now to place woman in her true position, making her primary and rags secondary." Elizabeth wrote. "The question is now to be not 'Rags, how do you look?' but 'Women, how do you feel?'" [18]

Such a reversal was intolerable to the fashion industry. "If a woman put on a short skirt, trousers, and a jacket, she would probably thrust her hands into the pockets, speak coarsely, and with a loud laugh. Dressed as a male, a woman could not help but behave like one in all his vulgarity," fretted *Godey's Lady's Book*. [19]

The clergy sided with the fashion magazines on this one.

"Have you seen the Reverend Mr. Sunderland's sermon from the text, 'a woman shall not wear anything that pertaineth unto a man,' etc.? The bloomers have made more impression than I thought, to be attacked by the pulpit," laughed Lucy Stone. [20]

Elizabeth Cady Stanton had been wearing the bloomer the first time Lucy met her at an activist meeting in New York. As soon as Lucy returned home to Massachusetts, she got to work making her own bloomer. Her sister, Sarah, tried to talk Lucy into at least putting some lace on the pants, but Lucy scorned the suggestion as frivolous. [21]

Lucy's appearance created a stir among her employers at the Anti-Slavery Society, who hedged about whether to allow Lucy to speak at the convention in such weird attire. How would it affect the cause?

"It is all fudge for anybody to pretend that any cause that deserves to live is impeded by the length of your skirt," insisted Lucy. "Audiences listen and assent just as well to one who speaks truth in a short as in a long dress."

"Well if Lucy Stone cannot speak at that meeting in any decent dress that she chooses, I will not speak," announced Wendell Phillips. That settled it, and Lucy took the stand in her bloomer. [22]

The *Frederick Douglass paper* reported that Lucy, "carried her audience above the earth, thrilled their hearts, and made herself their favorite." [23]

"I was greatly pleased that a Bloomer should have been the pet of the convention," Elizabeth Cady Stanton told Lucretia Mott. "Depend upon it, Lucretia, that woman can never be developed in her present drapery. She is a slave to her rags." [24]

"Do take care of your health, Nette, and to that end, I wish you would wear a bloomer. I had constant and hard meetings but I bore it well from the freedom and comfort of my dress. It is a great deal the best for health," Lucy proselytized to her best friend, Antoinette Brown. [25]

Nette had just started a speaking tour on behalf of the New York Women's Temperance Society, accompanied by Amelia Bloomer and Susan B. Anthony, and she was the only one of the three still wearing long dresses.

As the three traveled together, men stared and gangs of boys followed them, mocking Amelia and Susan for their bloomers. [26]

Reporters seemed obsessed with Susan's ugliness. "Mrs. Bloomer was pretty and gentle and was not much pitched into, though she wore bloomers. I wore long dresses and was not pitched into. But poor Susan did not look well in bloomers. She was a sort of scapegoat for all of us," Nette told her family. [27]

Like Amelia, Lucy had the advantage of being pretty and petite, so she didn't fully experience the kind of harassment her taller, homelier friend Susan endured—unless she was with Susan. Walking to the post office one day, a group of men blocked their path. Lucy and Susan backed up and turned a different direction, only to be stopped by other men. They frantically searched for an escape route, but soon realized that men and boys had completely surrounded them.

The laughter and catcalls of their captors attracted the attention of other men in the busy square. The crowd trapping the two, bloomer-clad ladies grew by the minute until, at last, a friendly onlooker called for a police officer to break up the crowd and a carriage whisked them away, their errand forgotten. [28]

It wasn't long before Elizabeth Cady Stanton surprised Susan by wearing yet another new style, longer than her first bloomer but shorter than more fashionable dresses with long trains. She did not wear pants with it. [29]

Elizabeth hoped that without the pants, dress reformers would be less conspicuous. As a bonus, with the "bloomers" part of the outfit gone, it wouldn't make sense any more for boys and men on the street to scream, "Here comes my Bloomer," as they walked past. [30] As much as the ladies liked Amelia Bloomer, the word *bloomer* was becoming odious to them. [31]

Amelia didn't like it either. "I never called it the bloomer costume," she insisted. [32]

Dress reformers had tried to find a new name—they liked *freedom dress*, but it did not catch on. [33]

Elizabeth offered to gift Susan the fabric if she would make a similar, no-pants outfit, but Susan refused.

"It will only be said, 'The Bloomers have doffed their pants the better to display their legs,'" Susan told Elizabeth.

Elizabeth tripped over her new dress. Susan knew she had made the right decision. [34]

About three years after dress reform was first heralded on the pages of the *Lily*, Elizabeth Cady Stanton filled her closet with long dresses and petticoats, throwing away every short skirt. She was fed up with fighting with her family about her unusual clothes. [35] Her cousin Elizabeth was still wearing the bloomer, but she had moved to Washington, D.C. when her father, Gerrit Smith, was elected to Congress. Dress reform was working out well for Cousin Elizabeth; both her husband and her father were big fans of the bloomer she had designed and she felt less conspicuous in that large city than in the smaller community of Seneca Falls. [36]

Meanwhile, Elizabeth Cady Stanton was left at home with less enthusiastic relatives. There was her father, who had threatened to bar her from his house when she started wearing the bloomer; her sister, who had cried when she first saw it, and her embarrassed little boys. [37] Her son Daniel had asked her not to visit him at boarding school because of her bloomer.

"Now why do you wish me to wear something that is uncomfortable, inconvenient and many times dangerous? I'll tell you why. You want me to be like other people," she told her son, before instructing him to "learn not to care what foolish people say." Her stern words did not betray to him that her children's humiliation was the "bitterest drop" for her. [38]

"When the dress is not a matter of trouble to them, your ultraisms will become more obvious to them," Susan warned Elizabeth.

Susan glumly reported Elizabeth's desertion to Lucy. "Everyone who drops the dress makes the task a harder one for the few left. I have been so pressed by those who are perhaps better and wiser than myself to lay aside the short dress, so implored for the sake of the cause, etc. etc., that for the last ten days my heart has almost failed me and, but for my reliance on my own convictions of right and duty, must have sat down disheartened and discouraged. It is hard to stand alone." [39]

"No, no, Susan, it is all a pretense that the cause will suffer," Lucy reassured her, but she had a confession.

Several weeks earlier, she had stayed at Lucretia Mott's house. Lucretia's daughters had begged Lucy to wear something else and refused to walk beside her until she did. Lucretia reprimanded them but their faces betrayed their mortification whenever anyone saw them with Lucy. It was one thing to bear catcalls from indolent street boys—it was something else when even the family of the great women's rights activist Lucretia Mott couldn't tolerate her appearance.

After leaving the Mott home, Lucy bought some fabric.

"I have had it a month, and it is not made because I can't decide whether to make it long or short. Not that I think any cause will suffer by a short dress, but simply to save myself from a great deal of annoyance," Lucy told Susan.

Lucy described her grievances:

> I am annoyed to death by people who recognize me by my clothes, and when I get a seat in the cars, they will get a seat by me and bore me for a whole day with the stupidest stuff in the world. Much of that I should escape if I dressed like others. Then again, when I go to a new city, where there are many places of interest to see, and from which I could learn much, if I go out a horde of boys pursue me and destroy all comfort. Then, too, the blowing up by the wind, which is so provoking when people stare and laugh.

Lucy hadn't made up her mind yet. There was a principle at stake, after all.

> Then, too, I have this feeling: women are in bondage. Their clothes are a great hindrance to their engaging in any business which will make them pecuniarily independent; and since the soul of womanhood can never be queenly and noble so long as it must beg bread for its body, is it not better, even at the expense of a great deal of annoyance, that they whose life deserves respect and is greater than their garments should give an example by which woman may more easily work out her own emancipation? [40]

"But Lucy, if you waiver and talk—yea, and resolve—to make a long dress, why then, who may not?" asked Susan. "If Lucy Stone, with all her reputation, her powers of eloquence, her loveliness of character, that wins all who once hear the sound of her voice, cannot bear the martyrdom of the dress, who, I ask, can?"

Susan ran back to the Stanton home to talk to Elizabeth about this unexpected turn of events.

"I now feel a mental freedom among my friends that I have not known for the two years past," Elizabeth told Susan. She encouraged Susan to give up the bloomer too, preferably before any reporter could make fun of her again. Susan had a speaking engagement the very next night, alongside Ernestine Rose.

"Let the hem out of your dress today, before tomorrow's night meeting," Elizabeth told Susan as she left.

Elizabeth sent a note to Lucy with the same advice.

> I've but a moment to say, for your own sake, lay aside the shorts. I know what you suffer among fashionable people. Not for the sake of the cause, nor for any sake but your own, take it off. We put the dress on for greater freedom, but what is physical freedom compared with mental bondage? By all means have the new dress made long.

Susan headed over to the printing office, pestered by rude, vulgar, staring men the entire way.

"There comes my Bloomer!" a man yelled at her as she opened the office door.

"Oh hated name!" grumbled Susan. [41]

In desperation, Susan called on an even less likely ally than Elizabeth to help her persuade Lucy to keep the bloomer: Nette Brown, who had never converted to bloomers in the first place. [42]

While Nette appreciated dress reform as an act of conscience, she believed it "a mistaken emphasis to cause so much discussion about mere clothes." Nette believed the negative attention directed at women in bloomers posed a "danger to the work the women were engaged in…prejudicing our plea for temperance and justice to women." [43]

"Don't suffer martyrdom over a short dress or anything else that can be prevented. Sorrow enough will come," Nette told Lucy. "There are many years in the distance waiting yet with greater burdens for your spirit, so let every avoidable thing go and good riddance to it." [44]

Susan wrote to Lucy a few weeks later to update her on the campaign.

> Dear Lucy:
>
> Where are you and why are you so long silent? We have had a most glorious hearing before our Assembly Committee, the one to whom was referred our Petition for the Just and Equal Rights for Women. All the members, save one, are quite liberally disposed. …Mrs. Rose made one of her very best arguments. I enclose the written statements as published in the *Tribune*. [45]

Instead of reporting any of the merits of their arguments, the news stories focused on the women's clothes, which allegedly proved the activists to be "unsexed women." [46]

According to the press, "the only effect produced was a determination more fixed than ever in the minds of the committee to remain bachelors in the event of the success of the movement. And who can blame them?" [47]

The last line of Susan's letter read, "Lucy, I have let down some of my dresses and am dragging around in long skirts. It is humiliating to my good sense of cleanliness and comfort." [48]

"I am amazed that the intelligent women engaged in the woman's rights movement see not the relation between their dress and the oppressive evils which they are striving to throw off. I am amazed that they do not see that their dress is indispensable to keep in countenance the policy and purposes out of which those evils grow," complained Gerrit Smith, when he learned that most women's rights activists had given up the bloomer, excepting his own daughter. [49]

With her famous father making such a public show of support for the movement she had begun, Elizabeth Smith Miller was too loyal to give it up. [50] She continued to wear the short dress for another three or four years after her cousin and most other reformers had abandoned it.

When questioned about her return to long dresses years later, she was embarrassed to admit she had become a victim to her own "love of beauty." In her own defense, she added that she still wasn't a complete slave to fashion:

I do not wear a heavy, trailing skirt, nor have I ever worn a corset. My bonnet shades my face. My spine was preserved from the bustle, my feet from high heels, my shoulders are not turreted, nor has fashion clasped my neck with her choking collar. [51]

Amelia Bloomer sold her newspaper and moved to Ohio, where she found that she preferred living without the notoriety of her New York life, and kept it that way by dressing inconspicuously in public. [52]

Years later, younger suffragists reintroduced the matter of dress reform at a women's rights meeting, proposing that suffragists wear bloomers again. Susan turned to Nette and whispered, "They may do it, but I shan't. I've suffered enough." [53]

Everyday, we choose our battles. Should I go for the big win or work toward incremental change? Woo powerful decision-makers or build grassroots support? Tell off that sexist pig or save my energy for Zumba class?

Dress reformers were absolutely, unequivocally right about the perils of those pretty but impractical corsets, long skirts and petticoats. Women couldn't move into male-dominated professions because they could hardly move at all. Basic household chores could be deadly if they dropped a candle or bumped into the hearth, setting their enormous skirts ablaze.

At first, dress reform seemed like a battle women could win. Unlike most causes suffragists supported, they wouldn't have to convince male politicians to agree with them; they had control over their own clothes. And yet, the earliest suffragists walked away from dress reform in the end, dragging their long skirts behind them.

It wasn't a battle worth fighting.

I can find no evidence that any women of color participated in the dress reform movement. If the street harassment was demoralizing to white women, that kind of attention could have been fatal for blacks. The dress reform movement took place at a time when the Fugitive Slave Act gave slaveholders free reign to hunt black people and force them into slavery in the South.

"I frankly confess that I do not expect any speedy or widespread change in the dress of women, until as a body they feel a deeper discontent with their present entire position," said Lucy about forty years later, when younger activists, still wearing long skirts in the 1890s, asked her about dress reform. She listed several issues she saw as higher priority, such as suffrage, property rights, custody rights and bodily autonomy, and encouraged them to work on those first. A woman's "miserable style of dress is a consequence of her present vassalage, not its cause," Lucy told them. "Woman must become ennobled in the quality of her being. When she is so, and takes her place, clothed with the dignity which the possession and exercise of her natural human rights give, she will be able, unquestioned, to dictate the style of her dress." [54]

During the 1920s, Lucy Stone's daughter, Alice Stone Blackwell, who was comfortably dressed in a fashionable short skirt exposing her "emancipated legs," saw an image of the bloomer and couldn't understand why it had been so offensive. Yes, it was ugly, but so was everything her mother's generation wore. [55]

More than a decade after most suffragists had given up dress reform, and a few months after the Thirteenth Amendment abolished slavery, the New York Anti-Slavery Society gathered to discuss their next challenge: eliminating the word *white* as a voting requirement. Elizabeth Cady Stanton made a bold suggestion— get rid of the word *male*, too.

The other delegates burst into laughter.

Elizabeth turned and addressed the crowd. "Why should a woman go about the state and ask for suffrage for the negro and not demand it for herself? In a cause for which women have labored for 30 years, I do not see the justice of securing suffrage to the negro and denying it to women."

"It would be an insult to ask a woman to go over to the state and make such a demand for the negro and not include herself, but that is simply an act of her own volition," Abby Kelley Foster answered diplomatically. Abby was a veteran of both movements, but she didn't want to discuss women's rights today. "I don't think such a subject should be introduced into an anti-slavery meeting. We have other organizations for the advocacy of those rights. Just as soon as the civil rights of the negroes are secured in the South, we cease to be an anti-slavery society and then I am ready for an organization for universal suffrage."

Wendell Phillips, the society president, declared Elizabeth's amendment out of order.

"I believe it is the business of this society to resist all oppression, the oppression of women as well as others," protested Robert Purvis. [56] Removing the word *white* might secure voting rights for himself, but not for his wife, Harriet Forten Purvis, who had been one of the organizers of the Fifth National Woman's Rights Convention in Philadelphia. As a woman of color, she could not vote until prohibitions based on both race and sex were removed. [57]

"How is Mrs. Stanton's amendment out of order?" asked Abby's husband, Stephen Foster.

"The sole object of this society is the abolition of slavery in the United States," said Wendell.

"My motion is merely that the constitution of the state of New York should be amended so as to give it a republican form of government and I expressed my opinion that that would strike out the word *male*. As long as any form of oppression is tolerated, even you are not secure in your liberty, Mr. Phillips," said Elizabeth.

As a white male, Wendell happened to be one of most secure people in the room. He called for a vote to strike Elizabeth's motion. The majority voted in Wendell's favor, but then Stephen raised the motion again.

"Mr. Phillips says on this platform we can demand only the right of the negro to the suffrage. But you can demand everything that goes to secure that suffrage to the negro," said Stephen. Without naming her, Stephen started talking about Abby. [58] Stephen married Abby five years after she became the first female officer of the American Anti-Slavery Society. Her appointment had been so controversial that some of the other officers had resigned and formed a separate organization. [59] While their daughter was young, Stephen supported his wife's activism as the stay-at-home parent. [60] "Twenty-five years ago, it was asked if woman had a right to speak in public on behalf of the slave. That right was conceded, although it caused a division of the Society. The question now comes, has woman a right to strike off the shackles of the slave by her vote as well as by her tongue? I say she has."

The audience applauded; it was not the reaction Elizabeth had received when she brought up the idea in the first place.

"I will fight to the death for it," continued Stephen. "And I tell you that you will never see the negro voting until woman cast her ballot for him."

Another man, Mr. Lee, doubted that. "I believe the most intense hatred of the negro in the city is held by the women. In the theater, the omnibus, the church, everywhere, this is manifested."

Lee finished up with a wee disclaimer. "Still I have a respect for the women, for I remember that my mother was a woman, and though I am in favor of woman's rights, I think it is right that they should have the truth told of them."

"It has been asserted that the black man should have the right to vote because he is not sure of his freedom without it. If this is the case, why should not the women who were lately slaves have the same right? Why should we be afraid of this question?" asked Charles Remond.

"The women who are so prejudiced against the black men are not the women who now demand universal suffrage. I entertain Frederick Douglass or Charles Remond the same as I would any other gentleman of education and culture," said Elizabeth, invoking the oft-used "black friend" defense that is still a staple among white people today.

Elizabeth's resolution, which had now become Stephen's, was adopted. [61]

Four months later, women's rights advocates gathered for the Eleventh National Woman's Rights Convention. It would be their first in six years, since the Civil War interrupted their work.

Susan presented their proposal to merge with the Anti-Slavery Society, but not until after clarifying that the universally popular Lucretia Mott would have done so herself, if it weren't for a nasty cold.

> Our demand must now go beyond women; it must extend to the farthest bound of the principle of the "consent of the governed," the only authorized or just government. We therefore wish to broaden our women's rights platform and make it in name what it ever has been in spirit: a human rights platform.

Susan explained the reasons for the change.

> As women, we can no longer seem to claim for ourselves what we do not for others, nor can we work in two separate movements to get the ballot for the two disfranchised classes, the negro and woman, since to do so must be a double cost of time, energy and money.

There was already a great deal of overlap between the two movements anyway, with many of the same people supporting both racial and gender equity.

> We were roused to the work by the several propositions still to permit negro disfranchisement in the rebel states and at the same time to put up a new bar against the enfranchisement of women. [62]

A year before, Wendell Phillips had warned the Anti-Slavery Society that the Thirteenth Amendment, ending slavery, would not be enough to liberate former slaves from their white oppressors in the Southern states. He called for a Fourteenth Amendment to prevent states from disfranchising voters on the basis of race. "I hope some day to be bold enough to add sex," he added. "However, my friends, we must take up but one question at a time and this hour belongs exclusively to the negro." [63]

"Do you believe the African race is composed entirely of males?" asked Elizabeth. [64]

Congress heard Wendell's call to action and was now considering a Fourteenth Amendment—but the wording of the Amendment was the "bar against the enfranchisement of women" that Susan was talking about. [65]

"Do you see what the sons of the pilgrims are doing in Congress? Nothing less than trying to get the irrepressible *male citizen* into our immortal Constitution," exclaimed Elizabeth when she read the proposed Fourteenth Amendment. The Amendment would grant citizenship to former slaves, require equal protection under the law and penalize states that did not enfranchise all male citizens. The word *male* had not been in the Constitution before, but the proposed Amendment repeated it three times, codifying that men—not women—had the right to vote.

"What a shame it would be to mar that glorious bequest of the fathers by introducing into it any word that would recognize a privileged order," continued Elizabeth. "As our Constitution now exists, there is nothing to prevent women or negros from holding the ballot but state legislation, but if that word *male* be inserted as now proposed by Broomall, Schenck and Jenckes, it will take us a century at least to get it out again." [66]

Elizabeth, Susan and Lucy Stone responded with a petition drive, calling for an amendment to grant women the right to vote. [67] They asked Senator Charles Sumner of Massachusetts to present the petition to Congress. He had recently given a speech on the Senate floor calling for universal suffrage.

"We can not add one line or precept to the inexhaustible speech recently made by Charles Sumner in the Senate, to prove that 'no just government can be formed without the consent of the governed,'" explained Susan. "We propose no new theories. We simply ask that you secure to all the practical application of the immutable principles of our government, without distinction of race, color or sex." [68]

When the Senator said, "universal suffrage," he had actually meant, "universal male suffrage," but it was hard to refuse a group of ladies quoting his own speeches at him. He agreed to submit their petition, but his delivery left much to be desired. He apologized as he handed it over and said, "I do not think this a proper time for the consideration of that question." [69]

When Congressional approval of the Fourteenth Amendment seemed imminent, Lucy and her husband, Henry Blackwell, went to Washington, D.C. to discuss their concerns with Senator Sumner in person. [70]

He told them that including women would make the amendment too controversial to pass. [71]

"Suffrage for black men will be all the strain the Republican party can stand," other senators had told him when the Amendment was discussed in Committee.[72]

"I sat up all one night and rewrote that clause of the Amendment fourteen times, so unwilling was I to introduce the word *male* into the Constitution, but I could in no other way embody my meaning," Senator Sumner told Lucy and Harry. [73]

The congressional committee had discussed substituting the word *person* for *male*.

"That will never do," someone said. "It would enfranchise all the Southern wenches." [74]

While extending the vote to black men would most likely increase Republican ranks in the South, enfranchising women would extend the vote to scores of Southern white women—likely Democrats. Republican concern wasn't entirely self-interested. Increasing Republican ranks in the South seemed to be the best way to combat racist laws supported by Southern Democrats.

At the National Woman's Rights Convention, Susan laid out her strategy for their new human rights campaign. They would start in her home state of New York.

> The state of New York is to hold a constitutional convention the coming year. We want to make a thorough canvass of the entire state with lecturers, tracks and petitions and if possible, create a public sentiment that shall send genuine Democrats and Republicans to that convention who shall strike out from the Constitution the two adjectives *white male*, giving to every citizen over 21 the right to vote and thus make the Empire State the first example of a true republican form of government. And what we propose to do in New York, the coming 18 months, we trust to do in every other state as soon as we can get the men and the women and the money to go forward with the work.

Susan's resolution was unanimously adopted and the women's rights advocates merged with abolitionists to advocate human rights together. [75]

The first order of business for the new American Equal Rights Association was to choose officers. Elizabeth Cady Stanton was nominated but deferred.

"I thank the convention for the honor proposed, but I should prefer to see Lucretia Mott in that office, that thus that office might ever be held sacred in the memory that it had first been filled by one so loved and honored by all. I shall be happy as vice president to relieve my dear friend of the arduous duties of her office, if she will but give us the blessing of her name as president."

The vote was unanimous. Stephen Foster escorted Lucretia to the front of the room for her acceptance speech.

My age and feebleness unfit me for any public duties but I rejoice in the inauguration of a movement broad enough to cover class, color and sex, and would be happy to give my name and influence, if thus I might encourage the young and strong to carry on the good work. [76]

The American Equal Rights Association established headquarters in New York. Lucy was there when a letter arrived from Samuel Wood, a Republican state senator from Kansas. The Kansas Legislature had approved a resolution to enfranchise women, pending voter approval, and he hoped the Association would send delegates to Kansas to campaign. It would be the first time American voters would consider extending voting rights to women and Lucy wanted to set the right precedent. [77] Lucy and Harry dropped off their nine-year-old daughter Alice with Harry's sisters, Elizabeth and Emily, and set off for Kansas. [78]

Sam Wood had announced in the local papers that a celebrity line-up of women's rights activists would come to Kansas to support the resolution: Henry Ward Beecher, Theodore Tilton, Ben Wade, Gratz Brown, Elizabeth Cady Stanton, Anna Dickinson, and Lucy Stone, among others. Reporters scoffed. The announcement was "one of Sam's shabbiest tricks," they said, accurately guessing that he hadn't actually booked any of them.

When famous Lucy Stone did show up, star-struck Kansas citizens were too elated to notice or care that the other half-dozen promised emissaries weren't in the wagon with her.

"I guess the thing will carry," people started to say.

"I fully expect we shall carry the state," Lucy wrote to Elizabeth. "Our meetings are everywhere crowded to overflowing." [79]

Lucy and Harry traveled across the state by wagon, holding meetings in log schoolhouses, stone churches and stores with planks brought in for seating. Once, they tried to use the construction site of an unfinished courthouse, but had to find another venue when it rained. The half-built structure didn't have a roof yet.

"We owe everything to Wood, and he is really a thoroughly noble, good fellow, and a hero," Harry wrote to Elizabeth and Susan. "The son of a Quaker mother, he held the baby while his wife acted as one of the officers, and his mother another, in a Woman's Rights Convention seventeen years ago. Wood has helped off more runaway slaves than any man in Kansas. He has always been true both to the negro and the woman. But the negroes dislike and distrust him because he has never allowed the word *white* to be struck out, unless the word *male* should be struck out also." [80]

Women's suffrage wasn't the only resolution on the Kansas ballot. Originally, the Kansas Legislature had considered a bill to enfranchise black men, not women. Senator Wood had amended the bill to also strike the word *male*, effectively halting the measure. Advocates for racial equity begged the Senator to remove his rider and allow the bill to pass.

"If we can have but one, let the negro wait," Sam told them. [81]

It wasn't the first time Senator Wood had stood in the way of suffrage for black men in Kansas. He had voted against it for five straight years. [82]

In the end, the House and the Senate compromised by dividing suffrage for (white) women and suffrage for (male) blacks into two separate resolutions, which Kansas voters would consider independently during the next election. [83]

Still, Harry predicted that "the woman and the negro will rise or fall together" and he felt confident about which way it would go. "Shrewd politicians say that with proper effort we shall carry both next fall." [84]

Lucy was delighted to find an active women's rights community in Kansas. "The women here are grand and it will be a shame past all expression if they don't get the right to vote," she wrote to Elizabeth. "One woman in Wyandotte said she carried petitions all through the town for female suffrage and not one woman in ten refused to sign. Another in Lawrence said they sent up two large petitions from there. So they have been at the Legislature, like the heroes they really are, and it is not possible for the husbands of such women to back out." [85]

Not every woman or husband had the noblest of motives for supporting women's suffrage. "I know my husband does not believe in women voting, but he hates the negroes and would not want them placed over me," one Kansas woman told a canvasser as she signed the women's suffrage petition. As newcomers, Lucy and Harry were naïve about these racial tensions.

Hoping for some positive press, Lucy sent an article by Sam to Elizabeth and asked her to get it printed in the *Independent*. [86] Edited by Theodore Tilton, the *Independent* was one of two Republican, East Coast newspapers widely circulated in Kansas. Horace Greeley's *New York Tribune* was the other.

Elizabeth couldn't get it published. She was having trouble of her own with the press. The *National Anti-Slavery Standard*, under the direction of Aaron Powell and Wendell Phillips, had recently printed a speech by Elizabeth, or rather, a bit of one. They edited out everything she had said about women's suffrage. What was left over appeared to be a speech supporting suffrage for black men only. [87]

Lucretia encouraged her friends to remain calm. "We cannot afford to quarrel with seeming unfairness and I would swallow a good deal that is distasteful rather than stand in an antagonistic relation with our friend and editor, Aaron Macy Powell. I presume he was ignorant of the important omissions in Elizabeth's speech. I was glad to see it in the *Standard* and never dreamed of any unfairness." [88]

"The *Tribune* and *Independent* alone could, if they would urge universal suffrage, as they do negro suffrage, carry this whole nation upon the only just plane of equal human rights," said Lucy.

> What a power to hold and not use! I could not sleep the other night just for thinking of it, and if I had got up and written the thought that burned my very soul, I do believe that Greeley and Tilton would have echoed the cry of the old crusaders, "God wills it," and rushing to our half-sustained standard, would plant it high and firm on immutable principles. They must take it up. I shall see them the very first thing when I go home.

After two months of campaigning in Kansas, Harry and Lucy needed to get back to their daughter. They would arrive back East just too late to attend the annual convention of the American Equal Rights Association, but Lucy sent Susan instructions. "Now, as I cannot be in New York next week, I want you to see Aunt Fanny and Anna Dickinson and get them pledged to come here in the fall. We will raise the pay somehow. You and Mrs. Stanton will come, of course. I wish Mrs. Harper to come." [89]

Frances Harper was not available to come to Kansas, as Lucy had hoped. She was in South Carolina. Curious fellow travelers asked Frances why a Northern black woman like herself would be traveling alone in the South.

"I'm on a lecture tour."

"What are you lecturing about?" someone asked.

"Politics, among other topics," said Frances, and surveyed the train car for reactions. So soon after the Civil War, white people were nervous. They kept talking about their fears that someone would "put the devil in the nigger's head."

One of her fellow passengers revealed that he was a former slave dealer. It is not worthwhile to show any signs of fear, Frances thought to herself. She started a conversation with him and soon, other travelers were crowding into the car to hear. [90]

Frances had come south to be part of reconstruction. "The South is to be a great theater for the colored man's development and progress. There is brainpower here," she said. [91]

She was touring the southern states, lecturing at churches on Sundays and schools on weekdays, sometimes twice in one day, and rarely taking a day off. [92] "I meet with a people eager to hear, ready to listen, as if they felt that the slumber of the ages had been broken and that they were to sleep no more," she wrote to friends in the North.

Frances was traveling alone, a circumstance that made many nervous on her behalf. [93] At one of the venues on her schedule, someone had punched the lecturer, they told her, and a black man had been shot.

Frances was determined to fulfill all of her committed appointments. "I do not feel any particular fear," she insisted. [94]

Her lectures were free of charge. She would pass around a collection plate but proceeds were often small. [95] She didn't expect more. Many of the black people attending her lectures were still living on the plantations where they had been enslaved before the war. Their cabins had doors but no windows or plaster. When offered, Frances saved money by staying with them in their homes instead of in hotels—she rarely had the luxury of a private room to herself. [96]

In Alabama, Frances's host was a man whose son had been murdered for marrying a white woman. There had been no police investigation into the crime. While she was there, Frances met a woman who was recovering from a severe beating. A group of white men had been out fox hunting a few days before and arrived at the woman's home, demanding that she let them in and make them a fire. She told them she had no wood, so they broke down the door and attacked her. [97]

"The condition of the women is not very enviable in some cases. They have had some of them a terribly hard time in slavery, and their subjection has not ceased in freedom." Frances told activists in the North. [98] Frances devoted part of her lectures to "preaching against men ill-treating their wives." [99] She took a lighter tone when she addressed this sensitive topic.

> Why, I have actually heard since I have been south that sometimes colored husbands positively beat their wives! I do not mean to insinuate for a moment that such things can possibly happen in Mobile. The very appearance of this congregation forbids it, but I did hear of one terrible husband defending himself for the unmanly practice with "Well, I have got to whip her or leave her." [100]

Frances decided to devote some of her time to private meetings with women. She wouldn't pass around a collection plate for these meetings; some of the washerwomen didn't even know how to count change. [101]

"I am going to talk with them about their daughters, and about things connected with the welfare of the race. Now is the time for our women to begin to plant the roots of progress under the hearthstone," she said. [102]

"Oh, friend, perhaps sometimes your heart would ache if you were only here and heard of the wrongs and abuses to which these people have been subjected," she wrote to William Still. "Things, I believe, are a little more hopeful. At least, I believe some of the colored people are getting better contracts and I understand that there's less murdering." [103]

There were signs of progress. Frances met a brick maker who now owned the home that used to belong to the white man who had enslaved him. He owned more than 60 acres of land and the former slaveholder was in the poorhouse. She met a woman who had been prostituted by the white man who enslaved her, who was now working as a schoolteacher. [104]

"Oh, if some more of our young women would only consecrate their lives to the work of upbuilding the race!" she wished. "Oh, if I could only see our young men and women aiming to build up a future for themselves which would grandly contrast with the past with its pain, ignorance and low social condition." [105]

"I am above eighty years old; it is about time for me to be going," Sojourner Truth told her audience at the American Equal Rights Association convention. "I have been forty years a slave and forty years free, and would be here forty years more to have equal rights for all. I suppose I am kept here because something remains for me to do; I suppose I am yet to help to break the chain. I have done a great deal of work; as much as a man, but did not get so much pay."

Sojourner used her address to remind delegates about black women like herself. "There is a great stir about colored men getting their rights but not a word about the colored women; and if colored men get their rights, and not colored women theirs, you see, the colored men will be masters over the women and it will be just as bad as it was before." [106]

Still in Kansas, Lucy Stone missed Sojourner's speech. Susan had asked her to send a telegram to read aloud at the convention—something to cheer up the masses. Instead, Lucy pulled out a piece of paper and started writing a letter. She knew it wouldn't arrive in time for the convention, but it was just as well, because it didn't have the cheerful news Susan was hoping for.

"I cannot send you a telegraphic dispatch as you wish, for just now there is a plot to get the Republican party to drop the word *male* and also to agree to canvass only for the word *white*," wrote Lucy. "There is a call, signed by the chairman of the State Central Republican Committee, to meet at Topeka on the 15th to pledge the party to the canvass on that single issue."

Lucy told Susan that a group of black men, led by a preacher named Twine, were leading the call to eliminate women's suffrage from the Republican platform.

"These men ought not to be allowed to vote before we do, because they will be just so much more dead weight to lift," wrote Lucy. She added a postscript. "P. S. The papers here are coming down on us and every prominent reformer and charging us with being free lovers." [107]

"It might be that colored men will obtain their rights before women but if so, I am confident they would heartily acquiesce in admitting women also to the right of suffrage," Charles Remond told the other delegates the next day, the second day of the American Equal Rights Association convention. After all, he was a black man, and a fervent supporter of women's suffrage.

Lucretia Mott wasn't so sure. "Woman have a right to be a little jealous of the addition of so large a number of men to the voting class, for the colored men would naturally throw all their strength upon the side of those opposed to woman's enfranchisement."

"Am I understanding right, that Mrs. Stanton and Mrs. Mott are opposed to the enfranchisement of the colored man unless the ballot should also be accorded to woman at the same time?" asked George Downing.

"We do not take the right step for this hour in demanding suffrage for any class. As a matter of principle I claim it for all," said Elizabeth. "But in a narrow view of the question as a matter of feeling between classes, when Mr. Downing puts the question to me, 'Are you willing to have the colored man enfranchised before the woman?' I say, 'No, I would not trust him with all my rights.' Degraded, oppressed himself, he would be more despotic with the governing power than even our Saxon rulers are. I desire that we go into the kingdom together, for individual and national safety demand that not another man be enfranchised without the woman by his side."

"Even if the enfranchisement of the colored man would probably retard the enfranchisement of woman, we have no right for that reason to deprive him of his right," said Stephen Foster. "The right of each should be accorded at the earliest possible moment; neither being denied for any supposed benefit to the other."

"If I were to lose sight of expediency, I must side with Mrs. Stanton," said Charles. "Although to do so is extremely trying, for I cannot conceive of a more unhappy position than that occupied by millions of American men bearing the name of freedmen while the rights and privileges of free men are still denied them."

"That is equaled only by the condition of the slave women by their side. There is a depth of degradation known to the slave women that man can never feel. To give the ballot to the black man is no security to the woman," said Elizabeth.

"No man in this country has made such sacrifices for the cause of liberty as Wendell Phillips," said Samuel May, although Elizabeth hadn't mentioned Wendell, yet. "And if just at this moment, when the great question for which he has struggled seems about to be settled, he is unwilling that anything should be added to it that might in any way prejudice the success about to crown his efforts, it is not to be wondered at. I am of the opinion, on the contrary, that by asking for the rights of all, we should be much more likely to obtain the rights of the colored man than by making that a special question."

"I must say a few words in relation to a remark recently made on this platform, that the negro should not enter the kingdom of politics before woman, because he would be an additional weight against her enfranchisement. Were the negro and woman in the same civil, social, and religious status today, I should respond, 'Aye, with all my heart,' to this sentiment." said Abby Kelley Foster. "What are the facts? …It has been well said, 'He has the title deed to liberty, but is not yet in the possession of liberty.' He is treated as a slave today in the several districts of the South. Without wages, without family rights, whipped and beaten by thousands, given up to the most horrible outrages, without that protection which his value as property formerly gave him. Again, he is liable without further guarantees, to be plunged into peonage, serfdom or even into chattel slavery. Have we any true sense of justice, are we not dead to the sentiment of humanity if we shall wish to postpone his security against present woes and future enslavement till woman shall obtain political rights?"

"As I understand the difference between abolitionists, some think this is harvest time for the black man, and seed-sowing time for woman. Others, with whom I agree, think we have been sowing the seed of individual rights, the foundation idea of a republic for the last century, and that this is the harvest time for all citizens who pay taxes, obey the laws and are loyal to the government," said Susan B. Anthony.

"In an hour like this I repudiate the idea of expediency. All I ask for myself I claim for my wife and sister," said Charles. "Let our action be based upon the rock of everlasting principle. No class of citizens in this country can be deprived of the ballot without injuring every other class. I see how equality of suffrage in the state of New York is necessary to maintain emancipation in South Carolina. Do not moral principles, like water, seek a common level?"

Someone complained that this philosophy discussion had diverted the group away from the agenda. Shouldn't they be getting some business done during the last few minutes of the meeting?

Susan took the hint. She had the perfect distraction in her hand: the requested telegram from Lucy Stone, which had arrived that morning. Lucy had apparently had second thoughts and visited a telegraph office after all. Susan didn't know yet that a long, depressing letter from Lucy was also slowly working its way to her door.

Susan read aloud:

> Atchison, Kansas, May 10, 1867.
> Impartial Suffrage, without regard to color or sex, will succeed by overwhelming majorities. Kansas leads the world!
> Lucy Stone

It seems that Lucy couldn't bear to impart bad news across the country through a medium that allowed no more space than a modern tweet.

Josephine Griffing stood up next to request that the Association send delegates to Washington, D.C. Before she sat down, she added, "I welcome the enfranchisement of the negro as a step toward the enfranchisement of woman."

Susan intercepted this return to that touchy subject by calling out, "We seem to be blessed with telegrams with cheering news from Kansas!"

She whipped out another one and started reading.

> Atchison, Kansas, May 10, 1867.
> With the help of God and Lucy Stone, we shall carry Kansas! The world moves!
> Sam Wood

After the applause subsided, it occurred to someone that they should ask a black woman what she thought about enfranchising blacks and women. Where had Sojourner gone? They found her and called her into the room.

"I am glad to see that men are getting their rights, but I want women to get theirs, and while the water is stirring I will step into the pool. Now that there is a great stir about colored men's getting their rights, it is the time for women to step in and have theirs," Sojourner told them.

"It requires a rash man to rise at this stage of the meeting, with the hope of detaining the audience even for a few moments, but in response to your call I rise to add my humble word to the many eloquent words already uttered in favor of universal suffrage," said Charles. He addressed the New Yorkers in the room, who would be with him at the State Constitutional Convention. "I demand that you so amend your Constitution as to recognize the equality of the black man at the ballot box." [108]

As soon as Lucy Stone arrived back in New York, she went to the *New York Tribune* office to beg Horace Greeley to cover the women's suffrage question in his paper.

The meeting didn't go well. Lucy became emotional and couldn't hold back tears.

"When you have been whipped as many times as I have, you won't cry about it," said Horace. Lucy left with the promise of only "a finger's length" of space in the *Tribune*. [109]

Soon after, Susan and Elizabeth also called on Horace to lobby for his support at the upcoming New York Constitutional Convention. He had been selected as a Republican delegate and appointed chairman of the Committee on Suffrage.

"This is a critical period for the Republican party and the life of the nation. The word *white* in our constitution at this hour has a significance which *male* has not," Horace told them. "It would be wise and magnanimous in you to hold your claims, though just and imperative, I grant, in abeyance until the negro is safe beyond peradventure and your turn will come next. I conjure you to remember that this is the negro's hour, and your first duty now is to go through the state and plead his claims." [110]

"Does the North consider it absurd for its women to vote and hold office? So views the South her negroes. Does the North consider its women a part of the family to be represented by the white male citizen? So views the South her negroes. Example is better than precept," countered Elizabeth. "Would New York, now that she has the opportunity to amend her own constitution, take the lead by making herself a genuine republic, with what a new and added power our representatives could press universal suffrage on the Southern states." [111]

On the day the Committee on Suffrage was scheduled to announce its recommendation to the delegation, Susan and Elizabeth marched to the capitol, carrying with them 20,000 signatures in support of universal suffrage. Theodore Tilton and Wendell Phillips walked alongside them.

"We should urge the amendment to our Constitution to strike out the word *white* as the thing to be accomplished by this Convention," said Theodore. "The question of striking out the word *male* we shall of course, as an Equal Rights Association, urge as an intellectual theory, but we cannot demand it as a practical thing to be accomplished at this Convention."

Wendell agreed. Elizabeth politely disagreed. Susan also disagreed, but not politely.

"What ails Susan?" asked Theodore. "I never saw her behave so badly before." [112]

They arrived at the capitol, where women filled the galleries. Suffragists presented each delegate with the signatures from their jurisdiction, saving Horace's for last.

"Mr. President, I hold in my hand a petition from Mrs. Horace Greeley and three hundred other women citizens of Westchester, asking that the word *male* be stricken from the Constitution," George William Curtis announced as he passed Horace his petition. Nearly everyone, Horace excepted, erupted into laughter.

An uncomfortable Horace Greeley then read the committee's report, which did not support women's suffrage. "However defensible in theory, we are satisfied that public sentiment does not demand and would not sustain an innovation so revolutionary and sweeping." [113]

The delegation voted in support of the Committee's recommendations, rejecting women's suffrage but removing a discriminatory provision that had required black men, but not white men, to own property before they could vote. [114]

After the Convention adjourned, Susan and Elizabeth looked for Horace, but he managed to sneak out a side door without speaking to anyone.

He explained himself through a *Tribune* editorial, clarifying that although his committee had not supported women's suffrage, it was not meant "as a verdict against a participation in public affairs by women."

> On the contrary, we hold that woman's influence not only is, but should be felt in legislation and government, and must increase in power as the race becomes more enlightened and humane. We only insist that she shall speak and be heard distinctly as woman, not mingled and confused with man. [115]

Elizabeth described it differently: "Says the New York Suffrage Committee, 'We will do the voting; let women pay the taxes. We will be judges, jurors, sheriffs; and give woman the right to be hung on the gallows.'" [116]

A few weeks later, at an evening party, Elizabeth and Susan saw Horace coming toward them. They stood and said, "Good evening, Mr. Greeley," and extended their arms to shake hands. He kept his arms down at his side.

"You two ladies are the most maneuvering politicians in the state of New York," he said. "You set out to annoy me in the Constitutional Convention and you did it effectually. I saw in the manner my wife's petition was presented that Mr. Curtis was acting under instructions. I saw the reporters prick up their ears and knew that my report and Mrs. Greeley's petition would come out together, with large headings in the city papers, and probably be called out by the newsboys in the street."

Turning to Elizabeth, he asked, "You are so tenacious about your own name, why did you not inscribe my wife's maiden name, Mary Cheney Greeley on her petition?"

"Because I wanted all the world to know that it was the wife of Horace Greeley who protested against her husband's report."

"Well, I understand the animus of that whole proceeding, and now let me tell you what I intend to do. I have given positive instructions that no word of praise shall ever again be awarded you in the *Tribune*, and that if your name is ever necessarily mentioned, it shall be as Mrs. Henry B. Stanton!" [117]

With the New York battle over, the American Equal Rights Association focused on Kansas.

"Don't publish it, but if Anna E. Dickinson's health is equal to it I think she will give September and November to Kansas," Susan wrote to Sam Wood. "Now don't let it get into the papers," she repeated. (Lucy had told her about Sam's tendency to namedrop unconfirmed speakers to the press.) "But what I want you to do is this, make a course of lectures in each of the towns of size to warrant, or perhaps better mass meetings, with Miss Dickinson, Mrs. Stanton, Mrs. Gage, Mr. Pillsbury, Mr. Douglass, Mr. Remond, all of whom I am almost sure we can induce to go to Kansas. Mr. Remond is real black, and fully a match for Douglass. But you see, the money, the money. ...I now think I shall be ready to go to Kansas by first of September. Shall trust to luck for myself but I can't promise anyone else will do so." [118]

They had hired Charles Remond to lobby for universal suffrage at the New York Constitutional Convention, but had to scramble to pay his wages when Wendell Phillips withheld the funds they were expecting. [119]

Wendell was trustee of the Hovey fund. Philanthropist Charles Fox Hovey left a bequest of $8,000 annually to finance abolition efforts. Once slavery was abolished, funds would be divided to spend on other causes he supported, including women's rights. Women's rights advocates expected to start receiving their share of the fund after the Thirteenth Amendment abolished slavery, but Wendell and the trust committee redefined the parameters to keep the money with abolitionists as they worked toward suffrage for black men. [120]

It was a good thing Susan ordered Sam to keep quiet, because she did not manage to recruit any of the people she named, with the exception of Elizabeth and herself. Fortunately, Lucy Stone convinced Reverend Olympia Brown to take leave of her Unitarian congregation in Massachusetts and spend the summer in Kansas. [121]

When Olympia agreed to go to Kansas, she never suspected that she would spend so much of her time there begging for rides. Lucy told Olympia that Kansas Republicans would schedule the meetings and transport her from place to place, just as they had for Lucy and Harry. They had also promised to recruit a local woman to be Olympia's traveling companion, since Olympia would be coming to Kansas alone.

Kansas Republicans did schedule meetings—many meetings—two each day, for two straight months. They advertised them, too. The citizens of towns spread across the Kansas map were expecting her, but how would she get to them? There was no railroad in the new state, hardly any public transportation options at all, and the Republicans had bailed on their promise to provide a carriage and a traveling companion. After each speech, Olympia found herself searching the audience for a stranger willing to give her a wagon ride to the next venue, sometimes fifty miles away. [122]

Sam Wood, the man who had requested delegates to Kansas in the first place, became sick, along with his wife and children. He spent several weeks in bed in critical condition. Meanwhile, his local post office was robbed. It was six weeks before anyone from the American Equal Rights Association could get in touch with him. [123]

By the time Susan and Elizabeth arrived in Kansas, the Republican Central Committee had endorsed black suffrage, still maintaining an officially neutral stance on the woman question. However, they selected a group of men to canvass the state in support of suffrage for black men, none of whom supported women's suffrage, and told them "they would be allowed to express their own sentiments on other questions." [124] A group of Republicans had formed an Anti-Female Suffrage State Committee, quoting Horace Greeley's report to the New York Constitutional Convention as their rationale, but Susan appraised their organization as "the lowest kind." So low, that "it helps us rather than hinders," she said. [125]

Susan was more concerned about the condition of the treasury. There was no money, and several suffrage tracts were being held by the printer pending payment.

Susan sent an urgent letter to Lucy, who was camping with her family. Lucy cut her vacation short and went to American Equal Rights Association headquarters, where she set to work fundraising, supplementing the fund with money from her own pocket. [126]

During the last few weeks before the election, Susan and Elizabeth received a letter from someone who wanted to join them in Kansas to help with the campaign. "How funny that George Francis Train is coming into the state for a month to talk for woman. What sort of a furor he will make," said Susan. [127]

George had not been on their A-list, but none of the prominent men Susan and Elizabeth had asked had made the trip.

"We begged Theodore Tilton, Wendell Phillips, Henry Ward Beecher, Horace Greeley, and every man in all the East who has ever spoken in behalf of woman suffrage, as they had any regard for this movement, that they should come to Kansas in person and lecture in our behalf," said Susan. "But they said Beecher was writing—what was it? His *Norwood* for the *Ledger*, and that Tilton was editing his *Independent*, and that Phillips was at his summer retreat at the seaside, and that Greeley was in the Constitutional Convention—and you know he had very important business there in presenting reports against us." [128]

George explained his interest in women's suffrage to Susan and Elizabeth this way: "When muscle and color and ignorance are to have votes, I think it is time that beauty, virtue and intelligence should be equally respected." [129]

He was unlike their usual allies, most of whom were Republican abolitionists. He was a Democrat who had amassed a small fortune in ships and railroads and now he wanted to run for president. [130]

"You have made a terrific personal attack on Senator Wood, calling him everything that is vile," George told a Civil War general at a public meeting in Kansas. "I do not know Mr. Wood. Miss Anthony has made all my arrangements, but perhaps you will allow me to ask you if Mr. Wood is a Democrat?"

The Democrats in the audience burst into laughter and applauded.

The general laughed, too. "No, he is a Republican, and chairman of the Woman Suffrage Committee."

"Good. I understand you and your argument against Wood is so forcible. I believe with you that Wood is a bad man, a man of no principle whatever," George made himself heard over increasingly louder laughter. "A man who has committed all the crimes in the calendar, who, if he has done what you have said, ought to be taken out on the square and hung, and well-hung too. Having admitted that I am converted to the fact of Wood's villainy, and you having admitted that he is not a Democrat, but a Republican, I think it is time the honest Democratic and Republican voters should rise up in their might and wipe off all those corrupt Republican leaders from the Kansas State Committee. Democrats, do your duty on the fifth of November and vote for woman suffrage!"

The audience cheered.

Sam wasn't the only suffragist George liked to poke fun at. Susan's history as an agent of the Anti-Slavery Society was particularly amusing to him.

"The first woman I had to convert to woman suffrage was the eloquent speaker who has just addressed you, Miss Anthony. She commenced the campaign four-fifths negro and one fifth woman. Now she is four-fifths woman and only one-fifth negro," George told his audience, holding up his fingers to demonstrate. "Keep your nose twenty years on a negro and you will have hard work to smell a white man again."

Just in case anyone hadn't understood his allegiances, George said, "Woman first and negro last is my program." [131]

In New York, Lucy saw a newspaper ad about George Train canvassing with Susan and Elizabeth, paid for by the American Equal Rights Association, with Lucy's name at the bottom. "Of this I knew nothing until I read it in the *Tribune*," Lucy protested, but all she could do from New York was fire off a series of ineffectual letters. [132]

During his last speech of the campaign, the night before the election, George made an announcement.

> The woman suffrage association want a few thousand dollars to pay off this expensive canvass. Miss Anthony has distributed two thousand pounds weight of tracts and pamphlets. Mrs. Stanton, Miss Olympia Brown and Mrs. Lucy Stone have been for months in all parts of the State. Kansas has furnished no part of the fund that makes her tomorrow the envy of the world. For the benefit of the Association, I have promised…to make seven speeches in the largest cities; the entire proceeds to be given to this grand cause—I paying my own expenses, as in this campaign. We commence at St. Louis about the 20th, thence to Chicago, Cleveland, Cincinnati, Philadelphia, Boston and New York.

After the applause, George predicted that suffrage for Kansas women would pass the next day with a "startling majority." The audience cheered. He also predicted that black suffrage would fail—and the audience cheered for that too.

"The negro can wait and go to school," George yelled to the crowd. [133]

Both referenda lost, with about two-thirds of Kansas's white male voters voting against suffrage for women and black men alike. [134]

"My friends, it was not the woman suffrage question that killed the negro question; it was the Republican leaders—the Republican party leaders, who killed negro suffrage and woman suffrage, too," declared Susan. "No person can make an argument against another person's right, with equal intelligence, to vote, and expect that it will not rebound against himself." [135]

While Susan, Elizabeth and George were working their way back to New York, Lucy and other members of American Equal Rights Association leadership published an announcement clarifying that they did not endorse the tour and had no part in planning it. [136]

By the time they reached New York, Elizabeth had big news: "My dream for years is at last to be realized. A rich friend of ours, the much abused George Francis Train, who is the most wonderful man of the century in some respects, proposes to help us establish a paper." [137]

The newspaper would be called the *Revolution*. Elizabeth would be one of the editors, Susan would be the publisher, and in exchange for his financial backing, George would have large segments of print space to write whatever he wished. [138]

As soon as Susan and Elizabeth arrived back at American Equal Rights Association headquarters, they kicked Lucy out, "without so much as saying, 'by your leave,'" Lucy complained to William Lloyd Garrison. [139] In turn, William wrote to Susan.

Dear Miss Anthony:

In all friendliness, and with the highest regard for the woman's rights movement, I cannot refrain from expressing my regret and astonishment that you and Mrs. Stanton should have taken such leave of good sense, and departed so far from true self-respect, as to be traveling companions and associate lecturers with that crack-brained harlequin and semi-lunatic, George Francis Train!

...The colored people and their advocates have not a more abusive assailant than this same Train; especially when he has an Irish audience before him, to whom he delights to ring the charges upon the "nigger, nigger, nigger," ad nauseam. He is as destitute of principle as he is of sense, and is fast gravitating toward a lunatic asylum. He may be of use in drawing an audience, but so would a kangaroo, a gorilla, or a hippopotamus. [140]

Officers of the Equal Rights Association grilled Susan about why she had involved George Francis Train without checking with them first.

"I am the Equal Rights Association. Not one of you amounts to shucks except for me," said Susan. She turned to Lucy. "I know what is the matter with you. It is envy and spleen and hate because I have a paper and you have not." [141]

The Association president, Lucretia Mott, was in Philadelphia. She called to a girl who was sweeping the pavement ahead of her. Had she seen her bag?

"Yes, a woman picked it up and went into that court," she replied, pointing.

Lucretia hurried that direction, searching for the red, green and yellow bag. Nothing of value had been in it, fortunately, but she hated to lose it—she had bought it from Harriet Forten Purvis at an anti-slavery bazaar before the war, and it contained a letter from her sister, Martha, that Lucretia had intended to answer.

It was no use. Returning home, she pulled out a letter that she hadn't lost: an unwelcome epistle from the Universal Franchise Association in Washington, D.C., congratulating Lucretia on her selection for its Advisory Committee. It was an honor she had neither sought nor desired. Lucretia flipped it over and used the back as stationary for Martha's letter.

She had disappointing news for Martha about the Philadelphia chapter of the American Equal Rights Association. Susan B. Anthony had come out to Philadelphia to help organize it, the very capable Sarah Pugh was appointed president, and "several intelligent colored young men and women drawn in," but it was all downhill from there.

"I found it was all a sham and only met once or twice," Lucretia told Martha. Frances Harper had guest lectured for them once, but not much else had happened. The last meeting Lucretia attended adjourned early because only half a dozen people showed up. A month later, Sarah Pugh found herself presiding over a meeting of only three people and decided to close the chapter due to lack of interest.

"So my more than a hundred dollars contributed is thus sunk!" Lucretia concluded.

"I have not even replied to Lucy Stone's letter, which is also in the lost bag," she told Martha, as she braced herself to discuss American Equal Rights Association headquarters. "I didn't want to put on paper anything of complaint of our loved coadjutors 'til they had had more time for defense and explanation." [142]

Elizabeth Cady Stanton was actively campaigning against "manhood suffrage," her term for enfranchising black men, and invoking Lucretia's name in a way that made Lucretia cringe. "Think of Patrick and Sambo and Hans and Yung Tung who do not know the difference between a monarchy and a republic, who never read the Declaration of Independence or Webster's spelling book, making laws for Lydia Maria Child, Lucretia Mott, or Fanny Kemble." [143]

The first issue of the *Revolution* had just come out. The opening line announced that the paper would advocate "educated suffrage, irrespective of sex or color." [144] But education tests weren't colorblind. Many black people had been raised in slavery, with no right to an education.

"The *Revolution* is not satisfactory and I have not the littlest notion of being a subscriber, 'though I think James said he intended to," Lucretia told Martha. "I only wait for the May meeting to withdraw from every office. My age and infirmities are reason enough."

Lucretia was 75 years old and feeling it. But her age wasn't the most pressing problem.

"Lucy Stone feels bad to hear of such intention from me or anybody, when the cause needs all the aid it can have," Lucretia wrote, but combining the abolition and women's rights movements into one society had failed, as far as she could tell. "It was a great mistake to unite the two, or even to organize a society for women's rights. The several conventions held were far more effective and all that we ought to have attempted."

Lucretia identified one thing, in particular, that was ruining the American Equal Rights Association: "Elizabeth Stanton's sympathy for 'Sambo' is very questionable," she wrote, putting quotation marks around Elizabeth's epithet. [145]

Well after 10:00 pm on the evening of the second annual American Equal Rights convention, Olympia Brown and Frederick Douglass were still deep in discussion.

"The Republican party controlled Kansas and yet repudiated woman's rights in the canvass of last year," said Olympia Brown.

Olympia was fed up with male Republicans telling her to put women's rights on hold.

> Some of our leading reformers work for other objects first: the enfranchisement of the negro, the eight-hour law, the temperance cause; and leave the woman suffrage question in the background, but woman

will be enfranchised in spite of them. It is no use to tell us to wait until something else is done.

"I champion the right of the negro to vote. It is with us a matter of life and death, and therefore cannot be postponed. I have always championed woman's right to vote but it will be seen that the present claim for the negro is one of the most urgent necessity," said Frederick Douglass, who happened to be one of those Republicans Olympia was complaining about. "The assertion of the right of women to vote meets nothing but ridicule; there is no deep-seated malignity in the hearts of the people against her. But name the right of the negro to vote, all hell is turned loose and the Ku Klux and regulators hunt and slay the unoffending black man. The government of this country loves women. They are the sisters, mothers, wives and daughters of our rulers, but the negro is loathed." [146]

Susan B. Anthony hated Frederick's argument that women were fine because men loved them. Later, she would explain it this way:

> The fact is that the men cannot understand us women. They think of us as some of the slaveholders used to think of their slaves: all love and compassion, with no malice in their hearts, but they thought, "The negro is a poor lovable creature, kind, docile, unable to take care of himself and dependent on our compassion to keep them" and so they consented to do it for the good of the slaves. Men feel the same today. Douglass, Tilton and Phillips think that women are perfectly contented to let men earn the money and dole it out to us. We feel with Alexander Hamilton, "Give a man power over my substance and he has power over my whole being." [147]

At the time, Susan had no words. Frederick continued:

> Women should not censure Mr. Phillips, Mr. Greeley, or Mr. Tilton. All have spoken eloquently for woman's rights. We are all talking for woman's rights and we should be just to all our friends and enemies. There is a difference between the Republican and Democratic parties.

"What is the difference in principle between the position of the Democratic party opposing the enfranchisement of two million negro men and the Republican party opposing the emancipation of 17 million white women?" asked Olympia.

"The Democratic party opposes suffrage to both but the Republican party is in favor of enfranchising the negro and is largely in favor of enfranchising woman," said Frederick. "Where is the Democrat who favors woman suffrage?"

"Train!" called out a voice from the audience.

"Yes, he hates the negro and that is what stimulates him to substitute the cry of emancipation for women," said Frederick.

"Why did Republican Kansas vote down negro suffrage?" Olympia asked her Republican colleague.

"Because of your ally, George Francis Train!" exclaimed Frederick.

To Susan's relief, Lucy Stone jumped into the debate here. While Lucy had no good words to say about Democrat George Train, she wasn't feeling the love for his Republican adversaries, either. "The Republican party is false to principle unless it protects women as well as colored men in the exercise of their right to vote," she said, then she circled back to Frederick's comment about the government's alleged love for women, with a laundry list of discriminatory laws that proved otherwise—and only a man could assume that a woman could fight for her rights without persecution. [148]

Thomas Wentworth Higginson had left the meeting before Olympia and Frederick's late-night debate, so Susan wrote to him to fill him in on what he had missed.

> Dear Mr. Higginson,
>
> I was sorry you were not present Thursday evening to see and hear Lucy Stone outdo her old self even. It was most delightful I can assure you, to all of us. I felt as if I ought and would overlook her every word and insinuation against me personally. Indeed I had done that before, but that speech at the close of that last meeting at 10 ½ o'clock melted all hearts into a recognition of woman's urgent need of the power of self-protection in her own hands.

It was an unusually messy letter, with words scribbled out, edits interjected, and underlining everywhere; her angry pen betraying that she hadn't actually overlooked Lucy's personal insinuations against her, even if she had liked Lucy's rebuttal of Frederick. [149]

Earlier in the day, Harry and Lucy had surprised Susan by calling for a review of the treasurer's report. They objected to Susan's use of Association funds to advertise Train's racist speeches in Kansas. [150]

"From your talk with me in the morning, you must have been surprised at Mr. Blackwell's opening their chapter of complaints against me—as I surely was—for all that he recapitulated had been said over and over in committee meetings: accounts all thoroughly examined in the committee and in full numbers voted to pay them. Hence, I never dreamed of it being brought up in a public meeting, and surely, much less dreamed it after you and other of Lucy's friends came to me and begged me not to bring up anything unpleasant," wrote Susan. She added a particularly emphatic underline to that last line.

"It must have been very painful to you, as it was to me and every other friend of progress there," Susan told Thomas. [151]

At the convention, Susan had reminded her colleagues that non-reimbursement would be a blow to her personal finances.

> I have always been obliged to spend the money first and collect it afterwards. …My expenditures have never before been questioned or censured. I got up the posters for Mr. Train, and I consider him a good card. Suppose he did spell negro with two G's? He was in favor of enfranchisement of woman and drew crowds to the polls in Kansas.

Frederick had some words to say about that but the secretary chose not to record them. The group voted overwhelmingly in favor of reimbursing Susan. [152]

Susan devoted a few lines of her letter to reminding Thomas that reform work had not made her a rich woman, certainly not wealthy enough to finance campaigns in faraway states without reimbursement. She finished the letter like this: "I don't know why I trouble you with this scribble, but that I want you to know that it is impossible for me to lay a straw in the way of anyone who personally wrongs me."—she underlined that part—"if only that one will work nobly for the cause in their own way and time. They may try to hinder my success, but I never theirs." [153]

By the time the American Equal Rights Association met again, the Fourteenth Amendment had become law and states were considering ratification of a Fifteenth Amendment: "The right of citizens of the United States to vote shall not be denied or abridged by the United States or by any State on account of race, color, or previous condition of servitude."

In Elizabeth Cady Stanton's opinion, yet another constitutional amendment protecting voting rights for men while women remained disfranchised was "an open, deliberate insult to the women of the nation." She accused Congress of assigning their "own mothers, wives and daughters" to lower political status than "unwashed and unlettered ditch-diggers, boot-blacks, hostlers, butchers, and barbers." [154]

Frances Harper had spent time with the people who held such jobs in the South, and she couldn't feel the same way. "I am glad that the colored man gets his freedom and suffrage together; that he is not forced to go through the same condition of things here, that has inclined him so much to apathy, isolation, and indifference in the North." But history would prove her right when she added. "I don't know how the colored man will vote, but perhaps many of them will be intimidated at the polls." [155]

Frances saw voting rights as a vital first step toward reconstruction.

> While I am in favor of universal suffrage, yet I know that the colored man needs something more than a vote in his hand: he needs to know the value of a home life; to rightly appreciate and value the marriage relation; to know how and to be incited to leave behind him the old shards and shells of slavery and to rise in the scale of character, wealth and influence. Like the nautilus outgrowing his home to build for himself more "stately temples" of social condition. A man landless, ignorant and poor may use the vote against his interests; but with intelligence and land he holds in his hand the basis of power and elements of strength. [156]

Taking a break from her reconstruction tour in the South, Frances traveled to New York for the next American Equal Rights Association convention. [157]

By that time, Lucretia had officially resigned as president, which made vice president Elizabeth Cady Stanton the new presiding officer, to Stephen Foster's dismay. He called for Elizabeth to step down, on the basis that she had "publicly repudiated the principles of the society."

"I would like you to say in what respect," Elizabeth responded coolly.

"I will with pleasure. For, ladies and gentlemen, I admire our talented president with all my heart, and love the woman." These words eased some tension and many of the thousand people in the audience laughed. "But I believe she has publicly repudiated the principles of the society."

"I would like Mr. Foster to state in what way," Elizabeth repeated.

Stephen laid out specifics. Elizabeth's paper, the *Revolution*, supported educated suffrage instead of universal suffrage and had recently published an article opposing the Fifteenth Amendment.

Stephen admitted that Elizabeth had not been the author of the offending article, "yet it comes from a person whom she has over and over again publicly endorsed. I am not willing to take George Francis Train on this platform with his ridicule of the negro and opposition to his enfranchisement."

"Is it quite generous to bring George Francis Train on this platform when he has retired from the *Revolution* entirely?" asked Mary Livermore, a new delegate from Illinois. [158] George had gone to England, where he was arrested for supporting an Irish rebellion. His sponsorship of the *Revolution* had come to an abrupt and complete stop. [159]

"If the *Revolution*, which has so often endorsed George Francis Train, will repudiate him because of his course in respect to the negro's rights, I have nothing further to say. But it does not repudiate him. He goes out; it does not cast him out."

"Of course it does not," said Susan.

"My friend says yes to what I have said. I thought it was so," said Stephen. "I only wanted to tell you why the Massachusetts society cannot coalesce with the party here, and why we want these women to retire and leave us to nominate officers who can receive the respect of both parties. The Massachusetts abolitionists cannot cooperate with this society as it is now organized. If you choose to put officers here that ridicule the negro and pronounce the Amendment infamous, why, I must retire. I cannot work with you."

"I will agree that many unwise things have been written in the *Revolution*," said Henry Blackwell, as he tried to smooth things over. "But I know that Miss Anthony and Mrs. Stanton believe in the right of the negro to vote. We are united on that point. There is no question of principle between us."

"There is no name greater than that of Elizabeth Cady Stanton in the matter of woman's rights and equal rights, but my sentiments are tinged a little against the *Revolution*," said Frederick Douglass. He rattled off a list of racial epithets, such as "Sambo," that he had read in its pages. "I must say that I do not see how anyone can pretend that there is the same urgency in giving the ballot to woman as to the negro. With us, the matter is a question of life and death, at least, in fifteen States of the Union." [160]

Frances had been to most of those fifteen states during the last two years and had seen the violence. "How have our people been murdered in the South and their bones scattered at the grave's mouth! Oh, when will we have a government strong enough to make human life safe?" she wondered, but she kept quiet and let Frederick continue his speech. [161]

> When women, because they are women, are hunted down through the cities of New York and New Orleans; when they are dragged from their houses and hung upon lampposts; when their children are torn from their arms, and their brains dashed out upon the pavement; when they are objects of insult and outrage at every turn; when they are in danger of having their homes burnt down over their heads; when their children are not allowed to enter schools; then they will have an urgency to obtain the ballot equal to our own."

There was applause, but Susan observed that men were clapping, not women. Someone shouted out, "Is that not all true about black women?"

"Yes, yes, yes. It is true of the black woman, but not because she is a woman, but because she is black," answered Frederick, to more applause. He invoked the name of a respected white woman who agreed with him, but wasn't present at the meeting. "Julia Ward Howe, at the conclusion of her great speech delivered at the convention in Boston last year, said: 'I am willing that the negro shall get the ballot before me.'"

Frederick finished up with some conciliatory words supporting women's suffrage, and he had some nice things to say about Elizabeth, too. "Let me tell you that when there were few houses in which the black man could have put his head, this woolly head of mine found a refuge in the house of Mrs. Elizabeth Cady Stanton, and if I had been blacker than sixteen midnights, without a single star, it would have been the same."

"The old anti-slavery school say women must stand back and wait until the negroes shall be recognized. But we say, if you will not give the whole loaf of suffrage to the entire people, give it to the most intelligent first," said Susan. "If intelligence, justice, and morality are to have precedence in the Government, let the question of woman be brought up first and that of the negro last."

"Mrs. Stanton will, of course, advocate the precedence for her sex, and Mr. Douglass will strive for the first position for his, and both are perhaps right. We are lost if we turn away from the middle principle and argue for one class," said Lucy. [162]

But now that the Fourteenth Amendment had passed, Lucy had resigned herself to it. The last time someone complained to her about Senator Sumner, Lucy said:

> I wish he felt moved to give our cause, the great, brave help he rendered to the slave. Nevertheless we must be forever grateful for what he has done for human rights, even though it does not tell directly for us.

I think God rarely gives to one man, or one set of men, more than one
moral victory to win. Hence we see the old abolitionists generally shrink
from the van of our movement, though they are in hearty sympathy with
it. If Mr. Sumner "don't want to be in this fight" as he told me, in my
heart I yet say "God bless him!" Our victory is sure to come. [163]

Lucy told the other delegates about the wise but illiterate black men she had
met at Oberlin, where she had a part-time job teaching night school to fugitives
escaping slavery. "Let no man speak of an educated suffrage," she said, and
reminded them: "If one has a right to say that you cannot read and therefore
cannot vote, then it may be said that you are a woman and therefore cannot vote."

Lucy finished her remarks by endorsing the Fifteenth Amendment.

Woman has an ocean of wrongs too deep for any plummet, and
the negro, too, has an ocean of wrongs that cannot be fathomed. There
are two great oceans; in the one is the black man and in the other is the
woman. But I thank God for that Fifteenth Amendment, and hope that
it will be adopted in every state. I will be thankful in my soul if anybody
can get out of the terrible pit.

"I would not be altogether satisfied to have the Fifteenth Amendment
passed without the Sixteenth," said Paulina Wright Davis, referring to a potential
Sixteenth Amendment to enfranchise women.

Woman would have a race of tyrants raised above her in the South
and the black women of that country would also receive worse treatment
than if the Amendment was not passed. Take any class that have been
slaves, and you will find that they are the worst when free and become
the hardest masters. The colored women of the South say they do not
want to get married to the negro, as their husbands can take their children
away from them and also appropriate their earnings. The black women
are more intelligent than the men, because they have learned something
from their mistresses.

Paulina threw out some examples of black men whipping their wives in the
South and finished up by revealing that one of her sister's servants whipped his
wife every Sunday regularly.

"I do not believe the story that the slaves who are enfranchised become the
worst of tyrants," said Frederick.

The audience clapped and someone shouted, "Neither do I."

"Not another man should be enfranchised until enough women are admitted
to the polls to outweigh those already there," said Elizabeth. "I do not believe in
allowing ignorant negroes and foreigners to make laws for me to obey."

Frances finally spoke. "When it is a question of race, I let the lesser question of
sex go, but the white women all go for sex, letting race occupy a minor position."

Frances asked to review a resolution about working women proposed by Henry B. Stanton. "I like the idea of working women, but I would like to know if it is broad enough to take colored women?" she asked.

"Yes!" answered several people.

"When I was at Boston, there were sixty women who left work because one colored woman went to gain a livelihood in their midst," Frances told them. "If the nation could only handle one question, I would not have the black women put a single straw in the way, if only the men of the race could obtain what they wanted."

The room erupted into applause. [164]

Frances stopped speaking there, but after she left the convention, she let a character in a novel she had been writing explain more. Her character, Minnie, says, "I think the nation makes one great mistake in settling this question of suffrage. It seems to me that everything gets settled on a partial basis. When they are reconstructing the government, why not lay the whole foundation anew, and base the right of suffrage not on the claims of service or sex, but on the broader basis of our common humanity?"

Another character, Louis, immediately echoes the slogan, "This hour belongs to the negro."

"Is it not the negro woman's hour also? Has she not as many rights and claims as the negro man?" asks Minnie.

Louis points out that giving rights to black men helps black women and Minnie agrees with him, then says, "But I cannot recognize that the negro man is the only one who has pressing claims at this hour. Today our government needs woman's conscience as well as man's judgment. And while I would not throw a straw in the way of the colored man, even though I know that he would vote against me as soon as he gets his vote, yet I do think that woman should have some power to defend herself from oppression, and equal laws as if she were a man." [165]

Charles Burleigh stood to speak next but the audience booed him. Charles hadn't done anything to deserve such treatment, but recently, the mostly female audiences at women's suffrage meetings had started booing men off the platform as a matter of course, adopting the same tactic men had employed against female speakers when Maria Stewart and the Grimké sisters started giving speeches three decades before. [166] Long-time suffragists were mortified. "While we ask justice for ourselves, let us at least be as just to the noble men who advocate our cause," they wrote after booing had disrupted most of the male speakers at a suffrage meeting in Washington, D.C. a few months earlier. [167]

The crowd quieted when Susan spoke again. "The Fifteenth Amendment isn't Equal Rights. It puts two million more men in the position of tyrants over two million women who have until now been the equals of the men at their side," she said.

Charles responded to her but no one heard him over the crowd.

The audience respected Lucy, Susan and Mary Livermore enough to be quiet when each, in turn, scolded them for their rudeness toward Charles, but not enough to comply with their pleas to let Charles speak.

"I hope that this, the first attempt at gagging discussion, will not be countenanced," said Susan sternly.

At last, Charles could be heard, but all he said was that he was finished. He sat down and the audience hissed. Before any more commotion, the session was adjourned. [168]

The American Equal Rights Association never convened again and the long friendship of Elizabeth and Susan with Lucy was also coming to an end. For decades to come, they would rival and resent each other to an extent that only former best friends ever could. Elizabeth and Susan formed their own organization, the National Woman Suffrage Association, while Lucy formed a competing group, the American Woman Suffrage Association, together with her husband Harry, sister-in-law Antoinette Brown Blackwell and New England Suffrage Association leaders Thomas Wentworth Higginson and Julia Ward Howe. Frances Harper and Sojourner Truth joined Lucy's organization while Harriet Forten Purvis and Mary Ann Shadd Cary joined Elizabeth and Susan, in spite of their racial rhetoric in those years following the Civil War. [169]

The Fifteenth Amendment was ratified within the next year, but many states continued to discriminate against voters of color through poll taxes, literacy tests and other means. Elizabeth Cady Stanton's prediction that it would take a hundred years to get the word *male* out of the Constitution was off; it would take half that long, which was still much too long. [170] The Nineteenth Amendment, prohibiting states from denying voting rights on the basis of sex, was passed in 1920, 52 years after the Fourteenth Amendment introduced the word *male* into the Constitution. By that time, Elizabeth and most other suffragists of her generation were no longer alive. But they would see successes during their lifetimes—only a few months after that final American Equal Rights Association meeting, the Wyoming Territorial Legislature would be the first to enfranchise women.

Support for the cause had grown during the three decades since Maria W. Stewart first took the stage to speak out on behalf of women, morphing from a bold but unpopular idea into a movement so large and diverse that differences of opinion were inevitable. Moving forward, advocates for women's rights would be less unified, but there would be more of them. Priorities would clash, heroes would fail, and biases would be exposed over and over again as passionate, inspired and flawed people worked to change the world. They would learn some lessons from the past; other mistakes would stubbornly repeat themselves.

In the words of Lucretia Mott: "The progress that we see in every work of truth and reform ought to lead us to hail each step in the advance-field of woman's duties and rights. Look back to the days of our grandmothers and be cheered." [171]

Thank you for reading.

We hope you enjoyed *Ask a Suffragist: Stories and Wisdom from America's First Feminists*. Help us get the word out. **Please leave a brief review** on Amazon or your favorite book website. Reviews are crucial for any author, and even just a line or two can make a big difference.

Want more inspiration? Check out the next book in the *Ask a Suffragist* series.

Ask a Suffragist: Activists Who Built a Movement covers the 1870s-1880s, when suffragists organized into thriving (but competing) groups and achieved early success in the West. It looks to suffragists for answers to modern questions such as:

- How do we cope with setbacks?
- Must a movement be united?
- Is it true that all press is good press?

...and more!

Visit askasuffragist.com for more information about *Ask a Suffragist* books and projects.

At askasuffragist.com, subscribe to our mailing list so you'll be the first to know when new Ask a Suffragist books are released.

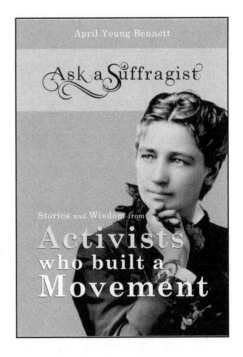

About *Ask a Suffragist* Books

Instead of droning on like an encyclopedia entry about dates, meeting minutes, and genealogy charts, *Ask a Suffragist* books emphasize relationships, strategies and activism, focusing on how suffragists addressed challenges that concern activists today, such as making our voices heard, balancing activism with our personal lives and choosing our battles. The events described in each book are organized by theme, not by chronology, with each chapter considering a question that modern activists might like to ask our feminist forebears. The narrative lists very few dates; few people like to read date salad. Check out the timeline at the end of the book to see when these events transpired in order.

Within American culture, we have a patriarchal naming system that places women at a considerable disadvantage. As I have studied and written about first wave feminism, I've become more aware than ever of how women's ever-changing names have obscured their place in history. Many history books respectfully refer to people by their last names. However, many history books focus on the male experience. Most of the women I am writing about had more than one last name over the course of their lives.

Ask a Suffragist books focus on women, so I level the playing field between men and women by primarily using first names. This saves me from continually writing parentheticals to clarify that differing surnames are referencing the same person. I also like the casual tone using first names gives my books. Frances, Nette and Mary Ann feel like friends to me and I hope my readers will feel the same way.

One of my goals in writing the *Ask a Suffragist* series is to learn from suffragists directly—hearing their words in their voices. I wanted the books to read more like novels than history texts, so I have included lots of dialogue, taken from meeting minutes, newspaper accounts, diary entries and letters. Some suffragists, such a Susan B. Anthony and Angelina Grimké, wrote detailed diaries which recorded long passages of dialogue. In some cases, the tense from the written record has been adjusted to match what the words probably sounded like when they came from the speakers' mouths, instead of how the words were recorded. For example, if the person who recorded the dialogue wrote:

She said that she was thirsty.

In this book, it might appear like this:

"I'm thirsty," she said.

Many people of the time carried on long, on-going conversations via letter, in the same way that modern people might carry on a conversation by text or on social media. Because letters are a slow, long-form medium, they would often include many questions and many responses to a previous letter in one long letter instead of firing off a question, waiting for an answer, and then asking another, like we may do via text. In the interest of concise storytelling, most quotes are extracted from the original long-form versions, with answers to questions placed right next to the question that motivated the response, the way we talk in in-person conversations.

Spelling errors, grammar errors and outdated grammar and spelling have been corrected and modernized to improve the flow and readability of the narrative. Abbreviations and shorthand are spelled out.

I took care to make sure that any adjustments did not change the meaning of the content. I encourage everyone to check out the references for passages that particularly interest them and read them in their original context.

The *Ask a Suffragist* series is not a comprehensive history. Not every first wave feminist activist who made valuable contributions to the movement is featured within these pages. The suffragists who are included in these books were selected because they had interesting experiences that are relevant to modern activists and because they represent diverse points of view and backgrounds. *Ask a Suffragist* books celebrate diversity instead of neatly pointing readers into one right way of living, highlighting the stories of prominent suffragists as well as lesser-known suffragists from Western states and of racial minority backgrounds.

America's First Feminists shares stories and wisdom from suffragists who worked during the 1830s-1860s, when women's suffrage was a bold and unpopular new idea. Not limited to the issue of suffrage, *Ask a Suffragist* books cover first wave feminism more broadly. During the time period covered in *America's First Feminists*, suffragists were also working toward abolition of slavery, temperance, racial justice, expansion of educational and professional opportunities for women, the advancement of feminist theology in churches, and dress reform (the right to wear pants or bloomers instead of dresses and petticoats).

The next book in the series, *Activists Who Built a Movement*, covers the 1870s-1880s, when support had grown enough to organize into thriving (but competing) activist groups, achieving early success as women won the right to vote in some of the Western territories.

Learn more at askasuffragist.com.

Timeline

1830

- Catharine Beecher organizes a nationwide petition drive to protest Andrew Jackson's Indian Removal Act.

1832

- Maria W. Stewart is the first American woman to break a taboo against women giving speeches to mixed gender audiences.

1833

- The Connecticut Legislature passes the Black Law. Officials arrest Canterbury Female Boarding School principal Prudence Crandall for educating black teenagers.
- The Philadelphia Female Anti-Slavery Society holds its first meeting.

1835

- Harriot and Sarah Hunt open the first successful medical clinic operated by female doctors in the United States.
- William Lloyd Garrison is attacked by a mob during a meeting of the Boston Female Anti-Slavery Society.

1837

- Sarah and Angelina Grimké become the first female agents of the American Anti-Slavery Society.
- Female abolitionists convene in New York for the first Anti-Slavery Convention of American Women.
- The General Association of Congregational Ministers in Massachusetts issues a Pastoral Letter in opposition to public speaking by women.
- Oberlin College in Ohio enrolls women in its bachelor degree program, becoming the first coeducational college in the United States.

1838

- Abolitionists and other progressive activists open Pennsylvania Hall as a venue for reform conventions. A mob burns it down after only four days of meetings.

1840

- Abby Kelley is the first woman elected as an officer in the Anti-Slavery Society. After the election, several delegates resign the society and form a separate, male-only abolition society.
- Female delegates are barred from the World Anti-Slavery Convention in London.

1842

- The Northampton Association of Education and Industry organizes a utopian community for equal rights advocates in Massachusetts.

1843

- Harriot Hunt forms the Charlestown Physiological Society in Massachusetts.

1848
- The New York Legislature passes the Married Women's Property Act.
- Lucretia Mott, Elizabeth Cady Stanton, Martha Coffin Wright and Elizabeth McClintock organize the first Woman's Rights Convention in Seneca Falls, New York.

1849
- Elizabeth Blackwell is the first American woman to graduate from medical school.

1850
- Sojourner Truth publishes her memoir.
- Congress passes the Fugitive Slave Act.
- The first National Woman's Rights Convention is held in Worcester, Massachusetts.

1851
- Amelia Bloomer shares Elizabeth Smith Miller's design and starts the dress reform movement.

1853
- The first issue of the Provincial Freeman is published by Mary Ann Shadd, the first black woman to edit a newspaper in North America.
- Women's rights activists protest the exclusion of women at the World Temperance Convention by holding the Whole World's Temperance Convention in New York.
- A women's rights meeting in New York is dubbed the Mob Convention after protesters force the proceedings to a halt.
- Antoinette Brown is the first woman ordained as a protestant minister.

1854
- Henrietta Hughes is the first female officer elected by the New York State Teachers Association.

1855
- Henry B. Blackwell and Lucy Stone use their wedding as a forum to protest sexist marriage laws.

1857
- Elizabeth Blackwell, Emily Blackwell and Marie Zakrzewska open the New York Infirmary for Indigent Women and Children.

1859
- John Brown and a small guerilla army raid Harper's Ferry.

1860
- The Tenth National Woman's Rights Convention in New York City is the last before women's rights campaigns come to a standstill during the Civil War.

1861
- The Civil War begins.

1865
- The Civil War ends.
- Congress approves the Thirteenth Amendment to end slavery.
- The Thirteenth Amendment is ratified.

1866
- The American Equal Rights Association is formed during the Eleventh National Woman's Rights Convention.
- Congress approves the Fourteenth Amendment to grant citizenship to former slaves, require equal protection under the law and penalize states that did not enfranchise all male citizens. It introduces the word *male* into the Constitution.

1867
- Kansas is the first state to put the issue of women's suffrage on the ballot as a referendum. Suffrage for black men is also considered during the same election. Both resolutions fail.

1868
- The Fourteenth Amendment is ratified. (However, early Supreme Court decisions such as Plessy vs. Ferguson in 1896 would limit its protections on a state and local level.)
- Massachusetts suffragists organize the New England Woman Suffrage Association.

1869
- Congress approves the Fifteenth Amendment to prohibit states from barring citizens from voting on the basis of race.
- Wyoming Territory gives women the right to vote.

1870
- The Fifteenth Amendment is ratified. (But many states continue to discriminate against voters of color through poll taxes, literacy tests and other means.)
- The American Equal Rights Association dissolves.

1920
- The Nineteenth Amendment is ratified, extending voting rights to women in all states. (But women and men of American Indian tribes are still excluded from American citizenship and many states continue to discriminate against voters of color through poll taxes, literacy tests and other means.)

1924
- The Indian Citizenship Act is signed, making it possible for members of American Indian tribes to vote in American elections. (But some states continued to bar indigenous people from voting in spite of their citizenship.)

1965
- The Voting Rights Act is signed, making the voting rights promised by the Nineteenth Amendment a reality for women of color who had been disfranchised through discriminatory voting laws.

Citations

Abbreviations

ADG I: Gordon, Ann D. (1997) The Selected Papers of Elizabeth Cady Stanton and Susan B. Anthony: Volume I: In the School of Anti-Slavery, 1840-1866. Rutgers University Press.

ADG II: Gordon, Ann D. (1997) The Selected Papers of Elizabeth Cady Stanton and Susan B. Anthony: Volume II: Against an Aristocracy of Sex 1866 to 1873. Rutgers University Press.

ADH: Hallowell, Anna Davis (1884) James and Lucretia Mott: Life and Letters. Houghon Mifflin.

AHG: Grimke, Archibald H. (1891) William Lloyd Garrison, the Abolitionist. Funk & Wagnalls.

AHTS: Andover-Harvard Theological Seminary. Reverend Olympia Brown.

ASB: Blackwell, Alice Stone (1930) Lucy Stone: Pioneer of Woman's Rights. Little, Brown and Company.

AMK: Kerr, Andrea Moore (1992). Lucy Stone: Speaking Out for Equality. Rutgers University Press.

BH: Hugh, Brent (2018) More "About John Brown's Body". Digital History.

BOF: B.O. Flowers (1892) Symposium on Women's Dress. The Arena Volume VI.

BSA: Anderson, Bonnie S. (2017) The Rabbi's Atheist Daughter: Ernestine Rose International Feminist Pioneer. Oxford University Press.

BWP: Palmer, Beverly Wilson (2002) Selected Letters of Lucretia Coffin Mott. University of Illinois Press: Urbana and Chicago.

CAK: Kolmerton, Carol A. (1999) The American Life of Ernestine Rose. Syracuse University Press.

CF: Faulkner, Carol (2011). Lucretia Mott's Heresy: Abolition and Women's Rights in Nineteenth-Century America. University of Pennsylvania Press.

CHB: Birney, Catherine H. (1885) The Grimké Sisters Sarah and Angelina Grimké: the First American Women Advocates of Abolition and Woman's Rights. Lee & Sheppard.

CHD: Dall, Caroline H., ed. (1860) A Practical Illustration of "Woman's Right To Labor;" or, A Letter from Marie E. Zakrzewska, M.D. Late of Berlin, Prussia. Walker, Wise & Co.

CL & MDM: Lasser, Carol & Merrill, Marlene Deahl (1987) Friends and Sisters: Letters between Lucy Stone and Antoinette Brown Blackwell, 1846-93. University of Illinois Press.

DCB: Bloomer, Dexter C. (1895) Life and Writings of Amelia Bloomer. Arena Publishing Company.

EAB: Bartlett, Elizabeth Ann (1988). Sarah Grimké: Letters on the Equality of the Sexes and Other Essays. Yale University Press.

EB: Blackwell, Elizabeth (1895) Pioneer Work in Opening the Medical Profession to Women. Longmans, Green and Co.

EC: Cazden, Elizabeth (1983). Antoinette Brown Blackwell: A Biography. Feminist Press.

ECS, SBA & MJG I: Stanton, Elizabeth Cady, Anthony, Susan B. & Gage Matilda Joslyn (1881) History of Woman Suffrage Volume I.

ECS, SBA & MJG II: Stanton, Elizabeth Cady, Anthony, Susan B. & Gage Matilda Joslyn (1881) History of Woman Suffrage Volume II.

EG: Griffith, Elisabeth (1984) In Her Own Right: The Life of Elizabeth Cady Stanton. Oxford University Press.

EJR: Renehan, Edward J. (1997) The Secret Six: The True Tale of the Men who Conspired with John Brown. University of South Carolina Press.

EPS: Southall, Eugene Portlette. (April 1930). Arthur Tappan and the Anti-Slavery Movement. The Journal of Negro History, Vol. 125, No. 2.

ERH: Hays, Elinor Rice. (1961) Morning Star: A Biography of Lucy Stone 1818-1893. Harcourt, Brace and World.

ES: Showalter, Elaine (2016) The Civil Wars of Julia Ward Howe: A Biography. Simon & Schuster.

EWS & MRS: Small, Edwin W. & Small, Miriam R. (December 1944) Prudence Crandall Champion of Negro Education. The New England Quarterly. Vol. 17 No. 4.

GASC: Proceedings of the General Anti-slavery Convention: called by the committee of the British and Foreign Anti-slavery Society, and held in London, from Friday, June 12th, to

Tuesday, June 23rd, 1840. Southampton University Library.

GFT: Train, George Francis (1867). The Great Epigram Campaign of Kansas. Prescott and Hume.

GL: Lerner, Gerda (1967) The Grimké Sisters from South Carolina: Pioneers for Women's Rights and Abolition. The University of North Carolina Press.

GSW: Wormley, G. Smith. (January 1923) Prudence Crandall. The Journal of Negro History. Vol. 8 No. 1.

GV: Vale, Gilbert (1835) Fanaticism; Its Source and Influence, Illustrated by the Simple Narrative of Isabella, in the Case of Matthias, Mr. and Mrs. B. Folger, Mr. Pierson, Mr. Mills, Catherine, Isabella, &c. &c. A Reply to W. L. Stone, with the Descriptive Portraits of All the Parties, While at Sing-Sing and at Third Street.--Containing the Whole Truth--and Nothing but the Truth.

GW: Williams, Gary (1999) Hungry Heart: The Literary Emergence of Julia Ward Howe. University of Massachusetts Press.

HKH: Hunt, Harriot K. (1856) Glances and Glimpses; or 50 Years including Twenty Years Professional Life. John P. Jewett and Company.

HPH: History of Pennsylvania Hall which was Destroyed by a Mob on the 17th of May, 1838 (1838) Merrihew and Gunn: Philadelphia.

IHH: Harper, Ida Husted. (1899) The Life And Work of Susan B. Anthony including Public Addresses, Her Own Letters and Many from Her Contemporaries During Fifty Years. The Bowen-Merrill Company: Indianapolis.

IVB: Brown, Ira V. (April 1978). Cradle of Feminism: The Philadelphia Female Anti-Slavery Society. The Pennsylvania Magazine of History and Biography 102 (2).

JHB: Baker, Jean H. (2005) Sisters: the Lives of America's Suffragists. Hill and Wang: New York.

JR-1998: Rhodes, Jane (1998). Mary Ann Shadd Cary: The Black Press and Protest in the Nineteenth Century. Indiana University Press.

JR-2005: Rycenga, Jennifer. (Fall 2005). A Greater Awakening: Women's Intellect as a Factor in Early Abolitionist Movements, 1824-1834. Journal of Feminist Studies in Religion. Vol 21. No. 2.

JW: Winch, Julie. (2002) A Gentleman of Color: the Life of James Forten. Oxford University Press: Oxford.

JWH-1900: Howe, Julia Ward (1900) Reminiscences: 1819-1899. Houghton Mifflin Company.

JWH & GW: Howe, Julia Ward and Williams, Gary (2004) The Hermaphrodite. University of Nebraska Press.

KJS: Shamus, Kristen Jordan (January 10, 2018) Pink pussyhats: The reason feminists are ditching them. Detroit Free Press.

LDG: Ginzberg, Lori D. (2010) Elizabeth Cady Stanton: An American Life. Hill and Wang.

LER & MHE: Richards, Laura E. & Elliott, Maud Howe (1915) Julia Ward Howe, 1819-*1910*. Houghton Mifflin Company.

LJF: Friedman, Lawrence J. (Spring 1979). Confidence and Pertinacity in Evangelical Abolitionism: Lewis Tappan's Circle. The John Hopkins University Press.

LW: Wheeler, Leslie (1981) Loving Warriors: Selected Letters of Lucy Stone and Henry B. Blackwell, 1853-1893. The Dial Press: New York.

MHP: Bacon, Margaret Hope (January 1989). "One Great Bundle of Humanity": Frances Ellen Watkins Harper (1825-1911). The Pennsylvania Magazine of History and Biography, Vol. 113, No. 1.

MJB: Boyd, Melba Joyce (1994) Discarded Legacy: Politics and Poetics in the Life of Frances E.W. Harper 1895-1911. Wayne State University Press.

MR: Richardson, Marilyn (1987). Maria W. Stewart: America's First Black Woman Political Writer. Indiana University Press.

MRW: Walsh, Mary Roth. (1977) Doctors Wanted: No Women Need Apply. Yale University Press.

NIP: Painter, Nell Irving (1996). Sojourner Truth: A Life, A symbol. W.W, Norton & Company.

NNN: Nercessian, Nora N. (2005) Nineteenth Century Black Graduates of Harvard Medical School. The Journal of Blacks in Higher Education No. 47.

PDW: Doress-Worters, Paula. (2008) Mistress of Herself: Speeches and Letters of Ernestine L. Rose Early Women's Rights Leader. The Feminist Press.

PF: The Provincial Freeman. Black Abolitionist Archive. University of Detroit Mercy.

PLH: Hill, Patricia Liggins. (1981) "Let Me Make The Songs For The People": A Study of Frances Watkins Harper's Poetry. Black American Literature Forum, Vol. 15, No. 2.

RTP: Terborg-Penn, Rosalyn (1998) African American Women and the Struggle for the Vote, 1850-1920. Indiana University Press.

SG: Gilson, Sarah (Mrs. Claude U.). "Antoinette Brown Blackwell, The First Woman Minister." Blackwell Family Papers. Schlesinger Library, Radcliffe Institute, Harvard University.

SGM: McMillen, Sally G. (2008) Seneca Falls and the Origins of the Women's Rights Movement. Oxford University Press.

ST & OG: Truth, Sojourner & Gilbert, Olive (1850) The Narrative of Sojourner Truth.

TDM: Morgan, Tammy Diane (November 13, 2015) The Lily and its Impact on Feminist Thought in Nineteenth Century America. Saint Mary's University.

UUA: Unitarian Universalist Association. Olympia Brown.

WS: Still, William (1872) The Underground Railroad. Porter & Coates.

VF: Voice of the Fugitive. Black Abolitionist Archive. University of Detroit Mercy.

WWHP: Worcester Women's History Project, Assumption College.

WLS: Stone, William L. (1835) Matthias and His Impostures or the Progress of Fanaticism, illustrated in the extraordinary case of Robert Matthews and some of his forerunners and disciples. Harper and Brothers.

WRC: The proceedings of the Woman's Rights Convention, held at Syracuse, September 8th, 9th, & 10th, 1852. HathiTrust Digital Library.

WWTC: The Whole World's Temperance Convention held at Metropolitan Hall in the city of New York on Thursday and Friday Sept. 1st 2nd, 1853. Fowlers and Wells Publishers.

Preface

1   Letter from Susan B. Anthony to Lucy Stone, March 7, 1854. ADG I.

Chapter 1

1   Maria W. Stewart (October 8, 1831) Religion and the Pure Principles of Morality, the Sure Foundation on which We Must Build. The Liberator. MR.

2   Letter to Lucy Stone, winter of 1847. CL & MDM.

3   Letter to Henry Blackwell, July 27, 1853. LW.

4   1 Corinthians 14:34

5   MR.

6   Maria W. Stewart (September 21, 1833) Mrs. Stewart's Farewell Address to her Friends in the City of Boston. MR.

7   MR.

8   Hatton, Louise C,. (May 28, 1879) Biographical Sketch. Meditations from the Pen of Mrs. Maria W. Stewart, 1879

edition. & James W. Stewart, 1829, Last Will and Testament. MR.

9   Walker, David (September 28, 1829) Walker's Appeal Walker's Appeal, in Four Articles; Together with a Preamble, to the Coloured Citizens of the World, but in Particular, and Very Expressly, to Those of the United States of America.

10   MR.

11   Maria W. Stewart (October 8, 1831) Religion and the Pure Principles of Morality, the Sure Foundation on which We Must Build. The Liberator. MR.

12   Maria W. Stewart (September 21, 1832) Lecture delivered at Franklin Hall, Boston. MR.

13   Notice in the Liberator, March 2, 1833. MR.

14   Nell, William C. (Feb. 19. 1852) Letter. The Liberator.

15   Maria W. Stewart (September 21, 1833) Mrs. Stewart's Farewell Address to her

Friends in the City of Boston. MR.

16   Notice in the Liberator, September 28, 1833. MR.

17   Maria W. Stewart (September 21, 1833) Mrs. Stewart's Farewell Address to her Friends in the City of Boston. MR.

18   CF.

19   Johnson, William H. (February 1, 1854) Lucretia Mott. The Lily. CF.

20   CF.

21   IVB.

22   CF.

23   IVB.

24   JW.

25   Sumler-Lewis (1997). The Forten-Purvis Women of Philadelphia and the American Anti-slavery Crusade & Trotter, Joe William and Smith, Eric Ladell (1997) African Americans in Pennsylvania: Shifting Historical Perspectives. Pennsylvania State University Press: Pennsylvania.

26   Robert Purvis, August 23, 1834. JW.

27   James Forten to Nathaniel P. Rogers, March 29, 1839. JW.

28   JW.

29   Letter from Sarah Forten to Angelina Grimké, April 15, 1837. JW.

30   Letter from James Forten to Nathaniel P. Rogers, March 29, 1839. JW.

31   Letter from Samuel McKean to Mary Grew, Feb 15, 1836 & IVB & Sumler-Lewis (1997) The Forten-Purvis Women of Philadelphia and the American Anti-slavery Crusade. Trotter, Joe William and Smith, Eric Ladell (1997) African Americans in Pennsylvania: Shifting Historical Perspectives. Pennsylvania State University Press.

32   John Quincy Adams on the Gag Rule. Digital History & HPH.

33   GL.

34   HPH.

35   EAB.

36   Grimké, Sarah The Education of Women. EAB.

37   EAB.

38   CHB.

39   Angelina Grimké, diary, May 20, 1829. GL.

40   Angelina Grimké, diary, February 10, 1828. GL.

41   GL.

42   Angelina Grimké, diary, March 29, 1829 and February 7, 1829. GL.

43   CHB.

44   GL.

45   Angelina Grimké, diary, May 7, 1828. GL.

46   GL.

47   Angelina Grimké (May 16, 1838). Speech in Pennsylvania Hall. GL.

48   GL & Grimké, Angelina (1836) Appeal to the Christian Women of the South.

49   GL.

50   CHB.

51   AMK.

52   ECS, SBA & MJG I.

53   ASB.

54   ECS, SBA & MJG I.

55   ASB.

56   Sandberg, Sheryl & Scovell, Nell (2013) Lean In: Women, Work and the Will to Lead. Alfred A, Knopf: New York.

57   ASB.

58   Beecher, Catherine E. (1837) An essay on slavery and abolitionism: with reference to the duty of American females. Perkins and Marvin: Boston.

59   New York Historical Society. (2017) Women and the American Story Resource 11: Catharine Beecher's Campaign Against Indian Removal. & Onion, Rebecca. (August 14, 2013). The Band of American Women who Tried to Stop Andrew Jackson's Native American Removal Policy. Slate.

60   Sullivan, Patricia (September 5, 2016) Phyllis Schlafly, a conservative activist, has died at age 92. Washington Post & Encyclopedia Britannica. (September 27, 2016) Catherine Beecher.

61   GL.

62   Letter from Angelina Grimké to Catherine Beecher, August 2, 1837. JW.

63   Grimké, Sarah (September 1837). Letter XV Man Equally Guilty with Woman in the Fall. EAB.

64   EAB.

65   GL.

66   CHB.

67   GL.

68   CHB.

69   GL.

70 Grimké, Sarah (September 1837). Letter XIII Relation of Husband and Wife. EAB.

71 Proceedings of the Anti-slavery Convention of American Women, Held in the City of New York, May 9th, 10th, 11th, 12th, 1837. CF.

72 HPH.
73 CF.
74 JW.
75 HPH.
76 IVB.
77 HPH.

78 Proceedings of the third Anti-slavery Convention of American Women, held in Philadelphia, May 1st, 2d and 3d, 1839.

79 AMK.

80 Hegewisch, Ariane (September 13, 2018) The Gender Wage Gap: 2017; Earnings Differences by Gender, Race, and Ethnicity, Institute for Women's Policy Research.

81 AMK.
82 ASB.
83 AMK.
84 ASB.
85 EC.
86 ASB.
87 AMK.
88 ASB.
89 AMK.
90 EC.

91 New York Tribune, September 2, 1853. EC.

92 ECS, SBA & MJG I.
93 EC.

94 John Marsh, letter to the New York Daily Tribune, May 18. 1853. ECS, SBA & MJG I.

95 WWTC.
96 SG.
97 ECS, SBA & MJG I.
98 SG.
99 ECS, SBA & MJG I.
100 SG.
101 ECS, SBA & MJG I.

102 Proceedings of the Woman's Rights Convention, held at Broadway Tabernacle, in the city of New York, on Tuesday and Wednesday, Sept. 6th and 7th, 1853.

103 New York Express, as quoted in the Liberator, Sept. 16, 1853. CAK.

104 ECS, SBA & MJG I.

105 ADH. Note: Hallowell incorrectly places this story at an anti-slavery convention, but the following sources state that it actually occurred at the New York Woman's Rights Convention: Marsico, Katie (2008) Lucretia Mott: Abolitionist and Women's Rights Leader. ABDO Publishing Company: Edina, Minnesota. CF.

106 CAK and EC.

107 Greeley, Horace (September 7, 1853). New York Tribune. EC.

108 SG.
109 EC.
110 SG.

111 DeSilver, Drew (December 18, 2018) A record number of women will be serving in the new Congress. Pew Research Center.

112 Chira, Susan (July 21, 2017) Why Women Aren't C.E.O.s, According to Women Who Almost Were. New York Times & AAUW (2015) Solving the Equation: Variables for Women's Success at Engineering and Computing.

113 Hadfield, Joe (September 17, 2012) Study: Deciding by consensus can compensate for group gender imbalances. BYU News & Adamczyk, Alicia (August 12, 2016) Why Women Talk Less Than Men at Work. Money Magazine.

114 Axelrod, Jim (April 12, 2017). Female Supreme Court justices interrupted more than male colleagues, study says. CBS News.

Chapter 2

1 Sarah Grimké (1838) EAB.
2 ECS, SBA & MJG I.
3 Elizabeth Cady Stanton (September 1848) Address on Women's Rights. ADG I.
4 AHG.
5 EPS.
6 CF.
7 Garrison, William Lloyd, (April 28, 1832) Untitled, The Liberator.
8 JR-2005.

9   Garrison, William Lloyd. (July 14, 1832) Female Anti-Slavery Society. The Liberator.
10 GSW.
11 EPS.
12 JR-2005.
13 EWS & MRS.
14 EWS & MRS & GSW.
15 GSW.
16 EWS & MRS.
17 AHG.
18 GSW.
19 EPS & GSW.
20 AHG.
21 GSW.
22 Letter from William Lloyd Garrison' to Isaac Knapp, April 11, 1833. GSW.
23 EWS & MRS.
24 Garrison, William Lloyd (July 6, 1833) Prudence Crandall. The Liberator.
25 GSW.
26 EWS & MRS.
27 JR-2005.
28 EWS & MRS.
29 GSW.
30 EWS & MRS.
31 EPS.
32 GSW.
33 EWS & MRS.
34 EPS.
35 EWS & MRS.
36 GSW.
37 Garrison, William Lloyd (July 6, 1833) Savage Barbarity! The Liberator.
38 Name withheld, letter dated May 24, 1833. The Liberator (June 22, 1833).
39 EPS.
40 EWS & MRS.
41 EPS.
42 Brown, Ira V. (January 1981) An Anti-slavery Agent: C. C. Burleigh in Pennsylvania, 1836-1837. The Pennsylvania Magazine of History and Biography, Vol. 105, No. 1.
43 EWS & MRS.
44 GSW.
45 GSW.
46 JR-2005.
47 Prudence Crandall Museum, Canterbury, CT. Students at Prudence Crandall's School for African-American Women, 1833-1834. Citizens ALL: African Americans in Connecticut, 1700-1850.
48 EWS & MRS.
49 Garrison, William Lloyd (September 19, 1835) Christian Heroism. The Liberator.
50 GL.
51 Garrison, William Lloyd (September 19, 1835) Christian Heroism. The Liberator.
52 AHG.
53 GL.
54 LJF.
55 Letter from Lewis Tappan to Asa Mahan, February 13, 1848. LJF.
56 LJF.
57 LJF & CF.
58 LJF.
59 AHG
60 EPS.
61 7th Annual Report, American-Anti-Slavery Society, 1840. EPS.
62 EPS.
63 Cumbler, John T. (2008) From Abolition to Rights for All: The Making of a Reform Community in the Nineteenth Century. University of Pennsylvania Press.
64 EPS.
65 SGM.
66 ECS, SBA & MJG I & SGM.
67 EPS.
68 CF.
69 GASC.
70 Letter from William Lloyd Garrison to Helen E. Garrison, New York, May 19, 1840. SGM.
71 Brown, Ira V. (1991) Mary Grew: Abolitionist and Feminist. Susquehanna University Press.
72 ECS, SBA & MJG I & SGM.
73 SGM.
74 GASC.
75 SGM.
76 GASC.
77 Elizabeth Cady Stanton (May 13, 1858) Address to the Eighth Annual Woman's Rights Convention. ADG I.
78 AHG.
79 CF.
80 AHG.
81 Elizabeth Cady Stanton (May 13, 1858) Address to the Eighth Annual Woman's Rights Convention. ADG I.
82 CF.

83 Pennsylvania Freeman, November 26 and December 10, 1840. CF.

84 CF.

85 ECS, SBA & MJG I.

86 SGM.

87 ECS, SBA & MJG I.

88 CF.

89 Letter from Elizabeth Cady to Sarah M. Grimké and Angelina Grimké Weld, March 4, 1840. ADG I.

90 ECS, SBA & MJG I.

91 SGM.

92 Frederick Douglass (July 28, 1848) The North Star. ECS, SBA & MJG I.

93 Post, Amy (1870) Proceedings of the Woman's Rights Convention held at the Unitarian Church, Rochester, New York, August 2, 1848.

94 SGM.

95 Post, Amy (1870) Proceedings of the Woman's Rights Convention held at the Unitarian Church, Rochester, New York, August 2, 1848.

96 SGM.

97 Letter from Elizabeth Cady Stanton to Amy Kirby Post, September 24, 1848. ADG I.

98 JR-1998

99 New England Colored Citizens' Convention (August 1, 1859) & RTP.

100 Boston Daily Mail (October 25, 1850) Grand Demonstration of Petticoatdom at Worcester—The "Woman's Rights" Convention in Full blast—Important and Interesting Report: WWHP.

101 NIP.

102 Vetter, Lisa Pace (2017) The Political Thought of America's Founding Feminists. NYU Press.

103 NIP.

104 Garrison, William Lloyd. (June 7, 1850) Woman's Rights Convention. The Liberator.

105 Fadel, Leila (February 4, 2019) A First: Women Take The Majority In Nevada Legislature And Colorado House. NPR.

106 Douglass, Frederick (April 1888) Speech to the International Council of Women.

Chapter 3

1 Lucretia Mott (December 17, 1849) Discourse on Woman.

2 Letter from Elizabeth Cady Stanton to Susan B. Anthony, April 2, 1852. SGM.

3 Letter from Susan B. Anthony to Antoinette Brown Blackwell, April 22, 1858. ADG I.

4 ASB.

5 ERH.

6 LW.

7 ASB.

8 Letter from Henry Blackwell to Lucy Stone, June 13, 1853. LW.

9 Letter from Henry Blackwell to Lucy Stone, July 2, 1853 & Letter from Lucy Stone to Henry Blackwell, June 21, 1853. LW.

10 Letter from Henry Blackwell to Lucy Stone, June 13, 1853. LW.

11 Letter from Lucy Stone to Henry Blackwell, June 21, 1853. LW.

12 Letter from Henry Blackwell to Lucy Stone, June 13, 1853. LW.

13 Letter from Henry B. Blackwell to Emily Blackwell, June 3, 1850. AMK.

14 Letter from Henry B. Blackwell to Emily Blackwell, September 29, 1850. AMK.

15 CL & MDM.

16 Letter from Henry Blackwell to Lucy Stone, July 2, 1853. LW.

17 Letter from Lucy Stone to Henry Blackwell, July 27, 1853. LW.

18 Letter from Henry Blackwell to Lucy Stone, July 2, 1853. LW.

19 Letter from Lucy Stone to Henry Blackwell, July 27, 1853. LW.

20 Letter from Henry Blackwell to Lucy Stone, July 2, 1853. LW.

21 Letter from Lucy Stone to Henry Blackwell, July 27, 1853. LW.

22 Letter from Antoinette Brown to Lucy Stone, September 22, 1847. CL & MDM.

23 Letter from Lucy Stone to Antoinette Brown, August 1849. CL & MDM.

24 Letter from Lucy Stone to Henry Blackwell, June 21, 1853 & letter from Henry Blackwell to Lucy Stone, February 12, 1854. LW.

25 Letter from Lucy Stone to Antoinette Brown, July 11 1855. CL & MDM.

26 Letter from Lucy Stone to Antoinette Brown, August 1849. CL & MDM.

27 Letter from Lucy Stone to Henry

Blackwell, June 21, 1853. LW.

28 Letter from Lucy Stone to Antoinette Brown, August 1849. CL & MDM.

29 Letter from Henry Blackwell to Lucy Stone, June 13, 1853. LW.

30 GL.

31 CHB.

32 GL.

33 CHB.

34 GL.

35 Letter from Henry Blackwell to Lucy Stone, June 13, 1853. LW.

36 Letter from Henry Blackwell to Lucy Stone, July 2, 1853. LW.

37 Letter from Elizabeth Cady Stanton to Abigail Kelley Foster, January 1851. ADG I.

38 Letter from Elizabeth Cady Stanton to Pauline Wright Davis, December 6, 1852. ADG I.

39 Letter from Susan B. Anthony to Lucy Stone, May 1, 1853. ADG I.

40 Letter from Henry Blackwell to Lucy Stone, August 24, 1853. LW.

41 Letter from Henry B. Stanton to Elizabeth Cady Stanton, February 14, 1858. LDG & letter from Henry B. Stanton to Elizabeth Cady Stanton, January 5, 1854. EG.

42 ADG I.

43 Letter from Elizabeth Cady Stanton to Elizabeth J. Neall, November 26, 1841 & letter from Elizabeth Cady to Elizabeth Pease, February 12, 1842. ADG I.

44 Angelina Grimké, speech to the Massachusetts Legislature, February 21, 1838. GL.

45 CHB.

46 GL.

47 Colman, Penny (2011). Elizabeth Cady Stanton and Susan B. Anthony: A Friendship that Changed the World. Macmillan.

48 Letter from Elizabeth Cady to Elizabeth Pease, February 12, 1842. ADG I.

49 ADH.

50 Letter from Elizabeth Cady Stanton to Sarah Grimké and Angelina Grimké Weld, June 25, 1840. ADG I.

51 CHB.

52 Letter from Sarah Grimke to Sarah Douglass. GL.

53 CHB.

54 EAB.

55 GL.

56 CHB.

57 CHB.

58 GL & letter from Elizabeth Cady Stanton to Daniel C. Stanton, December 10, 1851. ADG I.

59 CHB.

60 Letter from Lucretia Mott to Elizabeth Cady Stanton, October 3, 1848. ADG I.

61 SGM.

62 Elizabeth Cady Stanton (June 25, 1883) On the Social, Educational, Religious and Political Position of Woman in America. ADG I.

63 ECS, SBA & MJG I.

64 LDG.

65 Judith Wellman (2004) The Road to Seneca Falls: Elizabeth Cady Stanton and the First Woman's Rights Convention. University of Illinois Press.

66 Letter from Elizabeth Cady Stanton to Susan B Anthony, 1858 Harper, Ida Husted. (January 1, 1903) Early Letters of Elizabeth Cady Stanton. The Independent. Volume 55 (2835-2847).

67 Elizabeth Cady Stanton Address on Women's Rights. (September 1848) ADG I.

68 Letter from Henry Blackwell to Lucy Stone, July 2, 1853. LW.

69 Letter from Lucy Stone to Susan B. Anthony, January 16, 1856 & letter from Antoinette Brown Blackwell to Susan B. Anthony, March, 12, 1856. ADG I.

70 Letter from Elizabeth Cady Stanton to Susan B Anthony, January 16, 1854. ADG I.

71 Letter from Henry B. Stanton to Margaret Stanton, January 16, 1857. LDG.

72 Elizabeth Cady Stanton (September 1850) Housekeeping. The Lily. ADG I.

73 Letter from Elizabeth Cady Stanton to Susan B. Anthony, April 2, 1853. EG.

74 Letter from Lucy Stone to Elizabeth Cady Stanton, August 14, 1853. ADG I.

75 Maria W. Stewart (October 8, 1831) Religion and the Pure Principles of Morality, the Sure Foundation on which We Must Build. The Liberator. MR.

76 Letter from Henry Blackwell to Lucy Stone, August 24, 1853. LW.

77 Letter from Henry Blackwell to Lucy Stone, June 13, 1853. LW.

78 Letter from Henry Blackwell to Lucy Stone, August 24, 1853. LW.

79 Letter from Lucy Stone to Henry Blackwell, April 26, 1854. LW.

80 Letter from Henry Blackwell to Lucy Stone, May 5, 1854. LW.

81 Letter from Henry Blackwell to Lucy Stone, February 12, 1854. LW.

82 Letter from Lucy Stone to Henry Blackwell, March 29, 1855. LW.

83 Letter from Lucy Stone to Elizabeth Cady Stanton, August 14, 1853. ADG I.

84 Letter from Henry Blackwell to Lucy Stone, September 9, 1853. LW.

85 Letter from Lucy Stone to Henry Blackwell, September 24, 1853. LW.

86 Proceedings of the National Woman's Rights Convention held at Cleveland, Ohio, on Wednesday, Thursday, and Friday, October 5th, 6th, and 7th, 1853.

87 LW.

88 Letter from Henry Blackwell to Lucy Stone, September 9, 1853. LW.

89 AMK.

90 Letter from Henry Blackwell to Lucy Stone, January 22, 1854. LW.

91 Letter from Lucy Stone to Henry Blackwell, December 30, 1853. LW.

92 Letter from William H. Channing to Elizabeth Cady Stanton, December 28, 1853. ADG I.

93 Letter from Elizabeth Cady Stanton to Susan B Anthony, January 16, 1854 & letter from Susan B. Anthony to Elizabeth Cady Stanton June 5, 1856 & letter from Elizabeth Cady Stanton to Susan B Anthony, June 10, 1856. ADG I.

94 Letter from Elizabeth Cady Stanton to Susan B. Anthony, July 5, 1859. ADG I.

95 Letter from Elizabeth Cady Stanton to Susan B. Anthony, August 20, 1857. ADG I.

96 Letter from Susan B. Anthony to Antoinette Brown Blackwell, September 4, 1858. ADG I.

97 Letter from Elizabeth Cady Stanton to Elizabeth Smith Miller, December 1, 1858. ADG I.

98 Letter from Susan B. Anthony to Antoinette Brown Blackwell, December 1858. ADG I.

99 JHB.

100 Letter from Elizabeth Cady Stanton to Elizabeth Smith Miller, December 1, 1858. ADG I.

101 Letter from Elizabeth Cady Stanton to Elizabeth Smith Miller, February 10, 1851 & letter from Elizabeth Cady Stanton to Lucretia Mott, October 22, 1852 & letter from Elizabeth Cady Stanton to Susan B. Anthony, April 10, 1859. ADG I.

102 Letter from Elizabeth Cady Stanton to Susan B. Anthony, April 10, 1859. ADG I.

103 Letter from Elizabeth Cady Stanton to Susan B. Anthony, August 20, 1857. ADG I.

104 Letter from Henry Blackwell to Lucy Stone, January 22, 1854. LW.

105 Letter from Henry Blackwell to Lucy Stone, February 12, 1854. LW.

106 Letter from Susan B Anthony to Lucy Stone, February 9, 1854. ADG I.

107 Letter from Lucy Stone to Henry Blackwell, October 8, 1854 & letter from Lucy Stone to Henry Blackwell, January 18, 1855 & letter from Henry Blackwell to Lucy Stone, March 18, 1855. LW.

108 Letter from Henry Blackwell to Lucy Stone, September 1, 1854. LW.

109 Letter from Henry Blackwell to Lucy Stone, February 12, 1854. LW.

110 Letter from Henry Blackwell to Lucy Stone, January 22, 1854. LW.

111 LW.

112 Letter from Henry B. Blackwell to Sarah Stone Lawrence, April 21, 1854. AMK.

113 ASB.

114 AMK and LW.

115 Letter from Henry B. Blackwell to Samuel C. Blackwell, June 2,1853. AMK.

116 AMK.

117 LW.

118 SG.

119 Letter from Antoinette Brown to Lucy Stone, February 1850. CL & MDM.

120 Letter from Lucy Stone to Antoinette Brown, June 9, 1850. CL & MDM.

121   ADH & CF.

122   CF.

123   Yellin, Jean Fagan and Van Home,
       John C. The Abolitionist Sisterhood:
       Women's Political Culture in Antebellum
       America. Cornell University Press: Ithaca
       & Nuermberger, Ruth Ketring (1942)
       The Free Produce Movement: a Quaker
       Protest Against Slavery. Duke University
       Press: Durham, North Carolina.

124   BWP.

125   Lucretia Coffin Mott, memoir, 1853 or
       earlier. BWP.

126   SGM.

127   Letter from James Mott to Lucy Stone,
       June 29, 1853. AMK.

128   Letter from Henry Blackwell to Lucy
       Stone, June 18, 1854. LW.

129   Letter from Lucy Stone to Henry
       Blackwell, July 23, 1854. LW.

130   Letter from Lucy Stone to Henry
       Blackwell, October 8, 1854. LW.

131   Letter from Lucy Stone to Henry
       Blackwell, January 18, 1855. LW.

132   Letter from Henry Blackwell to Lucy
       Stone, September 1, 1854. LW & ERH.

133   Letter from Lucy Stone to Henry
       Blackwell, September 10, 1854. LW.

134   Letter from Lucy Stone to Henry
       Blackwell, October 8, 1854. LW.

135   LW.

136   ERH.

137   Letter from Henry Blackwell to Lucy
       Stone, March, 18 1855. LW.

138   Letter from Lucy Stone to Henry
       Blackwell, October 8, 1854. LW.

139   Letter from Lucy Stone to Henry
       Blackwell, September 10, 1854. LW.

140   Letter from Lucy Stone to Henry
       Blackwell, October 8, 1854. LW.

141   Letter from Henry Blackwell to Lucy
       Stone, January 3, 1855. LW.

142   Letter from Henry Blackwell to Lucy
       Stone, May 5, 1854. LW.

143   Letter from Henry Blackwell to Lucy
       Stone, February 6, 1855. LW.

144   Letter from Henry Blackwell to Lucy
       Stone, March 18, 1855 & letter from
       Lucy Stone to Henry Blackwell, March
       29, 1855 & letter from Henry Blackwell
       to Lucy Stone, April 2, 1855 & letter
       from Lucy Stone to Henry Blackwell,
       April 25, 1854 LW.

145   Letter from Henry Blackwell to Lucy
       Stone, April 2, 1855. LW.

146   Letter from Lucy Stone to Henry
       Blackwell, March 29, 1855 & letter from
       Henry Blackwell to Lucy Stone, April 20,
       1855. LW.

147   Letter from Henry Blackwell to Lucy
       Stone, April 13, 1855. LW.

148   Letter from Thomas Wentworth
       Higginson to Louisa Wentworth
       Higginson, May 1, 1855. ASB.

149   ASB.

150   Letter from Thomas Wentworth
       Higginson to Louisa Wentworth
       Higginson, May 1, 1855. ASB.

151   LW.

152   Letter from Lucy Stone to Antoinette
       Blackwell, March 29, 1855. CL & MDM.
       University of Illinois Press: Urbana and
       Chicago and letter from Henry Blackwell
       to Lucy Stone, December 22, 1854. LW.

153   McMillen, Sally G. (2015) Lucy Stone:
       An Unapologetic Life. Oxford University
       Press.

154   Letter from Susan B. Anthony to
       Elizabeth Cady Stanton, June 1856.
       ADG I.

155   Letter from Elizabeth Cady Stanton to
       Susan B. Anthony, June 10, 1856. ADG
       I.

156   Letter from Henry Blackwell to Lucy
       Stone, January 22, 1854. LW.

157   Letter from Elizabeth Cady Stanton to
       Antoinette Blackwell, March 13, 1861.
       ADG I.

158   70% of the Nation's Poor are Women
       and Children. Legal Momentum: The
       Women's Defense and Education Fund.

159   Schulte, Brigid (May 7, 2015) Once the
       baby comes, moms do more, dads do
       less around the house. Washington Post
       & Parker, Kim & Livingston, Gretchen
       (June 16, 2016) 6 Facts about American
       Fathers. Pew Research Center.

160   2010 Census. United States Census
       Bureau.

Chapter 4

1   Maria W. Stewart (July 14, 1832) Cause
       for Encouragement. The Liberator. MR

2   Ernestine Rose (May 30, 1844) "A Word

to My Sisters" New England Social Reform Society Convention. PDW.

3   The New York Herald. (October 25, 1850) Woman's Rights Convention. Awful Combination of Socialism, Abolitionism, and Infidelity. WWHP.

4   The Boston Daily Mail (October 25, 1850). Grand Demonstrations of Petticoatdom at Worcester—The "Woman's Rights" Convention in Full Blast--Important and Interesting Report & Woman's Rights Convention at Worcester, Mass. New-York Daily Tribune (October 24, 1850) WWHP.

5   PDW.

6   Ernestine Rose speech at the Third National Woman's Rights Convention, September 8, 1852. PDW.

7   Call to Convention. (1850) Proceedings, 1850 Woman's Rights Convention: WWHP.

8   Woman's Rights Convention at Worcester, Mass. New-York Daily Tribune (October 24, 1850) Proceedings, 1850 Woman's Rights Convention: WWHP.

9   BSA.

10 Boston Daily Mail (October 25, 1850) Grand Demonstration of Petticoatdom at Worcester—The "Woman's Rights" Convention in Full blast—Important and Interesting Report: WWHP.

11 Woman's Rights Convention at Worcester, Mass. New-York Daily Tribune (October 26, 1850) Proceedings, 1850 Woman's Rights Convention: WWHP.

12 Letter from Antoinette Brown to Lucy Stone, August 13, 1850. EC.

13 Woman's Rights Convention at Worcester, Mass. (October 26, 1850) New York Daily Tribune. WWHP.

14 ST & OG.

15 NIP.

16 ST & OG.

17 WLS.

18 NIP.

19 ST & OG.

20 GV.

21 WLS.

22 GV.

23 WLS.

24 GV.

25 ST & OG.

26 NIP.

27 ST & OG.

28 NIP.

29 ST & OG.

30 NIP.

31 ST & OG.

32 NIP.

33 ST & OG.

34 NIP.

35 D'Héricourt (December 8, 1869) Madame Rose, Boston Investigator. BSA.

36 PDW.

37 D'Héricourt (December 8, 1869) Madame Rose, Boston Investigator. BSA.

38 PDW.

39 Seaver, Horace. (October 28, 1863) The Jews, Ancient and Modern. The Boston Liberator. PDW.

40 Rose, Ernestine. (January 29, 1864) The Jews: Justice to All. The Boston Liberator. PDW.

41 Rose, Ernestine. (February 29, 1864) The Jews: Justice to All. The Boston Liberator. PDW.

42 Seaver, Horace. (March 16, 1864) Remarks. The Boston Liberator. PDW.

43 Rose, Ernestine. (March 22, 1864) The Jews. The Boston Liberator. PDW.

44 PDW.

45 Almendrala, Anna. (August 29, 2016) Most Americans Still Think Women Should Do The Bulk Of The Housework. Huffington Post.

46 BSA.

47 Simkin, John. Journey to America. Sparticus Educational.

48 BSA.

49 PDW.

50 PDW & BSA.

51 Sandra J. Berkowitz and Amy C. Lewis (Fall 1998) Debating Anti-Semitism: Ernestine Rose vs. Horace Seaver in the Boston Investigator, 1863-1864 Communication Quarterly, 46(4) & Davin, Anna (Autumn 2002) Honouring Ernestine Rose, London, 1 and 4. History Workshop Journal, No. 54.

52 Pula, James S. (Autumn 2001). "Not as

a Gift of Charity": Ernestine Potowska Rose and the Married Woman's Property Laws. Polish American Studies, 58(2).

53 Rose, Ernestine. (March 28, 1860). Letter to the Editor. The Boston Liberator. PDW.

54 Elizabeth Cady Stanton (May 1850) Legislative Doings. The Lily. ADG I.

55 SG.

56 AMK.

57 SG.

58 Letter from Lucy Stone to Antoinette Brown, June 9, 1850. CL & MDM.

59 Letter from Antoinette Brown to Lucy Stone, July, 1850. CL & MDM.

60 Letter from Lucy Stone to Antoinette Brown, August 1849. CL & MDM.

61 Letter from Antoinette Brown to Lucy Stone, July, 1850. CL & MDM.

62 Letter from Lucy Stone to Antoinette Brown, August, 1849. CL & MDM.

63 SG & letter from Antoinette Brown to Lucy Stone, June 1848. CL & MDM.

64 SG.

65 Letter from Antoinette Brown to Lucy Stone, June 1848. CL & MDM.

66 Letter from Antoinette Brown to Lucy Stone, winter 1848. CL & MDM.

67 SG.

68 Letter from Antoinette Brown to Lucy Stone, July, 1850. CL & MDM.

69 Letter from Antoinette Brown to Lucy Stone, winter 1848. CL & MDM.

70 Letter from Antoinette Brown to Lucy Stone, August 7, 1851. CL & MDM.

71 SG.

72 Letter from Antoinette Brown to Lucy Stone, July, 1850. CL & MDM.

73 SG.

74 Letter from Antoinette Blackwell to Lucy Stone, December 9, 1650. CL & MDM.

75 Letter from Antoinette Blackwell to Lucy Stone, August 4, 1852. CL & MDM.

76 Letter from Antoinette Brown to Lucy Stone, February 1850. CL & MDM.

77 WRC.

78 New York Herald (October 26, 1850) Conclusion of the Incantation of the Old Women--The Infidels, Abolitionists and Fugitive Slaves—Postponement of the Petticoat Revolution: WWHP.

79 Letter from Antoinette Blackwell to Lucy Stone, August 4, 1852. CL & MDM.

80 WRC

81 Letter from Antoinette Brown to Elizabeth Cady Stanton (December 28, 1854). ADG I.

82 SG.

83 CL & MDM.

84 SG.

85 Letter from Antoinette Blackwell to Lucy Stone, August 16, 1853. CL & MDM.

86 ASB.

87 Letter from Antoinette Blackwell to Lucy Stone, August 16, 1853. CL & MDM.

88 PDW.

89 Letter from Antoinette Blackwell to Lucy Stone, August 16, 1853. CL & MDM.

90 SG.

91 EC.

92 AHTS & UUA.

93 EC.

94 Diary of Susan B. Anthony, March 24, 1854. PDW.

95 PDW.

96 Ernestine Rose (June 4, 1853) Speech at the Hartford Bible Convention: Trample the Bible, the Church and the Priests. PDW.

97 Diary of Susan B. Anthony, March 24, 1854. PDW.

98 Diary of Susan B. Anthony, April 9, 1854. ADG I.

99 BSA.

100 Diary of Susan B. Anthony, April 9, 1854. ADG I.

101 New York Herald, January 31, 1852. ADG I.

102 Diary of Susan B. Anthony, April 9, 1854. ADG I.

103 CL & MDM.

104 Letter from Antoinette Blackwell to Lucy Stone, August 14, 1854. CL & MDM.

105 PDW.

106 Rose, Ernestine. (April 10, 1861) A Defense of Atheism. PDW.

107 SG & CL & MDM.

108 Letter from Antoinette Brown to Horace Greeley, January 8, 1855. EC.

109 SG.

110 EC.

111 Rose, Ernestine. (February 19, 1864) The Jews. The Boston Liberator. PDW.

Chapter 5

1 EB.

2 Letter from Zakrzewska, Marie to Mary L. Booth (September 1857). CHD.

3 HKH.

4 Betty Friedan (1963) The Feminine Mystique. W.W. Norton & Company.

5 HKH.

6 MRW.

7 HKH.

8 Janik, E. (February 9, 2014) The Feminist Origins of "Eight Cups A Day." Slate.

9 HKH.

10 MRW.

11 HKH.

12 Walter Channing, (August 14, 1847) Minutes of the Meetings of the President and Fellows of Harvard College. MRW.

13 EB.

14 Smith, Stephen (1892) EB.

15 EB.

16 Smith, Stephen (1892) EB.

17 EB.

18 Smith, Stephen (1892) EB.

19 EB.

20 Smith, Stephen (1892) EB.

21 Elizabeth Cady Stanton (May 13, 1858) Address to the Eighth Annual Woman's Rights Convention. ADG I.

22 EB.

23 HKH.

24 Letter from Oliver Wendell Holmes to President Everett (December 11, 1847). MRW.

25 HKH.

26 Letter from Henry Blackwell to Blackwell family (January 23, 1849) EB.

27 EB.

28 Letter from Henry Blackwell to Blackwell family (January 23, 1849) EB.

29 Harriot K. Hunt (October 24, 1850). Proceedings, 1850 Woman's Rights Convention: WWHP.

30 HKH.

31 Harriot K. Hunt (October 24, 1850). Proceedings, 1850 Woman's Rights Convention: WWHP.

32 HKH.

33 Hays, Elinor Rice. (1967) Those Extraordinary Blackwells. Harcourt, Brace & World, Inc.: New York.

34 EB.

35 Harriot K. Hunt (October 24, 1850). Proceedings, 1850 Woman's Rights Convention: WWHP.

36 EB.

37 HKH.

38 Letter from Oliver Wendell Holmes to President Sparks, November 25, 1850. Harvard College papers. MRW.

39 NNN.

40 HKH.

41 NNN.

42 HKH.

43 NNN.

44 HKH.

45 JR-1998.

46 Editor (January 1, 1851) Schools for Colored People in Canada.. VH.

47 JR-1998.

48 Shadd, Mary Ann (June 8, 1849) North Star. JR-1998.

49 Editor (November 4, 1852) Shall we ask for help in vain?. VH.

50 Editor (April 23, 1851) What do the fugitives in Canada stand mostly in need of? No. III. VH.

51 JR-1998.

52 Shadd, Mary Ann (1852) A Plea for Emigration, Or, Notes of Canada West, In Its Moral, Social, and Political Aspect: with Suggestions Respecting Mexico, West Indies, and Vancouver's Island, for the Information of Colored Emigrants. George W. Pattison.

53 Editor (June 17, 1852) A Plea for Emigration. VH.

54 Editor (June 17, 1852) Schools in Canada. VH.

55 JR-1998.

56 Henry Bibb (July 15, 1852) Voice of the Fugitive. JR-1998.

57 Letter from Mary Ann Shadd to George Whipple, June 21, 1852. JR-1998.

58 JR-1998.

59   Editor (October 21, 1852) The Refugee's Home. VH.

60   Letter from Mary Ann Shadd to George Whipple (undated). JR-1998 & Editor (October 21, 1852) The Refugee's Home. VH.

61   Editor (December 16, 1852) Colored People's Meeting in Windsor. VH.

62   Letter from Horace Hallock to C. C. Foote, January 12, 1853. JR-1998.

63   Letter from Mary Ann Shadd to George Whipple, January 13, 1853. JR-1998.

64   Letter from Mary Ann Shadd to George Whipple, December 28, 1852. JR-1998.

65   Minutes of the Committee on Canada Missions of the American Missionary Association, January 14, 1853. JR-1998.

66   JR-1998.

67   MacLean, Maggie. (February 7, 2012) Emily Blackwell: Doctor and Educator in the Civil War Era. Civil War Women.

68   EB.

69   Diary of Susan B. Anthony, November 1853. ADG I.

70   IHH.

71   PBS. Only a Teacher.

72   Susan B. Anthony (Sept 7, 1853) Speech to the New York Woman's Rights Convention. ADG I.

73   Susan B. Anthony (Sept 7, 1853) Speech to the New York Woman's Rights Convention. ADG I & IHH.

74   Susan B. Anthony (Sept 7, 1853) Speech to the New York Woman's Rights Convention. ADG I.

75   New York Teachers' Association (August 2, 1854)). ADG I.

76   IHH.

77   New York Teachers' Association (August 2, 1854)). ADG I.

78   EB.

79   Letter from Zakrzewska, Marie to Mary L. Booth, September 1857. CHD.

80   EB.

81   Letter from Zakrzewska, Marie to Mary L. Booth, September 1857. CHD & HKH.

82   Letter from Zakrzewska, Marie to Mary L. Booth, September 1857. CHD.

83   Editor (February 26, 1852) Colored Schools, etc. in Canada.. VH.

84   Editor (February 12, 1852) Colored Schools, etc. in Canada.. VH.

85   Shadd, Mary Ann (January 3, 1857) C.C. Foote Begging Operations. PF.

86   Provincial Freeman (March 23 1853) JR-1998.

87   JR-1998.

88   Shadd, Mary Ann (March 25 1854) Mr. Ward's Tour. PF.

89   Provincial Freeman (March 25 1854) JR-1998.

90   JR-1998.

91   Editor (June 1, 1851) Look out for imposition. VH.- & the Provincial Freeman. (April 14, 1855, September 9, 1854, November 25, 1854, June 23, 1855, April 18, 1857, May 2, 1857) Black Abolitionist Archive. University of Detroit Mercy.

92   Shadd, Mary Ann (July 15, 1854) What We will do, and what We will not do. PF.

93   Shadd, Mary Ann (October 28, 1854) To all whom it may concern. PF.

94   The Provincial Freeman August 26 or September 2, 1854 JR-1998.

95   JR-1998.

96   William Still (1855) JR-1998.

97   RTP.

98   Letter from Elizabeth Blackwell to Emily Blackwell, January 23, 1855. AMK.

99   EB.

100 Letter from Henry Blackwell to Lucy Stone, April 2, 1855. LW.

101 EB.

102 Letter from Marie Zakrzewska to Mary L. Booth, September 1857. CHD.

103 EB.

104 Susan B. Anthony. Educating the Sexes Together. (February 2, 1857) ADG I.

105 IHH.

106 Letter from Susan B. Anthony to Elizabeth Cady Stanton, June 5, 1856. ADG I.

107 IHH.

108 Letter from Susan B. Anthony to Elizabeth Cady Stanton, June 5, 1856. ADG I.

109 IHH.

110 Letter from Elizabeth Cady Stanton to Susan B. Anthony, September 29, 1857. ADG I.

111 IHH.

112 Letter from Susan B. Anthony to Lucy

113 IHH.

114 Letter from Susan B. Anthony to Lucy Stone, August 2, 1857. ADG I.

115 Letter from Elizabeth Cady Stanton to Susan B. Anthony, September 29, 1857. ADG I.

116 Remarks by Susan B. Anthony to New York Teachers Association, August 3, 1858. ADG I.

117 IHH.

118 Shadd, Mary Ann (June 30, 1855) Adieu. PF.

119 William E Newman (August 22, 1855) Salutory. PF.

120 Shadd, Mary Ann (June 30, 1855) Adieu. PF.

121 Shadd, Mary Ann (June 8, 1849) North Star. JR-1998.

122 Cary, Mary Ann Shadd (December 8, 1869) Proceedings of the Colored National Labor Convention held in Washington, D.C., December 6th, 7th, 8th, 9th, and 19th, 1869.

123 Minutes of the first meeting, Colored Women's Progressive Franchise Association. JR-1998.

124 Benjamin Artz, Amanda Goodall &Andrew J. Oswald (June 25, 2018). Research: Women Ask for Raises as Often as Men, but Are Less Likely to Get Them. Harvard Business Review.

125 Zarya, Valentina (January 31, 2018). Female Founders Got 2% of Venture Capital Dollars in 2017. Fortune.

126 Burns, Janet. (July 6, 2017) Women Get More Questions On Risk From Startup VCs Than Men Do--And Far Less Money. Forbes.

127 Hegewisch, Ariane (September 13, 2018) The Gender Wage Gap: 2017; Earnings Differences by Gender, Race, and Ethnicity, Institute for Women's Policy Research.

128 Robert Maranto, Kristen Carroll, Albert Cheng, and Manuel P. Teodoro (September 24, 2018) Boys will be superintendents: School leadership as a gendered profession. Phi Delta Kappen.

129 AAUW (2015) Solving the Equation: Variables for Women's Success at Engineering and Computing. & Chira, Susan (July 21, 2017) Why Women Aren't C.E.O.s, According to Women Who Almost Were. New York Times.

130 Laura Brown, Mary Clark, Margaret Dale, Nancy Meyer, Madeleine Mullin, Terri Rutter, Jocelyn Spragg, Eleanor Shore, Miles Shore, Elin Wolfe, Richard Wolfe (undated) History of Women at HMS: Matriculation of Women at Harvard Medical School. The Joint Committee on the Status of Women.

131 EB.

Chapter 6

1 Harper, Frances E.W. (1895) Poems.

2 LER & MHE.

3 JWH-1900.

4 JWH-1900. & LER & MHE.

5 JWH-1900.

6 The Dawning of Light, diary Julia Ward Howe, 1843. GW.

7 JWH-1900. & LER & MHE.

8 The Darkest Moment, Diary of Julia Ward Howe, 1843. GW.

9 JWH & GW.

10 JWH-1900.

11 Carradice, Phil (July 6, 2010) The Ladies of Llangollen. BBC & JWH-1900.

12 Letter from Julia Ward Howe to Louisa Ward Crawford, February 15, 1846. ES.

13 LER & MHE.

14 JWH-1900.

15 Letter from Julia Ward Howe to Louisa Ward Crawford, September 20, 1846. ES.

16 JWH-1900.

17 LER & MHE.

18 JWH-1900.

19 Letter from Julia Ward Howe to Louisa Ward Crawford, December 1, 1846. LER & MHE.

20 JWH-1900 & GW.

21 Letter from Julia Ward Howe to Louisa Ward Crawford, January 31, 1846. ES.

22 JWH & GW.

23 LER & MHE.

24 JWH & GW.

25 LER & MHE.

26 Letter from Julia Ward Howe to Annie Ward Mailliard, October 12, 1848. ES.

27 JWH & GW.

28 Letter from Julia Ward Howe to Louisa Ward Crawford, January 31, 1847. ES.

29 Letter from Julia Ward Howe to Louisa Ward Crawford, September 20, 1847. ES.

30 Julia Ward Howe, April 18, 1848. LER & MHE.

31 ES.

32 Letter from Samuel Gridley Howe to Louisa Ward Crawford, April 5, 1848, ES.

33 Letter from Julia Ward Howe to Louisa Ward Crawford, April 18, 1848, ES.

34 JWH & GW.

35 Letter from Julia Ward Howe to Louisa Ward Crawford, February 15, 1846. GW.

36 Letter from Julia Ward Howe to Samuel Gridley Howe, 1846. GW.

37 JWH & GW.

38 Diary of Julia Ward Howe, 1843. GW.

39 WS.

40 ExplorePAhistory.com. Frances E.W. Harper.

41 WS & MHP.

42 WS.

43 MHP.

44 Watkins, Frances Ellen (1853) Eliza Harris.

45 PLH.

46 Bellis, Mary. (August 20, 2018) The History of Microphones. ThoughtCo.

47 WS.

48 Watkins, Frances Ellen (1858) Bury Me in a Free Land. The Anti-Slavery Bugle.

49 Harper, Frances Ellen Watkins (date unknown). Our Greatest Want.

50 WS.

51 Watkins, Frances Ellen (June and July 1859). The Two Offers. The Anglo-African Magazine.

52 PLH.

53 Watkins, Frances Ellen (June and July 1859). The Two Offers. The Anglo-African Magazine.

54 ES.

55 JWH-1900.

56 ES.

57 Letter from Julia Ward Howe to Auguste Comte, February 15, 1853. ES.

58 JWH-1900.

59 Letter from Annie Ward Mailliard to Samuel Gridley Howe, April 29, 1851. GW.

60 JWH-1900.

61 Letter from Julia Ward Howe to Annie Ward Mailliard, December 8, 1853. ES.

62 LER & MHE.

63 JWH-1900.

64 LER & MHE.

65 ES.

66 Letter from Julia Ward Howe to Annie Ward Mailliard, February 1854. ES.

67 Howe, Julia Ward (1853). Passion-flowers. Ticknor, Reed, and Fields.

68 Letter from Julia Ward Howe to Annie Ward Mailliard, February 1854. ES.

69 ES.

70 Letter from Samuel Gridley Howe to Julia Ward Howe. ES.

71 Letter from Julia Ward Howe to Louisa Ward Crawford, July 23, 1854 and November 4 1854. ES.

72 ES.

73 LER & MHE.

74 Howe, Julia Ward (1860) A Trip to Cuba. The Atlantic Monthly.

75 Letter from Samuel Gridley Howe to Theodore Parker, March 25, 1860. ES.

76 Howe, Julia Ward (1860) A Trip to Cuba. The Atlantic Monthly.

77 Letter from Samuel Gridley Howe to Theodore Parker, March 25, 1860. ES.

78 JWH-1900.

79 EJR.

80 Letter from Julia Ward Howe to Annie Ward Mailliard, November 6, 1859. LER & MHE.

81 EJR.

82 Letter from Julia Ward Howe to Samuel Gridley Howe, November 21, 1859. ES.

83 Letter from Samuel Gridley Howe to Julia Ward Howe, November 24, 1859. ES.

84 LER & MHE.

85 DeCaro, Louis A. (June 8, 2011) Frances Ellen Watkins Harper and the John Brown Story. John Brown the Abolitionist—a Biographer's Blog

86 MJB.

87 Letter from Frances Ellen Watkins to Mary Brown, November 14, 1859. WS.

88 Letter from Frances Ellen Watkins to William Still, December 12, 1859. WS.

89 Letter from Frances Ellen Watkins to John Brown, November 25, 1859. MJB.

90 BH.

91 JWH-1900.

92 LER & MHE.

93 BH.

94 JWH-1900.

95 BH.

96 LER & MHE.

97 JWH-1900.

98 Howe, Julia Ward (February 1862) Battle Hymn of the Republic. The Atlantic Monthly.

99 LER & MHE.

100 Howe, Julia Ward (February 1862) Battle Hymn of the Republic. The Atlantic Monthly.

101 JWH-1900.

102 ES.

103 LER & MHE.

104 JWH-1900.

105 LER & MHE.

106 Speech by Frances Ellen Watkins Harper (May 10, 1866) The eleventh National Woman's Rights Convention, New York. MJB.

107 WS.

108 Speech by Frances Ellen Watkins Harper (May 10, 1866) The eleventh National Woman's Rights Convention, New York. MJB.

109 Watkins, Frances Ellen (June and July 1859). The Two Offers. The Anglo-African Magazine.

110 Speech by Frances Ellen Watkins Harper (May 10, 1866) The eleventh National Woman's Rights Convention, New York. MJB.

111 MJB.

112 Speech by Frances Ellen Watkins Harper (May 10, 1866) The eleventh National Woman's Rights Convention, New York. MJB.

113 Howe, Julia Ward (1866) Later Lyrics. J.E. Tilton & Company.

114 LER & MHE.

115 JWH-1900.

116 Letter from Samuel Gridley Howe to Julia Ward Howe, October 2, 1868. ES.

117 JWH-1900.

118 LER & MHE.

119 ES.

120 JWH-1900.

121 Harper, Frances Ellen Watkins (May 20, 1893) Woman's Political Future.

122 LER & MHE.

123 Lauter, Paul (Spring 1988) Is Frances Ellen Watkins Harper Good Enough To Teach? Legacy, Vol. 5, No. 1. & PLH.

124 Poirier, Agnès (May 14, 2018) #MeToo activists should stop trying to be film critics – they undermine feminism. The Guardian.

125 Waddell, Kaveh (January 23, 2017). The Exhausting Work of Tallying America's Largest Protest. The Atlantic.

126 KJS.

127 McLean, Bethany (March 13, 2017) The Backstory Behind That 'Fearless Girl' Statue on Wall Street. The Atlantic.

128 KJS.

129 Associated Press (April 11, 2017) 'Charging Bull' sculptor says New York's 'Fearless Girl' statue violates his rights.

130 Mullin, Amy. (Autumn/Winter 2003) Feminist Art and the Political Imagination. Hypatia. Vol. 18, No. 4.

Chapter 7

1 Maria W. Stewart (September 21, 1833) Mrs. Stewart's Farewell Address to her Friends in the City of Boston. MR.

2 Letter from Elizabeth Cady Stanton to Women's Temperance Meeting, Albany, January 28, 1852, Seneca County Courier. ADG I.

3 Susan B. Anthony (May 12, 1869) Speech at the American Equal Rights Association. ADG II.

4 Miller, Elizabeth Smith, 1892. BOF.

5 Letter from Elizabeth Cady Stanton, 1857. BOF.

6 ADG I.

7 DCB & Bloomer, Amelia, 1892. BOF.

8 Bloomer, Amelia, The Lily, (February 1, 1851) TDM.

9 DCB & Bloomer, Amelia, 1892. BOF.

10 Elizabeth Cady Stanton (March 1851) Sobriny Jane. The Lily. ADG I.

11 Letter from Antoinette Brown to Lucy Stone, April 28, 1851. CL & MDM.

12 Boissoneault, Lorraine (May 24, 2018) Amelia Bloomer Didn't Mean to Start a Fashion Revolution, But Her Name Became Synonymous With Trousers. Smithsonian.com & DCB.

13 DCB.

14 Bloomer, Amelia, 1892. BOF.

15   TDM & DCB.

16   Stanton, Elizabeth Cady, The Lily, (July 1, 1851) TDM.

17   DCB & Bloomer, Amelia, The Lily, (June 1851) TDM.

18   Stanton, Elizabeth Cady, The Lily, (July 1, 1851) TDM.

19   Godey's Lady's Book (1852) TDM.

20   Letter from Lucy Stone to Antoinette Brown. (November 24, 1852) CL & MDM.

21   AMK.

22   ASB.

23   Frederick Douglass' Paper, September 17, 1852. ADG I.

24   Letter from Elizabeth Cady Stanton to Lucretia Mott, October 22, 1852. ADG I.

25   Letter from Lucy Stone to Antoinette Brown, November 24, 1852. CL & MDM.

26   SG.

27   CL & MDM.

28   ASB.

29   Letter from Susan B. Anthony to Lucy Stone, May 1852. SG.

30   Letter from Susan B. Anthony to Lucy Stone, May 1852. SG. & Baker, Jean H. (2005) Sisters: The Lives of America's Suffragists. Hill and Wang.

31   Letter from Susan B. Anthony to Lucy Stone, May 1852. SG.

32   Bloomer, Amelia. BOF.

33   ASB.

34   Letter from Susan B. Anthony to Lucy Stone, May 1852. SG.

35   Letter from Susan B Anthony to Lucy Stone, February 9, 1854. ADG I.

36   Miller, Elizabeth Smith. BOF.

37   LDG.

38   Letter from Elizabeth Cady Stanton to Daniel Cady Stanton, October 14, 1851. LDG.

39   Letter from Susan B Anthony to Lucy Stone, February 9, 1854. ADG I.

40   ASB.

41   Letter from Susan B. Anthony and Elizabeth Cady Stanton to Lucy Stone, February 16, 1854. ADG I.

42   Letter from Antoinette Brown to Lucy Stone, February 18, 1854. CL & MDM

43   SG.

44   Letter from Antoinette Brown to Lucy Stone, February 18, 1854. CL & MDM

45   Letter from Susan B Anthony to Lucy Stone, March 7, 1854. ADG I.

46   Albany State Register (March 6, 1854) ADG I.

47   Albany Evening Journal (March 2, 1854) and New York Daily Tribune (March 7 1854) ADG I.

48   Letter from Susan B Anthony to Lucy Stone, March 7, 1854. ADG I.

49   Letter from Gerrit Smith to Elizabeth Cady Stanton, December 1, 1855. ECS, SBA & MJG I.

50   ASB.

51   Miller, Elizabeth Smith. BOF.

52   DCB.

53   SG.

54   Stone, Lucy. BOF.

55   ASB.

56   Minutes of the American Anti-Slavery Society, New York (May 8-9, 1866) ADG I.

57   Women History Blog (August 2016) Harriet Forten Purvis. History of American Women.

58   Minutes of the American Anti-Slavery Society, New York (May 8-9, 1866) ADG I.

59   EPS.

60   SGM.

61   Minutes of the American Anti-Slavery Society, New York (May 8-9, 1866) ADG I.

62   Minutes of the Eleventh Annual Woman's Rights Convention, New York (May 10, 1866) ADG I.

63   Phillips, Wendell. (May 9, 1865) Speech to the American Anti-Slavery Society, New York.

64   Letter from Elizabeth Cady Stanton to Wendell Phillips, May 25, 1865. ADG I.

65   Minutes of the Eleventh Annual Woman's Rights Convention, New York (May 10, 1866) ADG I.

66   Letter from Elizabeth Cady Stanton to Gerrit Smith, January 1, 1866. ADG I.

67   Elizabeth Cady Stanton, Susan B. Anthony and Lucy Stone (December 26, 1865) ADG I.

68   ECS, SBA & MJG II.

69   Equal Rights Convention, Rochester,

New York (December 12, 1866) ADG
II.
70 ASB.
71 AMK.
72 ECS, SBA & MJG II.
73 ASB.
74 ECS, SBA & MJG II.
75 Minutes of the Eleventh Annual
Woman's Rights Convention, New York
(May 10, 1866) ADG I.
76 ECS, SBA & MJG II.
77 AMK.
78 ASB.
79 Letter from Lucy Stone to Elizabeth
Cady Stanton, April 10, 1867. ECS, SBA
& MJG II & ADG II.
80 Letter from Henry B. Blackwell to
Elizabeth Cady Stanton and Susan B.
Anthony, April 21, 1867. ECS, SBA &
MJG II.
81 Helen Ekin Starrett, Reminiscences.
ECS, SBA & MJG II.
82 RTP.
83 Helen Ekin Starrett, Reminiscences.
ECS, SBA & MJG II.
84 Letter from Henry B. Blackwell to
Elizabeth Cady Stanton, April 5, 1867.
ECS, SBA & MJG II.
85 Letter from Lucy Stone to Elizabeth
Cady Stanton, April 10, 1867. ECS, SBA
& MJG II.
86 ECS, SBA & MJG II.
87 ADG II.
88 Letter from Lucretia Coffin Mott to
Susan B. Anthony (February 10, 1867).
ADG II.
89 Letter from Lucy Stone to Susan B.
Anthony, May 1, 1867. ECS, SBA &
MJG II.
90 Letter from Frances E.W. Harper to
William Still, May 13, 1867. WS.
91 Letter from Frances E.W. Harper to
William Still, June 17, 1867. WS.
92 Letters from Frances E.W. Harper
to William Still, March 29, 1870 and
February 20, 1871. WS.
93 Letter from Frances E.W. Harper to
William Still, May 13, 1867. WS.
94 Letter from Frances E.W. Harper to
William Still, July 11, 1867. WS.
95 Letter from Frances E.W. Harper to
William Still, February 20, 1871. WS.

96 Letter from Frances E.W. Harper to
William Still. undated. WS.
97 Letter from Frances E.W. Harper to
William Still, March 29, 1870. WS.
98 Letter from Frances E.W. Harper to
William Still. undated. WS.
99 Letter from Frances E.W. Harper to
William Still. December 29, 1870. WS.
100 WS.
101 Letters from Frances E.W. Harper
to William Still, March 29, 1870 and
undated. WS.
102 Letter from Frances E.W. Harper to
William Still, March 29, 1870. WS.
103 Letter from Frances E.W. Harper to
William Still, May 13, 1867. WS.
104 Letter from Frances E.W. Harper to
William Still, March 1, 1871. WS.
105 Letter from Frances E.W. Harper to
William Still, undated. WS.
106 ECS, SBA & MJG II.
107 Letter from Lucy Stone to Susan B.
Anthony, May 9, 1867. ECS, SBA &
MJG II.
108 ECS, SBA & MJG II.
109 ADG II.
110 ECS, SBA & MJG II.
111 Elizabeth Cady Stanton (February 19,
1867) Reconstruction ADG II.
112 Susan B. Anthony, (May 12, 1869),
Speech at the American Equal Rights
Association in New York. ADG II.
113 ECS, SBA & MJG II.
114 LW and Henry B. Blackwell, 1853-1893.
LW.
115 ECS, SBA & MJG II.
116 Stanton, Elizabeth Cady (July 18, 1867)
Constitutional Convention. Independent.
ECS, SBA & MJG I.
117 ECS, SBA & MJG II.
118 Letter from Susan B. Anthony Samuel N.
Wood, April 21, 1867. ADG II.
119 Letter from Susan B. Anthony to Gerrit
Smith, March 6, 1867. ADG II.
120 ADG II.
121 AHTS & UUA.
122 Letter from Olympia Brown to Susan B.
Anthony, March 16, 1882. ECS, SBA &
MJG I.
123 Letter from Henry B. Stanton to Lucy
Stone, October 25, 1867. LW.
124 ECS, SBA & MJG II.

125   Letter from Susan B. Anthony to Anna
      E. Dickinson, September 23, 1867.
      ADG II.
126   ADG II.
127   Letter from Susan B. Anthony to Anna
      E. Dickinson, September 23, 1867.
      ADG II.
128   Speech by Susan B. Anthony, St. Louis,
      Missouri, November 25, 1867. ADG II.
129   GFT.
130   Landers, Jackson (March 24, 2016) For
      Susan B. Anthony, Getting Support for
      Her "Revolution" Meant Taking on an
      Unusual Ally. Smithsonian.com
131   GFT.
132   Letter from Lucy Stone to William Lloyd
      Garrison, March 6, 1868. AMK & RTP.
133   GFT.
134   LW.
135   Speech by Susan B. Anthony, St. Louis,
      Missouri, November 25, 1867. ADG II.
136   ADG II.
137   Letter from Elizabeth Cady Stanton to
      Ellen D. Eaton, December 17, 1867.
      ADG II.
138   LW.
139   Letter from Lucy Stone to William Lloyd
      Garrison, March 6, 1868. ADG II.
140   Letter from William Lloyd Garrison to
      Susan B. Anthony, January 4, 1868. ASB.
141   Letter from Lucy Stone to Matilda Joslyn
      Gage. AMK.
142   Letter from Lucretia Mott to Martha
      Coffin Wright, January 21, 1868. BWP.
143   Elizabeth Cady Stanton (December 24,
      1868) Manhood Suffrage. ADG II.
144   Stanton, Elizabeth Cady, Pillsbury,
      Parker, and Anthony, Susan B. (January
      8, 1868). The Revolution; The Organ of
      The National Party of New America.
      The Revolution.
145   Letter from Lucretia Mott to Martha
      Coffin Wright, January 21, 1868. BWP.
146   ECS, SBA & MJG II.
147   Susan B. Anthony (May 12, 1869)
      Speech at the American Equal Rights
      Association. ADG II.
148   ECS, SBA & MJG II.
149   Letter from Susan B. Anthony to
      Thomas Wentworth Higginson, May 20,
      1868. ADG II.
150   Minutes of the American Equal Rights
      Association, Cooper Institute, New
      York, May 14, 1868. ADG II.
151   Letter from Susan B. Anthony to
      Thomas Wentworth Higginson, May 20,
      1868. ADG II.
152   Minutes of the American Equal Rights
      Association, Cooper Institute, New
      York, May 14, 1868. ADG II.
153   Letter from Susan B. Anthony to
      Thomas Wentworth Higginson, May 20,
      1868. ADG II.
154   Elizabeth Cady Stanton (December 24,
      1868) Manhood Suffrage. ADG II.
155   Letter from Frances E.W. Harper to
      William Still, May 13, 1867. WS.
156   Letter from Frances E.W. Harper to
      William Still, July 11, 1867. WS.
157   O'Brien, C.C. (2009) "The White
      Women All Go for Sex": Frances
      Harper on Suffrage, Citizenship, and the
      Reconstruction South. African American
      Review, Vol. 43, No. 4.
158   ECS, SBA & MJG II.
159   SGM.
160   ECS, SBA & MJG II.
161   Letter from Frances E.W. Harper to
      William Still, March 1, 1871. WS.
162   ECS, SBA & MJG II.
163   Letter from Lucy Stone to Mrs. Field,
      March 24, 1869. LW.
164   ECS, SBA & MJG II.
165   Harper, Frances E.W. (1869) Minnie's
      Sacrifice. The Christian Recorder.
166   ECS, SBA & MJG II.
167   Editorial Correspondence (January 22,
      1896). ECS, SBA & MJG II.
168   ECS, SBA & MJG II.
169   RTP.
170   Letter from Elizabeth Cady Stanton to
      Gerrit Smith, January 1, 1866. ADG I.
171   Letter from Lucretia Mott to Elizabeth
      Cady Stanton, October 3, 1848, Seneca
      County Courier. ADG I.

Index

About the Author

April Young Bennett began studying the lives of suffragists to inform her own activism. She has campaigned for better state and federal laws that affect children and families, addressing the wage gap, healthcare, education and juvenile justice; and for gender equity within her modern-day patriarchal religious community. As an organizer for the activist organization Ordain Women, she led hundreds of women and men in marches and demonstrations that attracted national attention.

April helps feminists of different faiths share ideas and collaborate toward common goals at the Religious Feminism Podcast. She blogs about Mormon feminism at Exponent II, an organization that began during the second wave feminist movement, that is named after a nineteenth century Mormon suffragist newspaper.

April is a motivational speaker who can speak at your event about what modern leaders, activists and change-makers can learn from bold women from history and what she has learned about changing hearts and minds as an advocate for women, children and underserved populations.

aprilyoungb.com

The *Ask a Suffragist* Book Series

America's First Feminists covers the 1830s-1860s, when the idea of equality for women was new and its supporters were vilified.

Activists Who Built a Movement covers the 1870s-1880s, when suffragists organized into thriving (but competing) groups and achieved early success in the West.

Leaders Who Mobilized for Change transitions from the 19th century to the 20th, when a new generation revitalized the stalled suffrage movement and expanded its human rights vision.

Fighters Who Won (and Lost) the Right to Vote covers the 19th Amendment victory and beyond, when women barred from voting by racial discrimination fought for their rights.

askasuffragist.com

CPSIA information can be obtained
at www.ICGtesting.com
Printed in the USA
BVHW041340160820
586437BV00009B/161